# YOUR OWN WORST ENEMY

ReganBooks  *An Imprint of* HarperCollins*Publishers*

KENNETH W. CHRISTIAN, PH.D.

YOUR

OWN

WoRSt

ENEMY

Breaking the Habit of
Adult Underachievement

Grateful acknowledgment is made to reprint from
*The Notebooks of Malte Laurids Brigge* by Rainer Maria Rilke,
translated by M. D. Herter Norton. Copyright 1949 by
W. W. Norton & Company, Inc., renewed © 1977 by M. D. Herter Norton
Crena de Longh. Used by permission of W. W. Norton & Company, Inc.

HarperCollins books may be purchased for educational, business, or sales promotional
use. For information please write: Special Markets Department, HarperCollins Publishers,
Inc., 10 East 53rd Street, New York, NY 10022.

FIRST EDITION

Printed on acid-free paper

Library of Congress Cataloging-in-Publication Data

Christian, Kenneth W.
Your own worst enemy : breaking the habit of adult underachievement /
Kenneth W. Christian.— 1st ed.
p.   cm.
ISBN 0-06-039392-0
1. Underachievement.   2. Success—Psychological aspects.   I. Title.

BF637.U53 .C47   2002
155.2'32—dc21
2002021376

02   03   04   05   06   WB/RRD   10   9   8   7   6   5   4   3   2   1

*I dedicate this book*

*to my mother and father,*

*who have always believed in me,*

*and even when they did not necessarily agree with me,*

*have always supported me.*

# Contents

# Introduction

I was driving home from my friend Mark's wedding weekend after spending the night with his family. I had met Mark during my freshman year of college, and we had grown close in the years since.

The previous afternoon and evening had been devoted to celebrating Mark and his bride, Susan, but my thoughts kept returning to Mark's younger brother, Pete. Seeing him had been unnerving. Pete was in sixth grade when I met him, and everyone had predicted great things for him. Intelligent, charismatic, enthusiastic, playful, he was adored by his family and drew people to him with his spontaneous zest for life. He took accelerated classes and played basketball competitively year-round.

I hadn't had regular contact with Pete since the family moved to the East Coast. Even though I knew from Mark that Pete had slipped from his pedestal—he had graduated in the bottom half of his high school class and later dropped out of college, struggling to "find himself"—the wedding was going to be the first time I'd seen him in years and I expected to see some of that former exuberance. I wanted to reconnect with him.

Nothing prepared me for what I saw. The bright light was extinguished.

Pete was distant at the rehearsal dinner. I approached him, but he said he was jetlagged, then went to his room. The next day he arrived at the last possible moment for the ceremony. At the reception he dutifully made the rounds but avoided my gaze. Instead of casting his former amiable spell on those around him, he looked like a cardboard cutout. He said the right things, but his remarks to family friends about future plans and how he was doing sounded too cheery.

In my heart I knew he had not grown up. Time had merely passed, and something shining had been lost. He still pretended the world lay before him. Perhaps the deadness I saw in him was caused by an awareness that the world had left him behind. The ambitious, imaginative, mesmerizing kid I had walked to the lake with on summer nights and taken for ice cream—the kid who called me "Doc" years before I got my Ph.D.—was gone.

The day after the wedding I took Pete aside. I needed to understand. At first he deflected my questions. I finally steered the conversation around to the past several years. Biting his lip, his head down and fighting back tears, he began to speak.

"Look," he said, "I screwed up, okay? I never thought I'd be where I am."

Pete stammered out his story. The year before the family moved he had wanted a break from being the "perfect student." He was sure he'd get back to normal in high school when it really counted—but he didn't. "I always told myself I'd study next year, but I could never quite get it going," he said. "It never quite seemed worth it when next year came. After a while I told myself I didn't care."

It never dawned on Pete that being engaged was not something he could just switch off then easily switch back on again. When he made his choice to take a break from being the perfect student, he began to move in a decisively different direction, leaving behind some part of himself. Before long he had forgotten who he had once been. The one thing he still cared about and excelled at was basketball. But he could no longer rise above the competition on talent alone. He made team practices but didn't work as hard in the summer leagues, and by his senior year he had encountered equally gifted athletes who worked more diligently. Still, he ranked third in scoring in the county that year.

Then he allowed something simply destructive to happen. His high school team qualified for the state championship tournament, but Pete, the linchpin player at point guard, was in trouble with his grades and in danger of failing his government class. His teacher gave him an unprecedented chance to pass by writing a two-page essay on any topic he chose related to the Constitution.

He never wrote it.

"What still kills me is that I didn't decide *not* to write it. I just let the deadline pass. Afterward I couldn't explain why. The guys went on to the tournament with my backup at point guard and got knocked out in the first round. I let down everybody—the team, my family, me."

After the basketball failure Pete went into a funk and never righted himself.

For the first time he looked directly into my eyes.

"Tell me, Doc, what kind of person does that?"

His question was a kick in the stomach, because I didn't have an answer. I took a deep breath and did what therapists are trained to do. I continued to listen.

The entire time we spoke Pete had a haunted look just behind his eyes. I started to offer to help him find a therapist. Even as I said it my jaw tightened at this automatic response. As a therapist, I knew what was possible, and I didn't really think therapy would help. Now I felt haunted too. Was his depression infectious, or was there something else right in front of me, something I was missing? I told him I would get back to him.

As I drove away from the wedding, I realized that Pete's situation seemed naggingly familiar. I thought of Vince, who had come to see me the previous year. Vince's story was so different from Pete's story. Or was it? What was I seeing? What was I *not* seeing?

Vince was not a sought-after star. He didn't have Pete's presence or natural charm. Though he was bright, he seemed lost, his face as drawn as Pete's had been. But there seemed to be something else about him that I could not put my finger on. I remembered how he had slumped resignedly in his chair, gazing at the carpet, young, yet already very old. He spoke of broken dreams and bad luck—none of the things he tried had worked out. A string of opportunities and shortcuts he couldn't pass up had turned out to be detours into blank walls.

I also thought of Elise, who had had everything going for her but during her first year of law school decided it was not worth it to continue because she no longer wanted that kind of life. When she quit, she thought that some time spent traveling would help her clear her head. But she found that she had no other calling, no other path she wanted to follow. Soon Elise felt aimless, consumed with self-doubt, and she became convinced that she had hit her high-water mark and was receding.

Instead of going home, I drove to my office and started pulling files. Here and there were names of other talented people like Pete, Vince, and Elise, who had been languishing in a similar way when I met them. Trying to find the way these people were connected, I began to look for similarities in their childhood experiences. Then I recalled Clarissa, one of my daughter's friends from preschool, who began school with enthusiasm and at some point faltered. Clarissa was bright and had no learning problems. As a consultant at a rehabilitation center, I had seen cases of serious learning disabilities. Clarissa did not suffer from any such disability. And I did not detect anything that would have interfered with her concentration. Like Pete, Vince, and Elise, she simply seemed to contract and stop putting out effort.

Scanning one file after another of adults, children, and concerned parents, I recognized that what I was seeing was not an isolated phenomenon. My practice was made up of adults, couples, and families. Perhaps 80 percent of the parents who had brought in their adolescents had expressed, among other concerns, worries about their children's school performance. Sometimes these kids were like Pete—children with potential, frittering it away. I had helped some of the children, but with others I was not satisfied with the results of my efforts. What was different about them, and what did they need? I didn't know, and I wasn't sure anyone else knew either.

It was late when I closed my files. I had been searching in vain for answers to Pete's haunting question. I was trying to give voice to something else too. Beyond my affection and concern for Pete and the others, their struggles touched something in me. These people had all arrested something vital within themselves. Seeing the similarities in their struggles made me determined to do something about what I saw and the incredible waste it represented. I wanted to find a way to reach these people—people like the faces that came back to me from my files—*before* they became as depleted and empty as Pete and Vince. But where to start?

In the weeks that followed I scoured the scientific literature for answers. Earlier in my career I had conducted research on self-esteem, focusing on what people consider important and the criteria they use to evaluate themselves. Beliefs about oneself and the world exert a powerful influence on goals and actions; I was sure that these issues must be involved.

Research on underachievement, I discovered, focused on external behavior, chiefly academic performance, and not on internal experience. Interest in the topic had hit a peak in the 1970s before waning. Theoretical concepts and methods of intervention became dated. Standard forms of psychotherapy yielded mixed results, stretching two years or more without reliable consequences. Group therapy showed more promise, but no results of any systematic use of family therapy were reported.

I widened my search to other areas, eventually coming across research from social psychology on self-defeating behavior: the paradoxical tendency of some people to respond to the possibility of failing by deliberately sabotaging their own efforts. Finally, I seemed to have a lead.

I knew by now that underachievement was an epidemic problem. Parents, educators, therapists, and others desperately needed a new perspective that would lead to hope and solutions. As I branched out from the research on self-defeating behavior, I began to develop an encompassing view of underachievement that offered new ways of intervening. I concluded that the best way to proceed would be to come at the problem with an intensive, multifaceted approach designed to shift the elements that kept underachieving behavior in place. To accomplish this, we simultaneously placed the child in a structured psycho-educational peer group, the parents in a parent education group, enrolled the family in family therapy, and consulted closely with school officials and teachers over a brief four and a half month period. With this approach, I founded the Maximum Potential Project in 1990. Using these specifically designed techniques we achieved unprecedented results. Children changed their fundamental orientation to schoolwork and their lives. We saw them become productive. We saw them become engaged.

In 1993 I was sitting in the studios of the San Francisco National Public Radio affiliate KQED, having just been interviewed about the Maximum Potential Project. As I started answering calls on the air, a curious thing happened. I presumed I would hear from concerned parents, but calls began to come in from listeners who said, "That's me you're describing. I was that kid who ducked out on assignments and toyed with school. I still duck out. I want to live differently, but I don't know how."

More than half of the callers that night were not parents wanting help for their children, but adults wanting help for themselves. Some of the calls were particularly wrenching. As I listened, I realized I had more work to do. In a matter of days I set out with my associates to understand how we could help Pete, Vince, Elise, and other adult underachievers change. I wanted to see *them* become productive. I wanted to see *them* become engaged.

I found that while some underachieving adults seemed to settle in and accept mediocre levels of functioning, many others, like Pete, Vince, and Elise, began a long, torturous slide backward into disappointment, bitterness, and regret. As I scrutinized more closely the issues they faced, I came to an inescapable conclusion: the basic elements of the style I saw in all these people were nearly universally present in the general population.

Everywhere I looked I found that people put limits on their lives. In fact, people seem embarrassed about having or articulating dreams and seem more devoted to squelching them than to pursuing them. They are bold about issues of scant personal import, but timid about the desires of their hearts; they secretly long to do more but remain frozen, passive. Furthermore, it became obvious that the widespread tendency for people to start a new program of self-development and then shrink back from its demands is in its own way a version of underachieving. In short, I saw that adult underachievment—even in its extreme forms—is an extension of such commonplace lapses as not finishing that book, putting off that change in diet, or repeatedly falling behind on correspondence.

Underachievement is widely accepted in the popular culture, which puts little value on persistence in the face of setbacks or on the unique pleasure of working long and hard on something personally important. We like things to be fun, quick, and easy. We are much more interested in prodigies and phenoms than in people who make steady progress toward goals. Folk heroes like Paul Bunyan achieve greatness through superior endowment rather than through hard work, while contemporary superheroes use gadgetry or superhuman powers and never break a sweat.

To avoid hard work we have lowered our standards. Low standards have infiltrated our institutions and become woven into public policy and the fabric of daily life. Advertisers routinely suggest that to be young and hip is to be clueless about history, literature, and world affairs and to be suspicious of the snobs who take an interest in them. In the 2000 elections an Ivy League graduate candidate for the United States Senate denied having heard of E. B. White in order to evince "just folks" appeal and avoid showing elite intellectual interests.[1]

The last vestiges of substance to concepts like excellence seem to have evaporated, particularly in academia. The Study of Higher Education, which traces an eighty-year decline in college general education requirements, demonstrates that nearly every major university now awards a severely diluted bachelor's degree.[2] Many university English majors are no longer required to read Shakespeare or Chaucer. In a particularly egregious move, the University of California at Irvine gave freshman English students the choice of writing a weekly essay about either a piece of assigned literature *or their favorite TV show.* Universities decry the problem of rampant grade inflation, but at Irvine instructors were told to grant senior English majors As no matter how they performed, since they would otherwise have trouble getting into graduate school owing to—you guessed it—grade inflation at other universities.[3] Ninety-one percent of Harvard seniors received honors at graduation in 2001, and one out of every two grades given was an A or A–.[4]

Standards and test scores for our public schools lag behind not only other nations but behind where they used to be.[5] Psychologists were alarmed, for example, when a revised form of the Minnesota Multiphasic Personality Inventory (MMPI) a test often used in hospital settings to diagnose serious mental illness, was released in 1998. The old version, from 1948, required patients with a sixth-grade-level reading comprehension; and the new version required an eighth-grade reading level. The ensuing controversy about the higher reading level was diffused only when the revision task force announced that the two versions actually require identical reading abilities, since what was considered sixth-grade level in 1948 is now considered eighth-grade level.[6]

In the midst of all this dumbing down, it should be no surprise that the term "overachievement" has come into play. Exactly what does this term suggest? Can a person actually achieve more than he or she is capable of? Or are overachievers people who achieve more than they *should*—that is, more than other people expect of them, or at a level that makes others uncomfortable? I believe it is the latter. We have come to a point where our expectations are so low that aspersions are cast when someone puts out exceptional effort. In that case, everyone should be overachieving!

Diminished standards surround us, encouraging us to lower our expectations for our own lives, and our emotional investment in them, even in life in general. We lower our expectations of, and demands for, relationships, self-knowledge, intellectual cultivation, and personal achievements. Virtually no one escapes these influences.

In a popular culture fascinated by the instantaneous, gadgets, and the promise of all things labor-saving, grand ideas wither and heroic pursuits pass from fashion. When I looked closely at my own life, I saw that I too sometimes delayed things that were important to me, postponing them for an indefinite future moment, that I also muted my passions or held too narrow a vision of what was possible.

I came to recognize that no matter how productive people eventually become, at some point nearly all of us deal with hesitancies or other obstacles on our way to later achievements. In fact, the biggest difference between those who achieve and those who do not is in how they choose to deal with the obstacles they face. Those who do not combat personal obstacles and cultural trends become numbed and disengaged, inured to lower quality, adept at settling for less, and, as in Plato's allegory of the cave, content with shadow approximations of what they actually need to satisfy their deepest longings.

Unfortunately, those who have the greatest potential for real accomplishment are especially vulnerable to underachieving, and the consequences are destructive not only to them but, cumulatively, to society. Underachievement may be eclipsed by serious drug use, violence, and other grave problems, but its insidious effects are more costly than may be apparent. How many philosophers, artists, and inventors have we lost? And how many individuals with multiple talents have thrown them away?

Underachievement has not gone unnoticed. Use of the term exploded in the 1990s. References to underachieving athletes, underachieving work teams, and underperforming corporations became commonplace in the media. Despite talent, assets, market position, or other obvious advantages, some individual or entity failed to produce outcomes in keeping with potential. People understood the concept, but no one could explain why it happened.

To label something is not to understand it. Too often inquiry and understanding stop once the label "underachiever" has been applied. Furthermore, the label sounds like a diagnosis when it is only a description. Underachievement is neither a disease nor a condition beyond personal control. Though limiting, habitual, tenacious, and destructive, it can be changed without adding "underachievement" to the bloated list of dysfunctions that emerged from popular psychology in the 1980s and 1990s.

All labels are problematic for the value judgments they imply. For that reason some ask, "What exactly is achievement? Who is to judge? Who says there is a right amount of achievement for each person? At what point can someone be said to *under*achieve? And who is to say that underachievement is a problem?"

To address these questions I suggest some alternative ways to think about problems concerning unrealized potential. Admittedly, the process is subjective, in large part because underachievement and achievement are matters of degree—of more or less—along a continuum.

With all these considerations in mind, my associates and I put together a focus group experience for underachieving adults that was part class, part practical coaching techniques, part group process, and part self-exploration. This combination of approaches, in conjunction with my work as a coach, a psychotherapist, and as a facilitator of workshops attended by hundreds of underachievers, is the basis for this book.

If the behavior I have been describing here feels familiar to you—or you see it in a brother, or mother, or son—then I urge you to read on. If you have picked up this book, I presume that you want to change or hope for change in someone dear to you. Change is possible. To simply desire it, however, is not enough. As a minimum it requires a clear-cut decision and a commitment to work hard for a while.

Unfortunately, those who limit their achievement have habitually avoided exactly such a commitment. To make the most of your potential, you must revise these ingrained habits and develop new skills. But you can only do that if you also have clear idea of where you are going and a planned approach to getting there. Otherwise, like a housefly that keeps hurtling itself against a windowpane, you will repeatedly encounter invisible barriers.

This book is a map, a plan, and a set of tools. A distillation of techniques from the Maximum Potential Project, combined with research findings and more than two decades of clinical experience, it provides a practical, effective method for overcoming blocks to realize potential.

Pulling back from your potential, at the most fundamental level, is a kind of abdication, an abandonment of your own best interests. Achieving self-development, on the other hand, is not only life's central mission—it can also be the most thrilling odyssey there is.

# Anatomy of
# a Problem

# Aiming Low

That is men all over. They will aim too low. And achieve what they expect.—Patrick White, *Voss* (1957)

. . . yielding to the small solicitations of circumstance . . . is a commoner history of perdition than any single momentous bargain.

We are on a perilous margin when we begin to look passively at our future selves, and see our own figures led with dull consent into insipid misdoing and shabby achievement.—George Eliot, *Middlemarch* (1871)

It is two days before Christmas, three-thirty in the afternoon. I am being driven across Paris by a personable new acquaintance, Auguste, who has kindly offered his assistance. Having only recently arrived, I am unfamiliar with the city. The apartment I rented must be painted before I can move in, and the painter—who has specified paint from a particular store on the north side of Paris—wants to start painting the day after Christmas. Our mission is to pick up the paint.

Traffic is dense, and it takes more than an hour to leave the heart of Paris. Auguste's lighthearted conversation makes the time pass quickly until we cross a particular intersection. Then I notice that his mood changes abruptly. He says we have missed a turn, and he is not sure how to get back. I ask if I can help by checking a map. He says he took it out of the car and left it somewhere in his house.

Five tense minutes pass. We barely move. Auguste breaks the silence by questioning whether we will make it to the store before it closes. Failing to understand the significance of his remark, I say I am sure we will make it easily. It is just past four-thirty, and even if the store closes at six, early for Paris, we have nearly an hour and a half.

We continue to creep. Abruptly Auguste sets the hand brake and without a word bounds from the car, threading his way through traffic to a taxi several cars ahead. He returns looking brighter and remarking on how helpful cabbies can be. At the next turn we leave the main flow of traffic in search of a particular street. Before long, however, it is clear that something has gone wrong. Auguste stops at a Metro station to study a display map and regain his bearings; we set out in a new direction. Minutes later, no closer to our destination, perhaps farther away, Auguste acknowledges that we are lost.

He hails a woman walking her dog, asks for help, listens, and nods. We now embark on a random, forty-five-minute course through the back streets of semi-industrial north Paris, following a path that, if diagrammed, would rival Moses wandering in the wilderness. Along the way Auguste consults a man working on his car, pedestrians, two policemen, other motorists, and yet another cab driver. On each occasion he writes nothing down but seems to listen carefully and nods knowingly as all point vigorously in various directions and assure us we are not far from our destination. When Auguste attempts to follow what he remembers of their directions, however, we get no closer. At 5:20 P.M. Auguste stops at a neighborhood bar. After loud debate among the patrons we are handed a complete set of written instructions—not on tablets of stone, but we are hopeful.

We complete the prescribed steps and at 5:35 P.M. find Canaan in the form of the long-sought street. Based on the street numbers, we turn left. In one block the street ends. Fatally, we decide to press on in search of where we hope the street will resume. We never find it. At five minutes before six, Auguste phones the store, explains the situation, and asks whether someone can wait for us. No takers, no directions, no mercy; sorry, holidays, already closing.

Auguste is extravagantly apologetic for the waste of time and for his failure to achieve the objective we set out to accomplish. By the time we get back to my apartment the pre-Christmas afternoon has become a four-and-a-half-hour object lesson in the seductiveness of shortcuts, their potential consequences, and how they can go awry.

The style was familiar. A former patient of mine, Charlie, once told me he would rather call ten times en route to ask for directions than bother carrying a map. Witty, engaging, enthusiastic, and perhaps the most charming man I ever met, Charlie pursued shortcuts with fervor. In the early days of computing Charlie became a self-styled computer expert and fix-it doctor—not by consulting instruction books or tutorials, but by plunging in and banging away when others retreated in bewilderment. With his bold approach, he often found seemingly miraculous cures for computer problems, but he could not say later exactly what he had done or why. His wife and dazzled friends began occasionally to report that, while his efforts had solved some immediate breakdown, their computers never functioned as well again. He experienced frequent software crashes and hard-drive meltdowns and spent massive amounts of downtime repairing or replacing equipment on his own computer, but undaunted, he continued to pursue this strategy.

Auguste's navigational strategy—heading in the right direction, then filling in the details as he went along—had functioned well enough to become his standard approach, despite its inherent flaws and occasional obvious failures. On a previous occasion, for example, Auguste had spontaneously set out to find a particular restaurant that served a regional specialty of which he was fond. Having neither the name nor the address of the restaurant, he drove me and our mutual friends on a zigzagging course in the direction of Champs-de-Mars, looking for a street he was sure he would recognize.

Finding the restaurant, albeit five minutes after the kitchen had closed, only validated Auguste's sense of talent for "seat-of-the-pants" navigation. That the kitchen was not reopened for pilgrims such as us he chalked up to sourpuss rigidity on the part of the restaurateur. Sitting down to a meal elsewhere at midnight, Auguste professed that if it had been his restaurant, he would have rewarded such devoted and creative efforts to get there and reopened the kitchen. I believed him.

Bright and talented people like Charlie and Auguste can be easily bored by routine and balk at the monotony of what they consider to be needless steps. To be fussily meticulous is surely one major way to lose time, while to eliminate truly unnecessary steps is efficient and creative. But simply to skip *bothersome* steps creates additional problems.

*Example:* You don't put down the drop cloth before painting, and you have to refinish your floor after painting the walls.

*Example:* You don't check your bank balance, incur overdraft charges, and lose time straightening out the mess.

In Jesus' parable of the five wise and five foolish virgins (Matthew 25), the wise prepare for a long night in advance by filling their lamps with extra oil. They ready themselves for contingencies. The foolish skip this step and run out of oil. Two days before Christmas, in an unfamiliar section of north Paris, true efficiency fell prey to Auguste's inflexible adherence to improvisation. He met his match. He ran out of oil.

Auguste was amiable, intelligent, and in many ways accomplished. Methodically planning a route was hardly beyond his abilities, but he believed he had other abilities on which he could rely if he skipped the map step. Using his method, he got where he wanted to go, sometimes a little late, but not without some interesting adventure that added a dash of color to getting from point A to point B. If he got lost or missed connections, he rolled with the punches and rebounded quickly. If he detained people who had been waiting for him, he was so genuinely sorry, apologized so charmingly, and told the story so disarmingly that few could hold a grudge for long.

Likewise, Charlie failed to appreciate the negative side of his strategy and viewed the problems he encountered fixing computers as due more to the instability of computer operating systems than to his methods. The missing piece of his logic, of course, was that if computer operating systems are unstable, then failing to take this into account is eventually more costly than using a more studied approach.

Devotion to shortcuts caused Auguste and Charlie to fail occasionally at straightforward tasks. But for each, the spice of an unconventional, slightly daring approach not only energized run-of-the-mill tasks but also served to distinguish them from ordinary, "play-it-safe" map- and manual-reading folks. When successful, they either felt brilliant or were convinced that they at least lived charmed lives. Otherwise, their attitude was, "Too bad; you can't win 'em all."

The risk of skipping steps as a strategy is that it becomes a limiting template when applied across the board. You do not strive for things you could rather easily attain if you are unwilling to be patient and systematic when necessary. All major undertakings have their monotonous aspects, and skipping steps does not work when your goals are complex or the stakes are high.

By adopting limiting patterns, High Potential Persons (HPPs) fail to reap the benefits of their exceptional talents and capacities. In this chapter, I sketch a basic introductory portrait of underachieving HPPs, define the problem of underachievement and identify its self-limiting aspects, cite the common characteristics of underachievers, and describe the major self-defeating, potential-inhibiting patterns that underlie the typical underachieving styles. I also demonstrate that even though self-limiting habits tend to lower our standard expectation for personal development, change is possible.

## Habitual Underachieving

Does any of the following sound familiar to you?

- Taking shortcuts and doing the minimum possible, even with important matters
- Spending more time getting ready to work, getting out of work, or getting others to do it, than working
- Inconsistent, insufficient effort
- A lack of real engagement, even in your most important life activities and relationships
- Ambivalence in making decisions
- Planning, scheming, and talking about things but not following through on them

- Difficulties organizing work and organizing your life in general
- Difficulties reaching distant goals due to a lack of appropriate planning and persistence
- Repeated initial excitement for new ventures, followed by disappointment when the novelty wears off
- False starts and frequent changes in direction and goals due to boredom and a desire to start something new
- Failure to complete important projects, whether pleasant or unpleasant
- A tendency to quit things just as you begin to achieve success doing them
- Procrastination
- Being involved with relationships, jobs, or other situations that demand less than your true capabilities and therefore provide less than full satisfaction
- Gravitating toward nontraditional, but unsatisfying, occupations in order to avoid traditional, structured work schedules or the demands of bosses or supervisors
- Being stuck in situations that you thought would be temporary
- Self-doubt and low or varying self-esteem
- Fears that you will not be able to live up to your own expectations or those of others
- Recurrent fears that you are "faking it" or are a fraud and about to be found out
- A paralyzing fear of striving for what you really want because you do not want to be disappointed or fail
- Unrealistic notions of what is actually required for success
- Keeping your options open by postponing serious commitments
- Difficulties in balancing risks and opportunities appropriately and a habitual tendency to take unnecessary risks, or play it too safe, or alternate between the two strategies

- Blaming failures on "bad luck" or other people instead of accepting personal responsibility for them
- A feeling that you are socially inadequate and have fallen behind your peers in reaching important milestones
- A feeling that time is running out, and you haven't gotten started
- Periods of depression

The list is a summary of the characteristics of HPPs with whom I have worked who fell into habitual self-limiting patterns. Your answers can alert you to ways in which you have limited your own possibilities and provide information that will help you begin to change your course. The greater the number of statements to which you said yes, the more likely it is that you have adopted at least some similar patterns. Identifying the tendencies can go a long way toward being honest with yourself about the degree to which you may have already cheated yourself of a fuller self-realization.

If you agreed with many of these items, you are not alone, and your situation is not hopeless. Self-defeating habits and mediocre expectations and efforts toward goals are commonplace. There are tens of millions of dancers who don't dance, writers who don't write, and athletes who quit and wonder what might have been—gifted people who shone briefly, then for one reason or another disappeared. They are everywhere. In boardrooms and bedrooms, in faculty lounges, from athletic fields to medical schools, in every age group, in every human activity, and across every racial, ethnic, and socioeconomic group, people achieve less than they could or abandon what they really want to pursue.

If you saw yourself in this list, it is not that you are down and out or do not achieve at all. To external observers, you may even appear to do well. You know, however, that you could have gone further but instead settled for something less—something easier, more conventional, or apparently more practical—and perhaps either never found or chose to leave behind what burned in your heart.

Perhaps your talents are abundant. You may have demonstrated extraordinary early capacities, learning more quickly at school or excelling more easily and expressively in dance, poetry, athletics, or music than many of your peers. Things that others struggled to learn perhaps came to you almost effortlessly. You had potential for real accomplishment, yet somehow, somewhere along the line, something unraveled. There is something you have never fully expressed in work, creativity, relationships, or other significant activities. Something in goals or follow-through has been lacking.

What is missing? What crucial internal capacity remains undeveloped and is undermining your real success? Is there something about talent itself that becomes a burden or otherwise contributes to your underachievement? Or is there some fear that prevents the expression of your talent and consequently your fulfillment?

Unfortunately, for reasons we will explore more thoroughly, the more gifted a person is, the greater is the likelihood he or she will fall into underachievement. Research on our very brightest high school students demonstrates that an astonishing 50 percent of them underachieve academically.[1] Though these statistics are startling and disturbing, academic underachievement is only one way in which potential is stifled and satisfactions are diminished.

When extremely gifted people carelessly squander their prodigious talents and make a lifestyle of minimal accomplishment, other people take notice. You may know someone who had a genius-level IQ, sailed through college, completed her dissertation and everything else for her doctorate except perhaps for her oral examinations, but at the last moment turned her back on what she had learned, became a bohemian, and drank herself to death at an early age. Or you may know an extremely gifted writer or astonishingly talented musician who also seemed to throw it all away.

Underachieving, however, is by no means confined to the extremely gifted or to the reckless, and sometimes it does not result in extreme gestures or actions. Many talented people slide into far less attention-getting patterns that nonetheless limit their accomplishment and fulfillment. I've met few people who did not feel that with minimal additional effort they could do much more, and I've met almost no one who felt he'd tapped his full potential.

Even if you agreed with only a few of the statements from the list of self-limiting patterns you may still know something about squelching potential. Whether by conscious choice or default, whether to an extreme or subtle degree, if you ignore personal ambitions, give less than your best, and accept less than you want, you cut back on your possibilities and limit who you are.

## Choice Points

Cindy, 37, has dated extensively but never married. She feels that her intimate personal relationships are a barometer of her inner feelings about commitment that she does not fully understand. Her relationships, other than one that spanned three years, have all been brief, eighteen months or less.

For a long time she felt that she was holding out for the perfect soul mate, but she recently met him, and a crisis has resulted. His genuine interest and caring and her attraction to him have provoked a series of mild panic attacks and an urgent review of her past relationships. She is beginning to take seriously the idea that a real relationship, not a perfect one, is possible.

Cindy feels that she has not done much that is truly significant with her life. Her on-again, off-again real estate sales career, though successful, is of no personal interest, and she feels that it is time to make some important decisions. She is at a crucial choice point.

▲ ▲ ▲

Gazing out a corner window, dark eyes casting about, Ronald strokes the stubble on his chin and announces that perhaps he should have stayed with the idea of becoming a professor. In a more animated voice, he says that once he had thought it was his true calling. He liked the working conditions, the atmosphere, the possibility of influencing young minds—he even liked college towns. In graduate school, however, he found his doctoral program in history to be "all about narrow, pedantic analysis" and the professors, arrogant.

He sampled various majors and dropped out several times, troubled by what he regarded as serious problems with "the whole philosophy of higher education." When he paused to reevaluate his goals, he worked at jobs he felt might teach him about real life—bartending in the Virgin Islands, driving a cab in Denver, serving as a courier to Thailand and Cambodia. He always maintained that there was plenty to learn on the street and through travel. He kept a journal that he still thinks could be the basis for an interesting travelogue.

While briefly pursuing premed studies, he met a nursing student, Tina, moved in with her to split expenses, then married her, because he suddenly realized "how wonderful she was." Tina's career has paid the bills and allowed them the flexibility to move, but he feels her growing impatience. He feels impatient too. He had hoped he would be much further along by now.

In the pharmaceutical sales job he took to pay off student loans, he often engages in long, philosophical discussions with physicians' receptionists when he should be moving on to other calls. He has not relinquished the idea of going back to graduate school but knows it would create further delays and more debt. At 38, he feels the clock ticking and wants to believe that his store of life experiences will serve him well at some point.

▲ ▲ ▲

► Stacy is attractive and animated, a youthful and trim 46-year-old. A vegetarian and organic gardener, she works out regularly. As a teen, she found many possibilities beckoning to her. Though a good student, an excellent graphic artist, an exceptional swimmer and diver, a gifted gymnast, and an excellent dancer, she dropped each of these activities one by one. She quit gymnastics, for example, when coaches encouraged her to enter serious competitions. She delayed college for a year to continue to study dance, then abruptly quit dance and started college when invited to join a professional company. She then dropped out of college and did not return for twenty years.

Stacy moved to San Diego from the East Coast for the climate and worked for varying periods as a flight attendant, cocktail waitress, real estate agent, and aerobics instructor, while selling skin-care products and dietary supplements on the side. A talented cook, she seriously considered opening a vegetarian restaurant but decided at the last moment that it would just be too consuming. Since moving to the Bay Area on her fortieth birthday, she has worked on and off at health clubs, done some catering, and completed coursework in both nutrition and massage therapy but pursued neither professionally. She rises to the top of everything she begins, but nothing holds her interest for long.

With some probing, Stacy confesses that her dream has always been to try her hand at choreography, but despite having maintained contacts in the dance world, she has not done so. When I ask why, she puts her hand to her chest and whispers, "What if—after all this time—I don't like it, or I'm not any good at it?"

Stacy's life has not been devoid of color or interest. She has chosen her own path and gained experiences she does not regret. But she has repeatedly played it safe at important junctures. She feels far behind her peers in terms of maturity and milestones that now seem belatedly important to her. Does she want to marry? Is it too late to bear a child? Does she want a serious career? She knows that she cannot delay these choices any longer.

People do not—and should not—necessarily always stay on a single path. We evolve. But the circuitous routes of Cindy, Ronald, and Stacy show that in pursuing anything you inevitably reach a point at which progress requires raising the bar and making a more serious commitment. When faced with this choice, each of these three people repeatedly stepped back from the brink and eventually paid a price.

I am told that for a staggering percentage of art school graduates, the last work of art they complete is their final project before graduation. After finishing school—away from instructors, assignments, expectations, fellow students, and an environment that supports their work—they stop. Though making a living as an artist presents problems, one would presume that art students knew this when they began their studies. How to explain their letting go of something that seems so central to their being? Do they finally tell themselves that they do not have sufficient talent, or does the leap from "art student" to "artist" seem too daunting?

Sometimes artists, athletes, writers, musicians, or mathematicians turn their back on a talent or passion because they have opened themselves to some other vital pursuit or form of expression. But often they do so because they have reached a choice point and decided to avoid the next level of commitment, thereby forsaking an interest or gift that had nourished them in ways of which they were not fully aware.

Everybody encounters choice points now and then. Should you seek a deeper, more demanding personal relationship or remain with someone shallow but seemingly safer? Should you take that new position with more complicated duties or stay put? Should you choose the course with the more challenging instructor or the one with the easy grade?

A decision to step back from an intense commitment may seem innocuous and even reasonable. You have only so much time and energy, you say. Why not take a breather? Besides, you cannot excel at everything. There are times to favor practicality over passion, leisure over exertion. Moreover, what if you put heart and soul into it and come up short—then where will you be? And anyway, you tell yourself, who wants to be a driven workaholic? Why not enjoy life?

One such choice, however, may define you if you follow it with a similar choice at the next juncture. Gradually it becomes your habit to take less demanding, less threatening paths, and relinquishing one possibility after another, you put an upper limit on your happiness and your life loses vividness. Enjoyment in life comes from many sources, and striving toward goals is one of them. If you systematically eliminate the particular pleasure of pursuing and mastering something meaningful, eventually you stagnate. Much of the celebrated restlessness that arises at midlife stems from the recognition that you have surrendered opportunities and jettisoned forgotten dreams for no good reason.

Sometimes it takes a while to realize just how far you have drifted and how often you have taken the easy way out. For some time you may have enjoyed resisting demands, found it clever to dodge work, and viewed yourself as brighter, more ingenious, and slyer than the slogging drones whose vapid lives are devoid of spontaneity. If you took a certain pride in a cool aimlessness or made slacking a conscious lifestyle choice, you may have thought of your resistance as principled. Some HPPs, well into midlife and beyond, continue to recount the stories of things they got away with and ploys they used to dupe others, as if those were life's finest moments.

Underachieving HPPs present a conundrum to those who wish to motivate them. Major corporations that invest heavily in staff development and incentive programs often find that the usual methods—seminars on organizational skills and time management, performance management reviews, heart-to-heart talks, appeals to reason, sanctions and rewards—fail to influence those with a habitually self-limiting style. Inspirational and motivational materials help only briefly; they may even backfire. All interventions fail or may even strengthen resistance when they do not address the underlying issues. Moreover, attempts by others to motivate an HPP can suggest indirectly that the problem *should* be resolved by someone else, if only they could supply the cure that would finally make a difference, but until then . . .

For this reason, people who try to help often withdraw their efforts and retreat to nurse vague hopes that the HPP will somehow blossom belatedly. Others give up and write off underachievers as terminal— uncoachable, unteachable, and unwilling to change. In 1998, for example, the Ford Motor Company dealt with the problem of gifted but low-achieving personnel by paying them bonuses to leave the company.[2]

If you feel you have been hounded about your potential and what you should have done with it, you too may have resisted attempts to change. It can be difficult at times to separate what you *don't* want—

more pressure from others—from what you *do* want for yourself. You do, however, need to keep them separate in your own mind. Once you do that, you may, like many others, search feverishly for a way to get going and close the gap in your life by finding a way to change.

No matter where you are at this moment or what else you have tried, this book provides the steps necessary to begin making real progress. To change most efficiently, you must understand exactly what you are up against.

## Putting Limits on Your Life

Having described the problem of unfulfilled potential, I turn now to definitions that provide an alternative way of thinking about it. These definitions focus on the underlying nature of the problem and the internal processes that produce underachievement. Clearly not all HPPs become underachievers in the extreme classic sense of the term. And there are HPPs who more or less fulfill their potential. But many HPPs underachieve by intentionally or unintentionally placing limits on their lives. For this reason I will, for the rest of the book, mostly refer to HPPs who underachieve as self-limiting HPPs or SLHPPs.

■ You set limits on your performance through your choices. When you have talent, as measured by tests or the appraisals of experts, and you do not develop that talent—to become a creative chef, a superb mechanic, a skilled gymnast, or an outstanding teacher—your behavior is *self-limiting*. If you score well on IQ tests, for example, you can expect to do well in school. If you do well in school, you can expect to perform well in a career that expresses your interests and aspirations. If you do not do what you are capable of doing well, you are engaging in self-limiting behavior.

The assumption in this definition, that self-limiting behavior is a choice, may run counter to your experience, and it may even feel like some kind of accusation. You may not recall ever having consciously decided either to limit your accomplishments or to sabotage your efforts. You may also feel that you would never have chosen your current situation; on the contrary, you may believe that you have knocked yourself out trying to make progress only to have encountered bad luck or unexpected circumstances. Both may be true. But choice is also an integral part of this equation.

First of all, you do not have to recognize or acknowledge that a choice exists in order for it to exist; you can choose and not know it. You can even choose by default—that is, choosing not to choose is also a choice.

Second, because most people consider whatever they do habitually to be normal, you may have accepted self-limiting behavior not as a choice but as simply the way you naturally are. It may not have occurred to you, therefore, that you made many choices in the process of becoming who you "naturally" are. That is, what feels normal and natural now *was* once a matter of choice. When you can recognize the element of choice, you have the opportunity to make a new one.

Try the following simple exercise. Take off your wristwatch and place it on the other wrist. Then leave it there for a day. Notice whether it feels unnatural or odd, and whether this feeling changes.

There is, of course, nothing "natural" about your choice of wrist on which to wear your watch; it is simply a matter of habit. Notice the way you apply hand cream or shave, or get into and out of the shower or bath. You always do these things in the same way. Change them, and notice how you feel. The point is that you can continue unhelpful, self-defeating habits because they feel "normal," and you can balk at very useful changes because they feel strange at first.

No matter how natural it may feel, limiting yourself and limiting your effort is self-defeating. What could be more self-defeating than betraying your possibilities of success by your own actions?[3] Anytime you avoid seeking a goal without paying sufficient attention to the consequences, a bullet from your own gun is likely to wind up lodged in your foot. We have already taken a long look at Auguste's and Charlie's shortcuts. Here are a few more simple examples of self-limiting, self-defeating choices:

► Certain she will fail her college chemistry final, Ophelia decides not to study for it. She fails.

► Chris, who hates public speaking, has waited too long to turn in the slides for an important presentation and is generally unprepared. He botches his delivery and is not asked to present again. At his next performance review, however, the incident is noted, and he is asked to develop a self-improvement plan. His bonus is less than he had anticipated.

► Damon, 19, is transferring to a new college and has three weeks to get in shape for a mile run that he must complete in under six minutes to be able to try out for the water polo team. He has never run a mile in under seven minutes. He has not yet gone to the track. In session I learn that he feels pressured by his mother, a former competitive swimmer, and he would rather play water polo only for fun.

► Ed, given a full athletic scholarship for baseball at a major university, has dropped out of school before the first season began because he has already had an argument with the coach and doesn't like the feel of the campus. He abruptly transfers to another school, forgoing his scholarship, but is unaware that the transfer entails sitting out a season. Angry about having to wait, he withdraws from school. When he enrolls in a two-year college a year later, he has not yet completed a credit or played an inning.

► Dan, a chronically unemployed computer programmer who has complained about being treated unfairly in employment interviews, realizes in therapy that though he is uneasy about continuing to live off his wife's income, he has been ambivalent and uncertain about returning to work. To avoid confronting these feelings or discussing them with his wife, he has systematically undermined his chances of being hired by subtly belittling job interviewers and the policies of their firms while telling himself and his wife that he would like to get a job.

Dan's self-sabotage allows him to attempt to convince his wife that he is being misunderstood and victimized, and that his failure to be hired is beyond his control or demonstrates a lack of appreciation for candor by the company. In fact, she understands his ambivalence and his desire to disguise it. But his lack of candor has damaged their relationship.

Self-sabotage like Dan's is a convoluted and calculated risk conducted slightly outside of conscious awareness.

Anything, however, that reduces your possibilities for success, happiness, growth, accomplishment, or well-being is self-limiting and self-defeating; some self-limiting choices bring immediate consequences, while others do not show up for some time.

Here are some everyday ways in which people limit themselves:

■ They have an inkling that something is missing and may feel empty and disappointed, but they do not look inside to seek a solution. Rather, some people prefer not to journey within to contact curiosities, interests, ambitions, a sense of vocation, or something that would inspire awe. Consequently, their lives lack force, a central axis, a mission, and passion.

■ Other people are aware of their wishes but leave them suspended and hypothetical, as if having the wishes were enough and actually taking steps to fulfill them would be an extreme move or even impossible. A family friend maintained a dream for over thirty years of traveling to Antarctica without ever taking one discernible step toward that end. He knew the stories of the Scott and Amundsen expeditions and their lessons: Scott was flashy, glamorous, a dashing adventurer with little sense of planning, and Amundsen was a plodder, but Amundsen got to the pole while Scott and all of his men died. My friend animatedly talked of whaling stations and wooden ships and of how great it would be to see it all. But his dream stayed in the "Wouldn't-it-be-great-to-see-Antarctica?" stage and became nothing more.

■ Some people go a little further and explore possibilities for pursuing their dreams before abandoning the extension class in French, the guitar lessons, or the workshop in ceramics as foolish. Instead of following through on their wishes, they dump them as if doing so were a sign of maturity or realism. Or they disqualify themselves as too old, too young, too married, too single, too divorced, or too timid to pursue those dreams.

■ Still other people are sure that, though they must delay what they want to do for now, when circumstances permit, they will act. New pressing circumstances continue to arise, however, and for some reason or another it is never the right time. They never decide *not* to go ahead, but they never begin.

▶ Deirdre, 42, has circled the same course offering, "Beginning Drawing," in the quarterly civic arts course catalog for four years. For sixteen consecutive quarters she has planned to sign up but then let the deadline pass. She once got as far as sending in a deposit, then backed out and had it refunded.

By contrast, some people who do achieve success, but by dint of talent and dutifulness more than enthusiasm, can reach milestone after milestone without being truly engaged and remain cut off from a life that is passionately meaningful to them or expresses their unique potential.

▶ Jim, a married, tenured university professor, says, "I'm nearly 45, and I've never done anything full-out with all my might, because what I have been doing is not really my idea.

I have cleared all the hurdles and done what I was supposed to, but I wonder if I have ever lived a single day as my own. It's time to change that. I want to find something I feel passionate about."

Jim achieved career success by adhering to the imperatives and conventions of his academic career. But by not tapping into what Sartre called the "frightening freedom" of inner sources of direction, he has left out something crucial.

All forms of self-limiting behavior are costly in terms of well-being. All forms of self-expression that tap into curiosities, talents, or deeply held interests, when pursued to excellence, are deeply nourishing. Despite this, people turn away regularly from the very things that satisfy them most. Sometimes they do it with the best of intentions. Sometimes they do it without even realizing they have. They awaken one day as if from a slumber and wonder how they reached this point.

Consider for a moment the ways in which you put limits on yourself and thereby defeat yourself. Take out a sheet of paper and list things you do that limit your effectiveness.

Now take a look at what you put on your list. How do you undercut yourself? Are you casual when the situation demands formality? Are you lax when you need to be strict? Are you strict when a more easygoing approach would serve you better? Do you procrastinate, give less than your best effort, or fail to meet deadlines? Your list could range from being unpunctual to deciding not to try in situations where you fear you won't succeed. Notice when and how you make these choices. Pay special attention to choices to escape situations that present some kind of threat to your competence and self-image.

## Self-limiting Styles

Self Limiting High Potential Persons (SLHPPs) etch enduring pathways over time by repeating their characteristic self-defeating methods. If you habitually limit your achievement in one significant area of activity, you are highly likely to limit your achievement in other areas, and this tendency in turn can evolve into a general *self-limiting style.* There is nothing fixed, however, about the following self-limiting styles. You may see characteristics of yourself or someone you know in more than one. The styles outlined here do not exhaust the possibilities. Each one represents a way in which what is possible and realizable in a person's life is habitually prevented or lost.

**Sleepers:** The style is seen most often in people from families or communities without models or traditions of high achievement. Sleepers lack accurate information about themselves, the extent of their talent, and ways to express it. Absent this background, they can go on for a long time without accurately perceiving their gifts, or they may never choose to investigate them.

> ▶ Dominique, 34, grew up in a small town in the rural South, and though she was a good student, her evangelically religious, working-class parents subtly discouraged college education. Not wanting to inflate her opinion of herself, they rarely spoke about her intelligence; as a result, though she knew she was smart and wanted to go to college, she did not have a clear measure of her real abilities. They could not afford to send her to a Bible college and were fearful of the effects of "Godless" secular education.
>
> Dominique joined the army and in her late twenties enrolled in college, testing high enough to take freshman honors classes. She began a career as an elementary school teacher but now wonders whether she has sold herself short in terms of her aspirations.

A lack of support, opportunities, and guidance often plays a role in the failure of sleepers' to make early contact with their possibilities, as does a parental preference not to spoil or inflate them. Many, like Dominique, eventually choose to take their own steps of discovery.

Sleepers who remain sleepers prefer to stay asleep and do not investigate the possibilities.

**Floater/coasters:** Floaters are aware of their capacities, see opportunities, and often are even pursued by others, but they rarely act on their possibilities. Some are temperamentally hesitant and slow to join in, while others can appear to be emotionally withdrawn or indolent and lacking in ambition. But the chief characteristics of floater/coasters are their passivity or lack of initiative and their disengagement.

▶ Dave, 38, feels that he is going nowhere and does not understand how he arrived at this point. He aimed no higher than to graduate from college with minimal effort. Without actively deciding to do so, he shut the door on curiosities, interests, and opportunities. Intrigued by the campus radio station, he intended to drop in and check things out, but he graduated without ever having made the time.

He passed on other things too—an invitation to join the debate team, a professor's offer to work on a research project, and two promising relationships with women he admired. All of these opportunities required taking actions that he simply never took. In retrospect, Dave says it pains him to think about all the possibilities he let slip away.

Dave majored in business for no particular reason and has worked mostly in sales without enthusiasm or much success. Over the years people have suggested to him that he has the ability to do any number of interesting things, but the opportunities always require more initiative than he feels he possesses, and he concludes that they "probably weren't meant to be."

Passive floater/coasters like Dave keep their aspirations low and settle into a groove for reasons of comfort or availability, or they drift from one marginal situation to another without distinction or satisfaction. They usually wind up taking jobs through the recommendations of friends or chance circumstances and almost never by mounting an intensive, self-directed job search. They entertain ambitions only briefly, because achieving them seems remote. Consequently, they fail to take actions that would, if pursued even a little more, make a significant difference.

**Checkmates:**   Because checkmates have multiple but contradictory ambitions that they cannot resolve, they feel hopelessly immobilized and unable, no matter how hard they struggle, to break free. Checkmates are not passive; they simply feel they cannot extricate themselves from their mutually neutralizing ambitions and wishes.

> ▶ Nadia, 35, is stuck in a paralyzing struggle involving four equally strong wishes, action toward any one of which will eliminate all the others as practical possibilities. She wants to have a child; wants to grow professionally and switch to a corporate environment; wants to leave advertising altogether, and go back to school for a master's degree in psychology and a marriage, family, and child counseling license; and wants to stay put because she feels loyal to the people with whom she works, who respect her creativity, gave her a start, and pay her well.

Checkmates like Nadia are often perfectionists who unconsciously fear change and arrange their lives so as to make change virtually impossible. Checkmates often come to therapy with very mixed feelings about actually finding a solution to their dilemmas, and they respond fearfully to suggestions that change is possible. Many SLHPPs—seeking to be checkmated so as not to have a reason to make a move—find something wrong with every solution, every path, every possibility.

**Extreme Non-Risk-Takers:**   Extreme non-risk-takers focus totally on minimizing risks in their lives. This does not mean necessarily that they lead totally inspired lives, though sometimes they do. But because they try to avoid situations in which they could possibly fail, they gravitate toward occupations, relationships, and activities that do not present serious challenges or reflect their real interests. Stacy, the vegetarian former dancer whom you met earlier, is one version of an extreme non-risk-taker, at least in terms of her ultimate potential.

Some extreme non-risk-takers idealize some activity or dream to such an extent that they do not allow themselves to pursue it for fear that doing so might spoil the image of perfection. They fear not only that they might not be worthy of the dream but also that it might disappoint them; in either case, they prefer not to know.

**Delayers:** Delayers make postponing major decisions and commitments their central life theme. Rather than avoiding actions with long-term consequences, delayers indiscriminately delay *all* choices and commitments, great and small. Their lives come to revolve around actions they prefer to put off until later, so that they procrastinate, miss deadlines, and accumulate stacks of things they have not dispatched.

Above all, delayers postpone the onset of adult life and instead drift, evading permanence, commitment, engagement, and seriousness. Delayers are SLHPPs who fear the demands of adult life and prefer to postpone settling down for as long as possible. Delayers often sample many things superficially. They are dabblers and dilettantes who keep trying out possibilities but do not engage fully in any of them.

**Stop-shorts:** Stop-shorts are aware of their abilities, entertain ambitions, and make significant progress, but firmly hold back from fully reaching their goals. Their arrested progress is often related to a fear of completing a life step or of taking on some role or responsibility that will be the outcome of fully realizing an aim toward which they have long striven.

Stop-shorts characteristically work hard up to a point but stubbornly keep their efforts just below the threshold necessary for success or completion, staying poised on the brink of a breakthrough. Stop-shorts take course requirements but do not complete the thesis, get a licensure or certificate but do not embark on the related career, finish law school but never pass the bar, suffer writer's block and fail to complete the novel, or in some other way take a marginal role within their field. As a result, they keep demands and expectations in check, assuage their fears, and avoid the possibility of becoming exhausted or overstressed.

Sometimes the barriers they fail to cross are incomprehensibly trivial.

> ► Marla, 31, has completed the requirements for a master's degree in education through a suburban satellite campus of a major university. When the university closed the satellite campus offices, it provided graduates with instructions on how to contact the education department at the main campus in order to have an official degree granted. Five years later Marla still has not contacted the department.

Some stop-shorts, wanting recognition for nearly completed efforts, attempt to create a special niche that lays claim to a special status. This is commonly seen among those who complete doctoral coursework but do not complete their doctoral dissertation and affix the label Ph.D. A.B.D. (All But Dissertation) to their name as if it were a recognized title.

Frequently perfectionist and anxious, stop-shorts prohibit themselves from actually attaining their goals out of fear they cannot quite define.

**Self-Doubters/Self-Attackers:** Self-doubters/self-attackers block their success by holding high standards they feel they can never possibly meet and for which they therefore seldom strive. But rather than rationalizing or blaming others for their lack of effort, they selectively attend to and mercilessly emphasize their own faults and failings to such an extent that they do not appreciate what they *do* accomplish. They are actually highly ambitious, but because they cannot tolerate anything but an idealized kind of perfection, they do not allow themselves to enjoy partial success, thus reducing their incentives to try.

Paradoxically, self-doubters/self-attackers use self-criticism to defend themselves. By attacking themselves, they say, "Though I did not achieve all I could, at least I do not accept myself," and by being their own worst critic they cast their minimal efforts as unwillingness to settle for mediocrity. They cannot escape knowing, however, that they have settled for a different kind of mediocrity, for which they still attack themselves.

If they make an effort and achieve distinction, they often feel that their accomplishment was a fluke or something insignificant. They feel that they do not deserve approbation, because their success came too easily or quickly, or because they achieved it without a mentor or validation by a luminary in their field. They therefore fear that because they have not paid their dues, they have cheated and will at some point be unmasked as frauds.

Self-doubters/self-attackers avoid demands and expectations because their fear of failing to meet their own standards makes it difficult for them to keep commitments in a timely manner. As a consequence, self-doubters often fall behind and attack themselves further for inconsistency and unreliability. Though they fear failure, success is equally punishing because it brings more demands and expectations. All of this leaves them anxious, overwhelmed, and exhausted—fugitives from their own talent and victims of their own success.

**Charmers:** Charmers are the kings and queens of good intentions. They generally mean well but are inclined to use their engaging interpersonal abilities as a substitute for effort. They travel light, do not take things as seriously as other folks, and often use a disarming sense of humor to diffuse criticism when they let things slide. As a result, they develop a pattern of unreliability that includes missed deadlines, inadequate preparation for meetings, and incomplete assignments for which they apologize profusely, or make you feel that things are simply not as important as you make them out to be.

Charmers often make promises that sound good to them at the time but that they cannot possibly keep. Consequently, they tend to disappear in the middle of projects without a phone call or word of explanation to those relying on them. They rationalize their disappearing act by finding fault with the other person or with the project and further justify their actions by touting their original sincerity in taking on the project. By putting the project out of mind, they hope it will disappear and that others will let the matter drop, because they really do not want to disappoint or to be seen as unreliable. Telephone calls and e-mails may go unanswered as they try to avoid an unpleasant conversation, but if called on their actions, they can react icily or counterattack.

On the strength of their convincing self-presentation in interviews, charmers occasionally secure positions for which they lack adequate or at least conventional preparation. They then use their unconventional preparation as a reason to avoid conventional rigor, claiming with a touch of humor that they approach things from a different paradigm and work "outside the box."

Charmers vary from those who are pleasant and mostly use charm as an asset to smooth difficult interactions to those who consciously use their charm to manipulate others and recruit them to step in and take over unpleasant tasks or cover for their lapses. The latter's conspicuous use of sweet talk, ruses, and petty cover-ups contains a distinct whiff of charlatanism. People enjoy being around the former type of charmer, but given enough time, people within organizations mistrust the latter type. Manipulative charmers who wish to remain within such a system resort to playing politics skillfully in order to survive.

**Extreme Risk-Takers:** Energetic, mercurial, and impulsive, extreme risk-takers limit their success by habitually taking unnecessary risks. Occasionally they achieve in dramatic fashion, but they are inconsistent because their reckless tactics minimize success and often ensure their own defeat. Extreme risk-takers would rather fail in a blaze of glory than succeed through patient effort. Charlie, the self-made computer expert, is an extreme risk-taker. Sometimes these SLHHPs take unnecessary risks to avoid a success they are not ready for. In the film *Tin Cup*, Kevin Costner plays just such a person, a club pro golfer who, through extreme risk-taking tactics, squanders his chance to win the U.S. Open.

**Rebels:** Rebels aggressively strike out at the world and go against authority. Often suspicious of what they feel are others' attempts to exploit or control them, they struggle fiercely or simply refuse to comply. The character portrayed by Jack Nicholson in *Five Easy Pieces* is a rebel. He comes from a patrician family devoted to the arts, and as a child he was a prodigy at the piano, but later, feeling that he could not meet his father's expectations, he abandoned the life he knew to work in the oilfields near Bakersfield, California.

> ► Michael, 31, remembers that as a high school senior, barely making the grades to stay eligible for football, he hated his 160 IQ because people expected him to perform well in school. Angry with his parents for imposing demands, he did not want to do well and give them the satisfaction of being able to say, "I told you so," or, "Isn't it nice the way he has finally come to his senses?" Instead, Michael avoided this concession in what he thought was a battle for his freedom.

All underachievers rebel to the extent that they refuse to comply with demands or give only the absolute minimum instead of seeing demands as opportunities to explore their strengths against a standard. Only a few, however, are as hostile as rebels in expressing their unwillingness to conform.

**Misunderstood Geniuses:** Misunderstood geniuses build a life around the notion that their talent sets them apart from others and that their lack of success is due to the misunderstanding, jealousy, and incompetence of others. Misunderstood geniuses are the ones who use excuses as a cover; they are the ones saying that their ideas are not mainstream or are too advanced for others to understand them, and therefore they cannot get the support they need. Authentic geniuses are often not appreciated or accepted in their time, but the real Van Goghs somehow find a way to work and create.

Misunderstood geniuses can be temperamental and storm off the set, court, or playing field, throw things, and generally engage in impressive displays of emotion designed to direct attention away from their shortcomings or failures and to suggest that something or someone else is causing their failure. At the same time, these theatrical displays are meant to demonstrate how desperately they want to succeed and how hard they are trying.

**Best-or-Nothings:** Best-or-nothings are highly talented individuals for whom success comes easily, or not at all. If there is the slightest hint that they could be other than the very best at something, they have no interest in participating at all. Best-or-nothings progressively drop one activity after another when something threatens easy supremacy. In this way, best-or-nothings are extreme low-risk-takers, but because they are characteristically very ambitious, they do not eliminate challenges if they feel they can succeed at the highest level. Best-or-nothings are closet perfectionists and holdouts who think they should save their abilities and efforts for something really worth doing rather than spend energy on ordinary tasks. They do not attack themselves but progressively narrow their lives down to a few activities at which they clearly excel and in the process leave behind many interests and enjoyable activities.

A re any of these patterns familiar to you? Have you known someone who stifles his or her potential? What about your own potential? Perhaps you recognize a glimmer of something, a stray thought or a tendency in your spouse or lover that you previously dismissed in yourself.

## Healthy Achieving

So what does it look like when people express their potential in a healthy way? Do they just stop having fun and lose all their charming idiosyncrasies? No. Rolling out an initial public stock option by age 30 does not mean you have achieved your potential, any more than obtaining degrees, or other external achievements. In Hermann Hesse's

*Siddhartha*, a young man, after a lengthy search for fulfillment, achieves self-realization as a mere ferryman taking passengers across a river. His achievement is an internal victory. Voluntary simplicity can be a reasoned choice, while climbing to the top of some heap may be someone else's dream but for you it's a ticket to unfulfilling loneliness.

There can be no formula—no recipe in this book or any other can dictate your goals, aspirations, happiness, and fulfillment. If someone tries to thrust such a formula upon you, run from it. Fulfilling your potential doesn't mean that you start living a perfect life, either. But when diverse SLHPPs with whom I have worked began to realize and express their potential, they spontaneously moved in some common directions.

■ They raise the bar. They set higher standards for themselves and others and devote greater attention and effort to things that matter to them. They become less acquiescent and stop settling for less—from others and for mediocrity from themselves.

■ They stop hoping and gambling that their lives will magically work out, relying on others to pick up the slack, and making excuses. Instead, they begin to follow through. They take risks, learn from their mistakes, and make peace with their fears in order to move toward realizing the ambitions that matter to them. They stop setting limits on themselves and on what is possible and also drop their self-destructively extreme risk-taking behavior.

■ They feel freer, lighter, happier, more passionate and childlike, and at the same time, curiously, often more sober, serious, and engaged. They move toward new adventures and challenge their limits for the sake of growing, testing, and experimenting. A life of fear becomes a life driven by learning.

■ To have time to do what interests them, they become methodical and businesslike in administering their legitimate obligations and responsibilities. They realize that time is the commodity they cannot buy or get back, and to live a life that matters to them, they take seriously what they do with their time.

■ They also accept that no matter how talented they are, or what path they choose, life inevitably presents dilemmas, riddles, and problems. They don't solve all, or even most, of them but instead of automatically retreating from problems that are difficult, they take them on as opportunities to learn.

This progression begins by seeing clearly the fundamental prerequisite for doing things differently. The commonplace cocktail party question, "What do you do?," could be a most intimate and searching one if truly answered. Responding honestly requires you to put a spotlight on your path and how you actually spend your time. If you are willing to look at your life clearly and unflinchingly, you will immediately gain from this kind of self-scrutiny.

The "What do you do?" question is usually an inquiry about your work and career, partly because work, for most of us, is the thing we do with the greatest amount of our time. Besides work, meals and grooming, management of ordinary affairs, and travel here and there, what is left?

Most of us want a personal life, and we devote at least some time and attention to relationships, finances, leisure pursuits, and perhaps self-development—to understanding ourselves and developing our faculties. In all of these areas, if you consciously aspire to a higher standard—one worthy of your possibilities—you leave the ordinary default position behind to pursue something more satisfying, not in career at the expense of your personal life, or in your personal life at the expense of career, but in everything you do. You have to *intend* to live this way, though. It does not occur on its own.

Are you an expert on your life, your happiness, your fulfillment? Do you know your talents? Is there something inside that you have thus far held back? Or does your life strike you as a series of empty patterns?

If you continue to aim low, you live a truncated version of your life. Like a feral child, you accommodate to a life alien to your nature, but by blending in, acquiring standards through fear or by osmosis, and adopting a kind of psychological protective coloration, you gradually lose your essential idiosyncrasies, set aside your possibilities, and do your best to howl like the rest of the pack, while barely noticing what goes unexpressed at your core.

More is possible. If you have read this far, you may be one of those who wants more.

# The Cradle of Mediocrity

I cannot tell how I entered it, so full of sleep was I about
the moment I left the true way.
> —Dante Alighieri, *The Divine Comedy* (1310)

There is no second such example of inevitability as that
offered by a gifted young man narrowing himself down
into an ordinary young man, not as a result of any blow of
fate but through a kind of preordained shrinkage.
> —Robert Musil, *The Man Without Qualitie* (1953)

**A** kind of charge fills the room as she enters, her family in tow like a celebrity's entourage. Animated, comfortable, and friendly, the family begins to talk, but it quickly becomes clear who is holding court. At 15, Amy is master of ceremonies for her family's very congenial talk show. She is funny, self-assured, and bright.

The family speaks openly and nondefensively about their concerns. They are there, they say, because Amy is doing poorly in high school. They mention her intelligence, which is easy to observe. Her grade point average for her first semester is a low 1.3 despite the fact that she vowed to get serious about her schoolwork once she got to high school. Amy's father, Doug, says that he doesn't want to fight with her and that because she is so likable it's hard to confront her.

Doug remarks that her friends are bright and do well. On cue, Amy recites the semester grade point averages of each friend, verifying her father's statement but pointing out that not all of her friends are doing well. There are more laughs.

I ask her whether she is embarrassed by her performance when it's compared to those of her friends. Her answer is quick and self-possessed. "No, they know I am bright; I'm just not trying."

Doug turns to me with a tone of seriousness. "It's so frustrating. She's got what it takes. Why won't she just *do* it?" I give him a nod, suggesting that he ask Amy that question, but when he turns to her, he drops the seriousness, whines exaggeratedly, and asks her why she forces him to play the role of heavy. "You know what I want you to do. Why don't you do it?"

Failing to understand what Amy needs from him, Doug wants his intentions understood without having to be direct and insistent. A Stanford graduate and owner of a Silicon Valley firm, Doug is both bright and skilled enough to handle this situation well. His predicament with Amy is illustrative of one particularly flawed response of parents who themselves underachieve when faced with the challenges of rearing HPPs. Amy's behavior also demonstrates the false steps SLHPPs take that can limit their success.

To understand why SLHHPs engage in perplexing, self-defeating behavior, we must map out its origins in the long period of early childhood dependence. Early displays of talent provoke potent reactions in parents and authority figures and establish the foundations for standards and expectations that have lasting effects, including an influence on the SLHHP's emerging view of the world and his or her place in it. Low demands and well-intentioned but mistaken efforts to help actually engender, then reinforce, certain outlooks that become the basis for a self-limiting style. Finally, the passage into adulthood becomes the first major and defining test of whether the SLHPP will accept the challenges of adult life or remain prey to the patterns of his or her youth.

The exchange between Doug and Amy in my office is replete with clues as to the kinds of things that go wrong on both sides of the parent-child equation. Doug is unwilling to play the heavy and asks

Amy *why* she doesn't do her work rather than insisting that she do it. Rather than risk damaging their warm relationship with a confrontation that could mushroom into estrangement, he prefers to finesse the situation.

But by seeking to avoid contention with Amy entirely, he capitulates to her resistance and undercuts his function. Parents, in addition to being supportive and affectionate, need to firmly guide adolescent children. Amy needs a clear sense of direction. Without it, she harbors questions about Doug's commitment to her progress and his opinion of her possibilities. Privately Amy asked me: "He always asks me why I don't do my work. Why doesn't he *make* me do it?" Without a clear directive, she behaves as if schoolwork were not a requirement when she clearly knows it is. Meanwhile, in typically self-defeating fashion, she ignores the harm she inflicts on herself. SLHPPs such as Amy face the same universal developmental tasks as other children but are endowed with extraordinary capabilities for making rapid progress. We must go back to early development to see what goes wrong.

## Out of the Starting Blocks

On paper, things look rosy. As a human, you are born with far fewer limits on your behavior than other species. Wired-in instincts do not dictate behavior, and a complex brain makes virtually limitless learning possible. But life does begin with some drawbacks. Whereas other species can move about within hours after birth, you are born physically helpless and unable to fend for yourself. Before you can survive independently, you have to mature physically and serve a long period as an apprentice human being engaged in two major efforts: learning how the world works, and acquiring the skills necessary to operate within it. You learn the world by observing, forming impressions, organizing them into discernible patterns, and, after acquiring language, receiving direct instruction. You acquire skills by trial and error, learning from mistakes, modelling, imitating, direct instruction, and practice.

At any given moment your ability to observe is limited. Though your brain is nearly limitless, your capacity for attention is not. You can tune into only a minuscule portion of the multitude of things happening around you.[1] You must focus and shift your attention repeatedly to form connections between things and selectively look for similar things to happen again under similar circumstances. This process of having to focus and shift inevitably causes you to miss certain things. As you continue to focus, shift, and observe again and again, however, you form concepts or templates—repeating sequences—and construct a picture of how things work.[2]

When your concepts are new and provisional, they remain in the foreground of your attention, ready for revision when further information comes in.[3] If patterns you perceived do not hold up, you adjust them or look for new connections between events. Conclusions that survive repeated observation become as building blocks for an evolving, ever more complete understanding. But since you do not know when you have observed enough, forming concepts always involves a leap of faith—of presuming or believing and reaching a conclusion. This is always going on with each new relationship and with each new situation.

Your concepts begin simply with basics like night and day, wakefulness and sleep, and hunger, thirst, and satiety. More subtle regularities take longer to discern, and some events easily lend themselves to mistaken interpretations. When does Mother come, and when does she not, and why? Hard to know exactly. Once you acquire language, you then learn from what you are told. Your caretakers share their understanding of the world and view of limits, and at first you lack a basis for refuting these notions. Eventually you learn that what people tell you is sometimes incorrect or applies only in certain circumstances.

Here we arrive at the heart of what you need to understand about your picture of the world. It is actually a working model, not a one-to-one representation of reality. You form concepts, and if they seem to work, they recede from conscious attention, no matter how accurate or inaccurate they are. Out of conscious awareness, they operate undercover and become increasingly resistant to change. In time what began as speculation becomes a given—like night and day, sleep and wakeful-ness, or the sound of your mother's voice—and you feel yourself *know-ing* it as a fact.

Each piece of the puzzle guides your interpretation of what you experience next. Thus, what you conclude first guides your selective attention and heavily influences what you look for and conclude next.[4] The earlier you develop a concept and the more central it is, the greater the number of other concepts that build on it.[5] As a result, your picture of the world, though subjective and inevitably inaccurate, becomes increasingly solid and more difficult to change. It is important, how-ever, to note the word *difficult*. Difficult does not mean impossible. With astute, well-thought-out efforts, you can revise long-held beliefs.

Part of the difficulty is that, with time, your ideas, thoughts, and skills—from feeding yourself to language, to tying your shoes or driv-ing a car—become habitual and function in a manner similar to instincts in other species: they are automatic and operate without conscious attention.[6] Habits, however, retain a major noteworthy advantage over instincts. With conscious attention, you can alter or replace them.

## Who You Are

When you learn the world and develop skills, you are anything but pas-sive. You are far from an inert lump of clay upon which events stamp their imprint. You engage in learning and actively direct it. And you are a formidable influence on your world. You certainly influence your parents, for example, at least as much as they influence you, if not more. (For a parent, having a child is a life-changing event; for a new-born, having a parent is a given from the beginning.) While you go about learning, you conduct your investigations and observations in your own characteristic and inimitable way.

Researchers Stella Chess and Thomas Birch have identified nine dimensions of temperament on which infants vary[7]—sensitivity, activ-ity level, adaptability, frustration tolerance, soothability or distractibil-ity, regularity rhythmicity, emotional intensity, mood, and approach withdrawal. Your particular profile of temperamental features provides a set of fundamental starting points for your personal way of exploring and reacting to the world.

Additionally, Herbert Gardner has identified eleven forms of intelligence—among them, the standard intelligence measured by IQ as well as interpersonal, intrapersonal, musical, and physical intelligence, which also lend themselves to preferred ways of learning.[8] Different combinations of temperamental features and types of intelligence influence what you express, attempt, and move toward or away from in different situations.

Temperament and intelligence have a genetic component, but their effects can be modified. For example, it is possible to increase your tolerance for frustration no matter where you start on this continuum. But temperament and intelligence are stable enough that they are fundamental givens for you and a steady point from which you move.

Your temperament and intelligence not only affect the way you learn but also influence people's reactions to you. Talent alone has a way of getting the grown-ups to stand up and take notice, but add a pleasant manner and you have them vying to play a role in this child's life, oversee his or her development, and perhaps even bask in some reflected glory. We have consistently noted that an extraordinary proportion of the SLHPPs with whom we have worked have been easygoing, personable, charming individuals. We observed these characteristics in both the adults and children in the project. Parents who have brought in their children often describe their gifted but inadequately performing offspring as "easy" or "wonderful," stating, "We don't have any complaints other than this school thing." We began to wonder if their easy manner and social pleasantness could somehow be part of the problem.

Psychologist James Cameron, a temperament expert and founder of The Preventive Ounce, notes that an easygoing disposition usually consists of a particular combination of three temperamental factors: high adaptability, low emotional intensity, and predominantly positive mood.[9] Highly adaptable children do not resist changes in routine and are therefore a less disruptive influence. Children of low emotional intensity have relatively milder reactions to frustration and fewer and briefer emotional upsets. Children with predominantly positive moods are less fussy. When the three factors combine, parents have a child who adapts easily to change, does not have strong emotional outbursts, and is not generally fussy. A parent can easily soothe such a child by distracting him or her from upsetting situations and directing the child toward a calming substitute activity.

This temperament combination also allows parents to remain calm and feel effective in their roles. If the child is also high in interpersonal and intrapersonal intelligence, he or she manifests sensitivity to and intuitive grasp of human relationships and a keen awareness of feelings and motivations. The result is a child who is highly skilled in human relationships and parents who are gaga over their luck in having such a child. This unbeatable combination of personal attributes would appear to afford both parent and child every possible advantage, but a little further down the line this same combination creates problems.

Here is what I came to understand: People with an easygoing temperament and good social skills are most likely to be granted favors, exemptions, and special considerations. People cut them slack, come to their rescue, and generally want to help out. As one SLHPP said, "I have learned that if I am pleasant and mean well, people make allowances." A winning smile has gained SLHPP's with whom we have worked everything from extended deadlines for papers to passing grades on driver's license tests. Objectivity and the state of gaga rarely go together. Those who are gaga over their beloved are rarely sober judges of that person, and gaga parents are often not realistic about their child's needs. Instead, they tend to remain enchanted and inclined to feel that the fairy tale simply *must* have a happy ending. Like Doug, parents of easygoing, adaptable SLHPPs usually want to stay on good terms with their exceptional child and tend to make their child's activities the central axis around which the family revolves. When the wrong person, no matter how outstanding, is in charge, even momentarily, the tail wags the dog, and predictable problems arise. Children easily draw unwarranted conclusions about their own significance, and this can have destructive implications. If you were such a child, a significant amount of work is required just to escape the corrupting influence of having been too indulged, too central, and too much in charge of the figures who should have guided you.

HPPs come in all stripes and can be of any temperament. But regardless of their particular combination of temperament and talents, gifted children—including those for whom social relations are difficult and who are singled out for ridicule by their peers—are usually a source of pride to their parents. Talents displayed early—before beginning school you may have already read, written, played a musical instrument, or shown precocious artistic or physical abilities—influence people's reactions. If you were like the SLHPPs with whom we have worked, you were extremely intelligent (a study of one group of fourteen, for example, showed an average IQ in excess of 150, where 100 is average) and had multiple talents. Such talents suggested that great possibilities lay ahead, and your parents celebrated their good fortune. And you, yourself, got used to things being easy.

These experiences of easy success along with your parents' pride and special attention, helped you acquire a particular emerging picture of the world and your place within it.

## Who You Think You Are

A central concept in your developing picture of the world, and one upon which many other concepts are based, is the one you come to hold of yourself: who you think you are. Your self-concept develops in the same way as other concepts about reality. You start from the backdrop provided by your temperament and talents, and then you observe, listen, and experiment. From birth you are always being scrutinized, discussed, and described, particularly in terms of your temperament and talents. You sense the interest of parents and other caretakers and from it gauge your importance. Although you are not able to sustain a stable picture of the world and an image and appraisal of yourself until about age nine, these descriptions and early experiences begin to give you early notions about yourself.[10]

A crucial fact about descriptions: they are never neutral, even if intended to be. They are always evaluative. No one is just a redhead, just athletic, or just gifted. Descriptions always implicitly mean something, positive or negative, or they would not be singled out for mention. A little girl in Charles Schulz's "Peanuts" comic strip, for example, says that people expect more of her because she has naturally curly hair.

The point is that what we react to most strongly is the implicit meaning of what is said, not the explicit content. The power of implicit communication is in fact at the heart of the effect of indirect hypnotic suggestions.[11] In a similarly indirect fashion, descriptions tell you not only what people think of you but implicitly what they *expect* from you. If you are described as "easy" or "wonderful" or "lazy," you understand that further easiness, wonderfulness, or laziness is expected from you. The attribution "lazy," for instance, primes you to (1) consider future behaviors as instances of laziness, (2) come to view yourself as lazy, and finally (3) behave lazily to fulfill the expectation or demand for further laziness. To be described as lazy injects the dimension of laziness into your world of meaning, and thus sensitized to it, you begin to deal with things in terms of it. Whether or not you wish to fulfill the expectation of more laziness, it is difficult to ignore the communication. If told you are bright, gifted, athletic, or beautiful, the internal process of being primed is the same, and demands and expectations come along as well.

Once you consider yourself lazy, however, laziness serves other purposes: you now have a justification for not mowing the lawn. The new concept also prompts you to find or create supportive evidence of this characteristic. That you are lazy is the explanation for any example of lazy behavior, and additional lazy behavior is proof that you are lazy. All descriptions operate in this circular, self-reinforcing fashion. Soon you see laziness as a personal attribute or inherent quality—like having blue eyes—that is enduring and seemingly unchangeable.

Of the thousands of thoughts you have in a day, a huge proportion are self-descriptive.[12] By repeating, "I'm a good cook," "I'm smart," "I hate getting organized," "I hate paperwork," "I'm an underachiever,"

"I'm shy," and acting accordingly, you impose continuity on your otherwise fluid existence and strengthen what you already believe.

The conventional wisdom is that when a child senses that he or she is important and special, that should be the basis for positive feelings and exceptional performance. But with SLHPPs something breaks down. How, more precisely, does this occur?

Being treated as special and seeing yourself that way, along with being able to do things with ease, become internal benchmarks from which you draw a wide variety of inferences. You can easily come to believe that life will always be like this—that you will always be able to do wonderful things with a flick of the wrist, that you are one of the lucky ones, one of the chosen few, and that you will continue to lead a charmed life.

But life is not so straightforward and "gifted" or "bright" as descriptions turn out to produce complicated and unexpected consequences, especially at school. As you prepare to make the transition to school, your pictures of the world and of yourself are sketchy, incomplete, and fluid. Most of what you have learned thus far, except from television, has come from experiences within your family. Primary and secondary school span the entire period of childhood dependency. Over this long formative period your picture of the world inevitably changes, and school itself is a basis for many defining experiences that can become a part of what else breaks down.

## Off to Conquer the World

On the day he broke a long-standing record by playing in his 2,131st consecutive baseball game, a feat spanning more than fourteen years, Cal Ripken Jr. was asked about his family's reaction. He replied that the record came on his daughter's first day of school, which, for the family, overshadowed everything else, including the record. Mr. Ripken's possible modesty aside, what makes a child's first day of school so significant?

School makes formal demands, sets standards, and renders evaluations. When a child begins school, he or she leaves the protective circle of family for the first time to go out into the world and see how he or she measures up. School represents both the child's first step in the long process that leads to leaving home and the parents' first step of letting go. Success in school has a meaning beyond simply learning skills. School performance is taken as early evidence of how you will fare in the world for this reason: at school you respond to the demands, standards, and evaluations and develop attitudes toward them that influence situations throughout much of your adult life.

Parents accustomed to their own success expect their gifted child to be successful too and communicate their confidence implicitly. It seems to them that they have only to pave the way or simply step back and watch the marvels unfold as their child realizes his or her promise. A child thus fortified leaves to take on the world with no reason not to expect the best from himself.

Once at school, HPPs' talent, temperament, physical skill, and even physical attractiveness usually work the same magic they did during the early years at home. Teachers covet gifted children for their classrooms, coaches want them on their teams, and adults in general vie for their attention. After all, being "gifted" means that things come easy, and schoolwork is no exception. HPPs experience few school challenges that they do not master with ease. For the bright person, reading is like breathing and math is a game. For those with other exceptional talents and gifts, life in this new extension of the world is a kind of paradise.

▶ Sofia understood quickly that she was smarter than others, and by the time she finishes fourth grade she has reached three fundamental conclusions. First, having learned things easily— horseback riding, the cello, speaking Italian—she is sure that learning will always, and should always, be magically easy. Second, knowing that she has special abilities, she feels that she will lead an exceptional, perhaps almost magical, life. And third, after receiving special treatment, including being excused from school and some assignments for her special activities, she has begun to expect special treatment and to feel that special rules and special exemptions apply to special people.

Sofia's conclusions are typical for SLHPPs in the primary grades. Not having to expend effort becomes the internal standard. Not opting to or wanting to expend effort often follows.

Over time school teaches a variety of lessons beyond the ABCs. School is Life 101, and the classroom is always open. Formal instruction has direct and intended effects, as well as indirect and unintended ones. School presents lessons in designated instructional periods, but much of what children learn in school is incidental to curriculum and outside designated instructional periods. That learning derives instead from the structure and the processes, both formal and informal, that school presents. HPPs draw conclusions about school and life from its tasks and requirements, rules and procedures, differences between what is stated and what is practiced, and from their interactions with school personnel, from instructors, janitors, and attendance secretaries to other children.

Attending school exposes children to all sides of reality, including unfairness, conventionality, uniformity, scapegoating, and cruelty. It also teaches cheating, taking shortcuts, jockeying for attention, and lobbying for delays and extensions on deadlines.

Indirectly, school teaches potentially valuable and essential lessons by exposing children to doses of boredom and frustration from which they can learn patience and persistence. Furthermore, at their best, schools provide children with opportunities for cooperation, tolerance and forbearance, vision, creativity, and expression of their ideas and their idealism. Unfortunately, however, schools often fail to capitalize on learning possibilities in exactly these areas.

At their worst, schools stifle autonomy and initiative and block personal engagement by other common practices that teach HPPs unintended lessons:

■ *Putting everyone on the same page:* Unintended lesson: be normal, adhere to a mediocre standard, rein in your intellect and your curiosity, slow down. Result: HPPs are not challenged, do not engage their intellects fully and spend long, unproductive blocks of time waiting for others to catch up. In the meantime they are disengaged and feel bored.

■ *Punishing efforts to work ahead:* Unintended lesson: everybody should be the same, don't be curious, fit the program, don't try math problems not yet assigned, don't read ahead in books. Result: curiosity and personal initiative are muzzled, school becomes absurd, trivial, and again, boring. HPPs lose respect for school as a serious endeavor.

■ *Granting free time as a reward for completing assignments:* Unintended lesson: study is unpleasant and something from which to escape as quickly as possible in order to do time-killing activities. Result: the bright are disengaged for significant periods of time instead of being given new, interesting, more challenging work with which to grapple.

■ *Giving homework that merely repeats classroom work:* Unintended lesson: learning is not a process of discovery, teachers are not imaginative, school has little to teach. Result: skipped assignments, habits of evasion, contempt for homework and for school.

■ *Giving massive amounts of homework rather than briefer, more intense, truly challenging assignments:* Unintended lesson: all of the lessons already mentioned, plus teachers are cruel and sadistic, and learning, at least at school, is a form of punishment. Result: anger, incomplete or skipped assignments, habits of evasion, hatred of homework and school.

■ *Using incentives like grades to encourage learning:* Unintended lesson: you would not want to learn what we teach for its own sake, you must be bribed or otherwise coerced into studying, we know of no other way of evaluating and encouraging improvement than giving you a grade. Result: cynicism.

HPPs report complicated reactions to school, ranging from appreciation to disappointment to regret and scorn. Essentially, they express appreciation for the brilliant individual teacher or two who inspired them, disappointment over the lack of intellectual stimulation or rigor, regret for the wasted time, and scorn toward a system too simple-minded and oriented to test-taking, right answers, and competition. HPPs often claim that school encouraged them to have low aspirations, teaching them to maneuver for grades rather than to appreciate the intrinsic pleasures of learning.[13]

This is generally not the attitude with which these children begin school. My second daughter could not wait to finish preschool, start real school, and have important homework to do like her older sister. Kindergarten and most of first grade disappointed her because they lacked serious assignments. When required to write her first story in second grade, she was ecstatic. Finally, something to sink her teeth into—something real! For the days she worked on her story she went about the house singing to herself and stopping by to talk about her story. On the night before the story was due she came to me with a problem I hoped she might always have.

"Daddy," she said, "I don't want to end this story. I like it too much."

Years later I remember wincing as I passed by her room and overheard her say to a friend in a weary tone on the phone that the English paper was supposed to be four pages but three would probably be enough. Fall from grace.

Most SLHPPs similarly began school with enthusiasm, then became gradually dismayed by the slow pace or some other feature of school that frustrated them or insulted their intelligence. By the time they reached middle school and adolescence, they had become critical of instruction, particularly in social science and government classes where they believed they were being fed a propagandized diet of conventional American values while school policies, classroom discussion, and freedom of expression were restricted and nondemocratic.

At some point SLHPPs abandon the joyous pursuit of learning and begin to simply go through the motions, more or less disengaged, and investing less and getting less than they could.[14] The larger problem, previously noted, is that cynicism, habits of resisting, and withdrawal of effort become engrained and carry over to all future situations involving assignments, demands, and standards.

## Balking

People experiment with resisting demands throughout life. Unreasoned noncompliance, a mistaken thrust toward independence, is noteworthy at age two, and then again during adolescence when the psychological processes that ultimately lead to leaving home begin. Underachievement in school—particularly among boys—begins as early as second grade, but during adolescence peers gain greater importance as we realize that we will assume our position in the world with them. Establishing credentials with them is therefore significant. One bogus shortcut to acceptance is to disparage or reject adult demands, and school is an available place to do it. Not surprisingly, the onset of poor school performance in HPPs most commonly occurs during adolescence.

You may remember becoming less cooperative about completing work or at some point balking at school demands. Tellingly, when HPPs balk, especially the first time, those in charge take a rosier view of that resistance than they do with those less bright, and they tend to see it as a temporary, understandable phase. The state of gaga, with its accompanying lack of objectivity, prompts parents and teachers to overlook indiscretions, become solicitous, or intervene to rescue rather than firmly nudge SLHPPs back into the correct mode. In the process the adults in charge implicitly suggest that perhaps the requirements do not always apply.

> ► Blake, a 42-year-old bicycle messenger, comedian, and comedy writer, remembers that when he forgot to finish a take-home math sheet in third grade, his teacher winked at him and said, "Well, you already know that, so don't worry." By fourth grade he had begun randomly filling in the boxes on answer sheets for class reading assignments because his teacher did not

check them. He could make a few marks in a row of boxes and skip reading stories that bored him.

Neither teacher intended Blake to develop a pattern of desultory responses to assignments that he then carried forward into adult life, but each encouraged it. When the people responsible for demanding the best from gifted young people grant exemptions, they become accomplices and co-conspirators in the petty crimes and cover-ups that soon follow as sorry substitutes for honest effort. In every case of stifled potential with which I am familiar, the people responsible for insisting that the SLHPP meet demands were not adamant, even if they wished or intended to be. By cutting slack, they modeled inconsistency and sanctioned a style.

And then there is the matter of dispensing the wrong kind of help. Sometimes it starts with a single, significant rescue.

► Kendra, 29, a temporary worker in computer-related fields, was consistently at the top of her class in the early primary grades. When her grandparents came for a visit just before a major fourth-grade assignment was due, she uncharacteristically lost track of time and waited until the last night to build a replica of a California mission. Since the situation was unprecedented and the assignment constituted a major portion of her social studies grade, her entire family, including Grandma and Grandpa, stayed up late, made popcorn, drank hot chocolate, and built the mission together in a cozy, memorable family project. Kendra could not have missed the message that she had the support of her family (a plus) and their wish that she do well (mixed).

Early the following autumn Kendra put off another assignment until the last night, but this time there were no houseguests and no real excuse. Her father and mother counseled her to get better organized, and then she and her family took another step toward a pattern of occasional last-minute rescues. Kendra continued to do well in school but sensed that her parents' wish for her to do well was even stronger than her own and that they were willing to do what was necessary to make it happen. Though her parents warned her that they would not continue to bail her out, if a class grade was riding on the outcome of an assignment, they stepped in.

When her family intervened the first time, Kendra learned something new about the way the world works: rescue is an option. Each ensuing rescue increased her balking because being rescued reduced her immediate anxiety. But it sabotaged an opportunity for her to learn skills related to managing long-term projects.

In a matter of three or four assignments over the next two years, Kendra missed enough crucial rehearsals of new skills to add a new conception to her view of herself: that she was not good at meeting deadlines and needed help with them.[15] Once Kendra was in the Maximum Potential Project, she realized that she had re-created the same pattern of good intentions and last-minute faltering at work.

We now come to something crucial. When, as a consequence of balking, expectations and demands falter, "gifted" as a description begins to produce complicated and unexpected consequences. Such a description is only positive when accompanied by a supporting context of *explicit* demands for excellence and the kind of specific support and encouragement that lead to accomplishment based on these abilities.[16] Real accomplishments provide a tangible reference for the "gifted" label and certify that the gifts have been road-tested and authenticated in real time. A history of achievement leads to a circular, self-reinforcing experience that builds real confidence and produces a willingness to approach new challenges.[17]

Without explicit demands and support, being labeled "bright" or "gifted" is akin to being conferred an aristocratic lineage—a heritage that exists independently of what you do with it. The difference is that the labels "bright" and "gifted" come with *implicit* demands, and when appropriate *explicit* demands are lacking, the labels sit there like ticking bombs.

On the one hand, these labels tell you that merely being bright or talented is enough, but on the other hand, the longer you go being praised for talent alone, the more anxious you become about the time when you will be required to deliver. *What if the time finally comes, and I do not live up to expectations? What if when the time comes, it is not so easy? What if others are just as good as I am, or better? What if I really do not have the stuff?* This is the double-edged sword of being known for having talent but having done little with it: the label exerts a steady force of expectations concerning an indefinite future moment. The result is a desire to escape.[18]

Furthermore, an easygoing temperament and keen social intelligence turn out to have unexpected drawbacks too.[19] Social skills and charm make it easy to finagle dispensations, and adaptability, low emotional intensity, and positive mood—the raw temperamental materials for the prized easygoing style—become liabilities by making it easy to switch activities when faced with difficulties instead of locking in on an objective and gutting it out. As a result, these qualities can work in tandem to provide a temperamental backdrop for fickleness, dilettantism, glibness, superficiality, and a lack of persistence.

Serious achievements require perseverance, which in turn requires tolerance for frustration. Tolerance does not develop if you habitually steer away when you encounter upsets and setbacks. Emotional intensity, despite its drawbacks for parents and occasional annoyance to others, can provide the boost that keeps you going in the face of setbacks—a fuel for persistence and a component of determination, stamina, and commitment. To abandon efforts beguilingly is no better than to abandon them any other way.

Those who learn to power their way through when things get tough learn the value of repetition, drill, and grunt work. Their successes, which stem from their ability to work implacably and consistently, eventually supersede those achieved on the basis of talent alone. If you previously neglected learning these skills, the good news is that it is not too late to learn them. You merely have to realize what you are up against. Temperament makes a strong initial contribution and provides starting points, but the effects are not absolute. They can be modified by surprisingly small amounts of consistent effort.

When a child like Kendra starts to experience a certain amount of drift and damage is done to his or her commitment, skills, and school performance, adults express concern about a problem they call under-achievement, and they apply the label "underachiever" for the first time. This label, like other labels, soon makes demands for more of the same behavior while serving simultaneously as the justification for it.

Does the label mean a child has been demoted from the top rung? Not usually, or at least not right away. Because the label says reassuringly that you have talent you aren't using, it is actually comforting. Unfortunately, however, it makes adults nervous and sets off a chain of events that often strengthen SLHPPs' resistance.

Usually the fix-it brigade is the first on the scene. To the adults involved, the label is a call to arms, and they embark on a kind of holy crusade for causes and solutions, while initiating further rescues. For you, being gifted has always meant perks and privileges that you are happy to retain. This is who you are, and what you have always been known for. Who would you be if you were not bright and gifted? Rather than relinquish your image, you turn your gifts over to the full-time defense of your status as gifted instead of deepening your dedication to developing your abilities.[20] As you take the path away from developing your abilities, however, your life begins to lose a certain luster as you bypass becoming accomplished.

## Defending an Image

To defend their image, SLHPPs eventually resort to tortured logic. The starting point is usually simple. Remember what Amy said when I asked her if she was embarrassed by her school performance when compared to her friends' performances? "No, they know I am bright; I'm just not trying."

The story Amy told to others was one she wanted to believe. She preferred to see herself as capable but unmotivated. Failing to try was familiar, and in the past it had usually not even prevented her from getting good grades. But Amy was on to something with her excuse. Social psychologists have found that on tests of mental ability, "not trying" is universally accepted as a valid explanation for poor performance.

The enticing internal justification for not trying follows these steps: *If I fail, but I wasn't trying, it doesn't count. If I don't try, I therefore can't fail. If I don't try, I can still maintain that if I had tried I could have succeeded. If I try and do not succeed, I cannot use that excuse. Therefore, it's better not to try.* In the extreme, even if you gain another label—slacker, lazy, late bloomer, or undependable—under no circumstances will you lose your membership in the HPP club.

Failing to try is a standard and commonplace way in which people defend an image of competence. Experimental subjects, told that they were performing poorly on a test of skill and that other subjects would be informed of their results, were observed to withdraw effort deliberately from that point on in the experiment. By withdrawing effort, they could explain their poor results later by saying, "I didn't try."

Roy Baumeister, a leading researcher on this ploy—dubbed self-handicapping—tells the following anecdote. A touring chess master used to take on all comers as long as he could start any match two pawns down. Reason? If he won, his victory demonstrated impressive skill. On the other hand, if he lost, the explanation for his defeat was set up in advance: the two-pawns-down start. Self-handicapping always involves building in some form of excuse ahead of time to explain a possible future failure.[21]

Self-handicapping strategies bear remarkable similarities to those developed in a classic experiment in which children were allowed to choose any strategy they wished to obtain success in a simple game.[22] Some chose to convert the game into a test of skill. Other children were focused on defending an image and chose to play the game in ways designed to protect themselves from the implications of negative results.

In the experiment, psychologist Stanley Coopersmith invited children one at a time into a large room, at one end of which was a screen with a clown's face and a hole for the clown's mouth. Handing each child six beanbags, he gave the simple instruction: "Toss as many bean-bags as you can into the clown's mouth."

In response, children spontaneously adopted one of three strategies: they took a position directly in front of the clown and simply dropped the beanbags into its mouth; they assumed a position farther away, where success was possible but required a skilled throw; or they went to the back of the room, as far from the clown as possible, and tossed from there. Results? The children throwing from directly in front of the clown were 100 percent successful; those in the middle were moderately successful; and those at the back rarely reached the clown, much less its mouth.

On the surface the groups standing away from the clown, either in the middle of the room or in the back, appear to have responded most similarly. In fact, however, the groups at the two extremes were most alike. Though their strategies appeared different superficially, the children in both of these groups were avoiding a test of skill at which they could fail.

Those in front stood so close to the clown's mouth that they could not miss. No one could contest the apparent success of the number of beanbags they put in the clown's mouth. But they reduced risk so thoroughly that their success could hardly be seen as an accomplishment. On the other hand, no one could say for certain that they could not have tossed in all six from anywhere in the room, had they wanted to. They eliminated the decisive test.

The back-of-the-room group disguised a self-protective wish by cloaking it in daring. Standing where they did, their lack of success was explained by the distance they chose rather than by any lack of skill. They were self-handicappers, so if others tossed in beanbags from a closer range, so be it. Anyone could make a few successful tosses from an easier range. Disdaining the lesser challenge set these children apart and defined them differently. To even attempt such a feat staked an implicit claim of greater skills or of more courage, or both. If they tossed one in, legendary status would await, and as with the group that stood in front of the clown, no one could prove that they might not have tossed in all six beanbags from a different distance.

The middle group treated the task differently. They created a trade-off between success and risk, standing far enough away to introduce difficulty, yet not so far away as to make success unlikely or accidental. They engaged in a contest that tested their skill and focused on the rewards of significant success. Though their choice of position reduced the number of successful tosses they made, each success meant something.

You may observe a relationship between these two self-protective strategies and the self-limiting styles I described in chapter 1. The close-to-the-clown strategy is related to the style of extreme low-risk-takers and to some degree sleepers, floater/coasters, stop-shorts, self-doubter/self-attackers, and best-or-nothings. The back-of-the-room strategy is the style of extreme risk-takers and, to some degree, misunderstood geniuses. Charmers, and others too, oscillate between front- and back-of-the-room strategies depending on the situation.

Coopersmith found that the self-esteem of the two groups at the extremes was low. Failure would have been confirming evidence of their self-estimate and would have made them feel worse. Each preferred to avoid a direct test of abilities—an overt comparison with others in which they could come up wanting. Their twin strategies for avoiding failure were prototypical and costly protective strategies. Each virtually eliminated the possibility of experiencing a satisfying sense of accomplishment. In this sense, extreme low and extreme high risk-taking are functionally the same.

The attempt to keep an image intact is a crucial underlying aim of self-handicapping. If you look closely at your own history, you will probably find that you have used all three beanbag strategies. In practice, HPPs who limit their success spend most of their time dropping beanbags from the front (avoiding risks entirely), heaving them from the back (self-handicapping or extreme risk-taking), or alternating between these two strategies depending on the situation.

There are, of course, many other ways to defend an image, such as offering an infinite number of explanations and excuses for poor performance.[23] All such defenses, however, are attempts to continue to lay claim to a special status. It is the same in basketball, gymnastics, music, or dance. Whether the excuses are completely accepted or not, making excuses becomes a new automatic habit. If you make excuses, rationalizations, and justifications, you step on a treadmill and employ your intellect and abilities not to toil and extend your skills but to grind out these same rationalizations and explanations, ploys and strategies, dodges and justifications: "I'm saving myself for later." "This wasn't my idea." "I don't get to do what I want." "The coach didn't like me." "The grading was unfair." "Everybody did poorly." "Traffic was heavy."

Note, however, that making excuses is immediately self-defeating and self-limiting. If you complain of unclear assignments, unreasonable demands, being misunderstood or treated unfairly by others, including teachers, mentors, supervisors, project coordinators, former lovers, and ex-spouses, you put not only the blame elsewhere but also the control over your life. Blame others, and you ignore possibilities for exerting control and keep your personal power under wraps. In the arts, for example, saying that your work is misunderstood or that it cannot get the attention it deserves quickly becomes the reason for not starting new projects.[24]

Beyond blaming, SLHPPs rationalize poor performance by denigrating the institution or activity, disparaging the work, or attaching some higher value to something else. The objective is to establish that the problem does not, and cannot, lie with them or their efforts. This chain of rationalizations eventually leads the SLHHP to say, "I don't care," or, "It doesn't matter." One SLHPP student made performing poorly a badge of dubious honor by announcing that his goal was to be class "maledictorian"—the student with the lowest grade point average who nonetheless still managed to graduate. The ironic, slightly elitist bent of the maledictorian is reminiscent of Paul Reubens's Pee-Wee Herman character in the film *Pee-Wee's Big Adventure:* upon falling off his bicycle, he gets up and announces, "I meant to do that."

To preempt criticism, the rationalizations go beyond disparaging the activity to disparaging those who do it well, those who try to do it well, and those who try to do well at anything. Over time rationalizations and justifications become more intricate, convoluted, and tortured.

▶ Tara, 34, remembers that as a high school sophomore she told her mother that she would rather get Cs by not trying than get As and risk having her friends think she might have worked to get them.

Tara's parents bought into her vaunted wish for acceptance by her peers, and they believed that she was still capable of As. But beyond that, Tara framed her choice as more insightful, more dignified, or perhaps more politically correct: she would neither grovel nor join with the philistines in their search for external validation, and she wanted to be certain that her friends knew she stood for something. Simultaneously she could maintain a slightly rebellious air of the unconventional. And while others worked, she had free time.

In reality, Tara *was* seeking validation of her abilities, but without having to demonstrate them. Like Kendra and most SLHPPs, however, the longer Tara skipped out on her work, the less certain she could really be about her capabilities. Putting out effort therefore had two major liabilities: if she worked on a term paper for weeks, like her friends, and received anything less than an A, in her mind she would have done the work for nothing, and the grade would cast doubts on her abilities.

On the other hand, though, Tara soon found herself surrounded by fresh wet paint. By withdrawing effort, by choosing to say, "I could have done it if I had wanted to, I just didn't want to," she froze herself at a particular level and did not develop further. By the time she reached high school she was finding it difficult to maintain her image. The rationalizations grew too complicated, then collapsed. She finally concluded that she was just not cut out for serious work. It was the final link in a chain. She made a stab at college, then settled for sales work at a department store.

▶ "I was pretty independent—maybe I threatened them." Denise, 37, a talented keyboardist and guitarist who is largely self-taught, is talking about some former music teachers—ones whom her parents had hoped would help her develop her musical talent. One by one, she says, they got frustrated and quit working with her. She acknowledges that she just couldn't get interested in boring music theory and formal composition when she could compose directly on the keyboard.

Denise's extraordinary talent made it easy for her to pass over music theory and repetitive drills and to see no immediate negative consequences. But she has never filled in the gaps in her skills and has not really advanced. It is not unusual for SLHPPs to feel brighter or more talented than their teachers and to then use that as the reason not take their suggestions to heart.

Others reach the point of making excuses more hesitantly.

▶ Brad, 34, who had been conscientious and always done well in school, felt that he was betraying his internal standard when he first made excuses. He continued the behavior, however, and gradually made an internal accommodation.

On graduating from middle school, Brad had straight As, not because grades were his objective, but simply because he was bright, took his work seriously, and consistently did it well. He was not a grind; he had a social life and friends and was respected and admired.

When he entered high school, his older brother suggested that if he continued to perform well he could graduate as class valedictorian. Studying had never been about external goals for Brad, and he did not like this new pressure. His internal standard required doing well, and he liked learning. One quarter later Brad got his first B, thus eliminating the burden of his brother's vision. But he knew he could have done better and felt that sense of self-betrayal.

In his sophomore year Brad's grandfather died and his parents separated. He concealed his sadness, confusion, and anger, but in an attempt to gain attention and support he stopped studying and got two Bs and one C. His high school counselor and a college adviser consoled him, telling him not to worry about the grades. They would write letters explaining the emotional distractions to the college admissions boards. With this vaguely sanctioned excuse for lesser performance, Brad reduced his effort consciously, as if it were expected because he had been given permission. More Bs followed in his junior and senior years.

In his second quarter of college, Brad came down with hepatitis, then broke up with his girlfriend just before finals. This time no one else had to make an excuse. He casually declared the poor grades to be "understandable" in light of his illness and emotional distress. The excuse rolled right off his tongue. He did not ask for incompletes so he could catch up because he did not want to ruin his spring break by having to study.

Brad proceeded to settle into a pattern of inconsistent effort and told anyone who asked that he received "As and Bs" in order to avoid directly stating a grade point average of which he was not proud. On entry, Brad's SAT scores had fallen in the 99th percentile. His college performance was decidedly mediocre for his abilities because he had backed away from his conscientious standard. When his father asked how he had done in his final quarter, the boy for whom excellence had once been a matter of course now only mustered, "I was doing pretty well in the beginning of the quarter, but I guess I just sort of ran out of steam." Ran out of steam? That answer never would have occurred to him eight years earlier.

Of course a variety of random events and experiences can contribute to bright HPPs' getting momentarily sidetracked, then drifting permanently from striving. Ask SLHPPs when and why they ceased putting out effort and their responses will vary. Some say they quit early with the first homework assignments in primary grades. Others will say they stopped due to a crucial precipitating incident, for example, a difficult encounter with a coach or teacher who ridiculed their performance, or a move to a new school followed by a loss of belonging, and extended emotional withdrawal or depression. More often than not, however, the withdrawal of effort comes as a slow drift into complacency followed by an inner flame finally dying out.

At the brink of adulthood your pattern of past choices colors your approach to this next defining step. Significant success requires talent. Talent, on the other hand, does not ensure success. More is required. If you coasted here and there but maintained some ongoing contact with goals and striving, you may shake off your torpor and rise to the occasion. On the other hand, if, like Tara, you developed a hardened resistance to striving, you may take any of a number of other paths.

Achievement is the result of continual cumulative effort and only occasionally yields glamorous, magical moments. Moving on from any stage requires taking certain risks.

A lyrically beautiful story from the Sufi tradition relates the dilemma faced by river water as it comes to the edge of the desert and is about to be transformed into vapor and carried away on the wind. The water knows what it is to be water and what it means to be part of a river. It does not know about this other state, vapor. But if it resists this change, it will end up brackish in the sands of the desert. Only if it accepts change will it be carried across the desert to the mountains, where it will condense and fall, to begin the cycle anew with more knowledge.

In life we move from what is known to what is unknown. If you resist this progression, you stop your evolution. If you thought you simply held back in school because you were saving yourself for when things would count, now things count. But if you coasted or skipped over requirements, questions arise about your ability to meet the inevitable challenges of adulthood.

# Settling for Less

For if we think of this existence of the individual as a larger or smaller room, it appears evident that most people learn to know only a corner of their room, a place by the window, a strip of floor where they walk up and down.
—Rainer Maria Rilke, *Letters to a Young Poet* (1962)

Only our concept of time makes it possible for us to speak of the Day of Judgment by that name; in reality it is a summary court in perpetual session.—Franz Kafka, *The Great Wall of China: Stories and Reflections* (1946)

I feel ashamed for all the things I did not take seriously. I had so many opportunities that I treated casually. I lacked humility. I lacked respect. I had the luck of being talented and I took it for granted. I didn't appreciate it.
—Robert, 51, Stockbroker

**M**agic has its limits. At some point you reach the edge of what you can do on talent alone or with minimum effort. At some point things stop being merely easy. Sometime, somewhere, somebody else is smarter, knows more, or works harder, or the task is more taxing and the standards are more rigorous. No one knows when this point will come, but whether it is in school or in your early career, you have to choose how you're going to play it. Just showing up is no longer going to be enough. If you are to remain among the best, you will be called on to extend yourself in new ways. Doing well in one stage of life does not guarantee doing well in the next; people with promise sometimes flame out and fail to make the next cut. Is this moment—the passage into adult life—the moment when you will fail?

# Defining Moments

Besides death and birth, the onset of adult life surely qualifies as the big enchilada of all defining moments. Whatever else adulthood may represent, it signals the completion of the long apprenticeship, the end of the process of preparing to face the world on your own. Now it's time to make good on all that preparation.

From a distance, it might be easy to pass off the difficulty of this passage. If absence of struggle is standard proof of giftedness (gifted = things are easy), does a different equation (things are tough = not gifted) now apply? Even asking the question puts you in new territory. Everything you took for granted is no longer certain. Does beginning work signal the moment when the wheat will be separated from the chaff? Should you quit now and cut your losses—retire and relinquish the mantle of the elite? When the smoke clears, two fundamental choices emerge: go all out, or go with one of the infinite possibilities for bailing and finding the softest landing possible.

If you go all out, you put yourself on the line. If you don't make it big, it could be hard to escape the interpretation that your capacities did not stack up in the real world. On the other hand, if you succeed, what awaits? More demands? And what if you can't step up to these demands, or don't want to? Being ordinary is not good enough for people with extraordinary talent. You could succeed moderately and be considered second-rate—a mere also-ran when you had worked your hardest.

Facing this transition, some settle for what they consider a reasonable compromise and opt for a position close to the clown's mouth, while others seek defiant or risky solutions. Still others attempt to avoid or postpone confronting these questions for as long as they can. In the film *High Fidelity,* three young men take refuge in the sheltered world of a music store, where they consider themselves superior, criticize and ridicule others, and mock those they consider less hip. In truth, they are frozen. It is only when they begin to take risks that their lives take on any color.

As you enter adult life you bring along your history of self-defeating choices and habits from youth. They may have provided momentary escape from uncertainty, but cumulatively they limited your success. What happens in adulthood, when it all counts? Will you shake yourself and awaken?

In this chapter, I examine the crucial transition to adult life to understand the fear it can evoke and the characteristic ways in which SLHPPs react. Newly minted adults face a momentous choice when deciding on a career. I explore in detail the career choices to which SLHPPs are drawn and the characteristic stances they develop toward work. All SLHPPs, whether or not they postpone beginning an adult life, build patterns of avoidance that affect their work, finances, relationships, and leisure pursuits. I consider these, then focus on SLHPPs who, at the end of the line, are consumed by regret and have nowhere else to go but up.

## A Dozen Wishes

HPPs ready to seek a career have plenty of choices. What might you want from a career, an activity at which you spend so much of your life? What would constitute the perfect ingredients for an ideal occupation? Get out a piece of paper and pause to reflect on your own priorities. Then make a list for yourself and compare it to the following one. (Numerous written exercises will follow throughout the book. You might want to write this one out in a suitable notebook in which you will keep other written exercises as well.)

Here are a dozen ways in which you can extract a sense of involvement and accomplishment from a career:

1. *Intrinsic interest:* engaging in activities that are personally interesting to you and worthwhile in their own right
2. *Challenge and stimulation:* solving problems of sufficient difficulty to require a satisfying exercise of mental agility
3. *Personal involvement:* doing work you care about for a cause that matters to you
4. *Significance:* doing tasks that make a real contribution and feeling that what you do matters

5. *Recognition:* having your efforts recognized and appreciated; being valued for your contributions and feeling that you matter

6. *Influence:* having a say in both the job and the enterprise

7. *Creativity:* having the opportunity to contribute ideas and solutions and to receive support for those contributions

8. *Independence:* being able to work independently and make decisions autonomously without constant scrutiny

9. *Control:* having a degree of choice over your work schedule and work activities

10. *Income:* earning a sufficient or comfortable income and benefits

11. *Security:* having the promise of dependable, ongoing employment

12. *Positive environment:* working in a positive environment with congenial coworkers

Significant observations can be made about this list. First of all, it is in no particular order. What you value most about your work could differ profoundly from what others value most. Second, since every career benefit involves trade-offs, the list may contain some that you would never seek. Third, there may be something you seek from work that does not appear on this list. And finally, seeking out certain benefits or all the benefits in one occupation requires a serious level of involvement.

Any list of what you hope to get from your work has a built-in risk: you can use it to avoid taking an imperfect but worthy job. Though ideally you might want all twelve qualities in a job, beware of initiating a long and pointless search for the perfect job. It is a delaying tactic that could cost you any number of positions in which you could learn and grow. On the other hand, beware of bypassing positions out of fear: you could miss opportunities to grow this way as well. Think of where you want to position yourself in relation to the clown's mouth.

Choosing a career is a serious and daunting task. How do you decide at age 22 or 23 what you want to do with the rest of your life? In reality, the process of finding a worthwhile job does not usually involve proceeding from a list like this one. It is a matter of juggling trade-offs. People search for ideal positions but wind up seeking certain qualities in a job that they consider indispensable. Obviously, your beliefs about yourself, about work, and about the trade-offs between rewards and demands weigh heavily as you determine your priorities. So what kind of career should you pursue? The answer to that question comes from tuning in to what is most important to you.

In the abstract, most professions can provide all or many of the dozen benefits I've described. But in reality, professions require advanced training, and poor academic performance can bar you from being accepted to graduate and professional schools. Once you complete the training, most professions make exacting demands and require that you shoulder serious responsibilities and stay abreast of developments in your field through continuing education. The serious demands of the work often cannot be simply turned off when you walk out the office door. Many SLHPPs have little interest in or patience for the regimented preparation and the intense demands.

Furthermore, running an independent professional practice is an entrepreneurial enterprise—a business whose product is each minute you spend applying your skills. And since most beginning professionals are in debt for their education and get a late start earning an income, many are tempted to work too much. If you do not control how much you work, you quickly accumulate deficits in the rest of your life. Professionals who have no interest in running and promoting a business can avoid entrepreneurial demands by joining large group practices, doing corporate work, or serving on panels, advisory boards, or regulatory agencies, where hours are predictable.

Of the professions, university teaching offers perhaps the greatest autonomy, control, and independence and can potentially provide all twelve benefits. The salaries vary, but once you achieve tenure, usually after five or six years, you are virtually assured lifelong employment. Teaching requirements, committee assignments, and thesis supervision differ, but SLHPPs arrange to reduce or avoid them and find other ways to minimize their workload, including doing little or no research.

Teaching at any level entails responsibilities different from those of other professions; indeed, teaching public elementary school and secondary school is fundamentally a form of civil service work. Salary restrictions and reduced education spending affect morale, but the appeal of this kind of teaching for SLHPPs stems from the relative autonomy of running a classroom, the reasonable hours, and the excellent paid vacations. Most serious teachers labor carefully to perfect what they offer their students. Some teachers work very long hours—in fact, they overwork—grading, preparing, making lesson plans, and holding parent conferences, while others simply do not. SLHPP teachers cut outside preparation to the minimum.

Any kind of public-sector work is appealing to SLHPPs who prize low demands and security more than direct control, independence, and influence. Civil service positions seldom require creativity or ingenuity, which, in fact, are frowned upon: decisions are made by the book. SLHPPs who prefer to minimize risks tolerate and accept that condition. And the pace of government work is legendarily slower than that of the workplace in private industry. If you have ever stood in a line at the post office or the DMV, you know to park your conventional notions of efficiency at the door before you enter.

Because of the relatively structured and sometimes humdrum quality of civil service work, the positions most highly prized by SLHPPs are those that provide a car or otherwise allow for off-site field visits as a way of breaking the routine. If you check out at 10:00 A.M. to visit an external site or facility across town, you are home free until one o'clock in the afternoon. It's accepted that you will stop for coffee, and if you run into traffic, well, everyone knows what that can be like. Despite the jokes about highway patrolmen at doughnut shops, spreading goodwill at Dunkin' Donuts and Krispy Kreme is an acceptable part of community relations work. Dropping by another government office to chat with colleagues about the vagaries of next year's budget decisions is also acceptable as long as it does not prevent you from completing your tasks.

What about work in the private sector? Corporate work can provide stimulation, variety, the opportunity to be a part of a team, and a chance to do interesting projects while making good money from salary or stock options. In short, depending on the position and situation, it can provide many or nearly all of the twelve benefits. Corporate cultures vary, however, and corporate careers can demand sacrifices in your personal life and extraordinary commitments of time. Corporate environments can also be notoriously cutthroat and unpredictable, and sometimes they present unexpected personal challenges.

► When recruiters came to campus, Derek heard an appealing story, did his part in the mating dance, received a flattering offer, and signed on with a creative consulting firm. The job provided Derek with most of the twelve career benefits and seemed too good to pass up.

During his first two years Derek impressed his superiors but noticed that a number of his colleagues approached their work differently. They were more proactive, maybe a little more gung-ho, and some seemed more mature and sure of themselves. Derek felt tentative and lucky that the projects on which he worked came out unexpectedly well.

After two years Derek was surprised when he was asked to manage a small, struggling division and offered a promotion and raise. His supervisor said that success at this assignment would bode well for Derek's chance to get an M.B.A. the following year on company time at company expense, an honor reserved for rising stars. The idea of managing did not bother him, but the sudden high-profile attention did. He could not depend on continuing to be lucky and wondered whether he should accept the position.

Derek searched for a way to turn down the position and still stay with the firm; if he were perceived to be trying to duck the assignment, it would be the kiss of death with upper management. Derek briefly fantasized that a lingering chest cold could lead to pneumonia and an ensuing extended medical leave, which would allow him, for the good of the company, to decline the new position. But wishing for pneumonia was, besides being bizarre, an unreliable solution.

Derek decided he would take a position somewhere else, whatever he could find and preferably out of state, and then use it as an opportunity to rethink his career. The position he took was a distinct step backward, and he followed it a year later with another dubious choice of jobs. In a matter of three years his CV now looks suspect: he is in a less attractive position in a less attractive firm than the one in which he began. He regrets his decision to leave the first job and views it as a fatal error. He did not consult with anyone, and now, his confidence shaken, he has begun a long slide into dead-end assignments from which he feels he cannot escape.

Derek considered sales as a way out but did not feel cut out for that field. Sales work, however, is a magnet for other SLHPPs for several reasons. If you have squandered past educational possibilities or made a mistake or two, as Derek did, sales looks like a great leveler, at least in terms of income, and a way to get back on track. Neither your college major nor your grades matter; the only thing that matters is closing the deal.

Independence is a major part of the allure. Once trained and given a territory, you are largely on your own. Ah, freedom. With no one looking over your shoulder, you can stop by the dry cleaners, get a book out of the library, have coffee or a long lunch, or go to the gym in the morning before making sales calls. Other than certain required sales meetings, you call the shots, set the appointments, and set the hours.

Being a sales rep is particularly attractive to SLHPPs with charm and social skills, who often feel as if they are getting paid without having to work. As Charlie says, "I make $250K for sitting around and talking on the telephone. How difficult can it be?" But the lack of intellectual demands can be a potential drawback of sales. Personal interest, challenge and stimulation, personal involvement, and significance are often low, and Charlie does not feel that he is challenged to be creative or self-expressive.

There is also a flip side to the independence of sales involving the lack of structure. By the time you get to the office, pick up e-mail and phone messages, look at correspondence, have more coffee, and shuffle some memos, it's time for a two-hour lunch. You may spend the afternoon making only one or two actual in-person sales calls.

Making a good income in sales requires disciplined effort. For those who do not develop that discipline, sales turns out to be a siren song. The tantalizing freedom of being able to set up anywhere with a cell phone and a laptop or sit around at home in your underwear and make money over the phone without sitting in commuter traffic runs smack into another reality: you must invest time in a systematic way to meet sales quotas. For this reason many SLHPPs attain only marginal success, but some cling to sales simply for the promise of freedom.

There are other sales possibilities for those who prefer less structure and more autonomy. Some veer toward self-employment or other opportunities that involve entrepreneurial risk. But successful pursuit of any of these possibilities requires perhaps even more disciplined, goal-directed personal effort because of the lack of structure.

For those wanting to avoid quotas or demands, real estate sales is enticing. The field of residential real estate has a slower pace than the corporate sales environment, and in a hot market it looks easy. To SLHPPs who enjoy pressing the flesh, the real estate licensing test looks like a small hurdle to conquer before arriving at such a Mecca of freedom and possible big bucks. As a Realtor, you come and go as you please, and everything you do, from Lions' Club and Chamber of Commerce meetings to breakfasts out, is promotion. Have one or two big months, and you can coast for the rest of the year.

Realtors, of course, must deal with demanding, nervous clients who want attention, hand-holding, and reassurance at all times; without these services, clients can pull out of deals. There is occasional floor duty at the office and pesky paperwork. In addition, weekends are often spent working, and true days off are rare. Finally, without systematic effort of course, no one consistently does well in real estate over time.

Multilevel marketing schemes pose as sales/enterpreneurial hybrids and present seemingly great opportunities. Again, there is the promise of independence and control—you are entirely your own boss, you can work when and how much you want, and theoretically you can get very rich very quick. The pitch of freedom and wealth usually involves some variant of pursuing the American Dream by selling vacuum cleaners or some elixir or another. Possibilities for intrinsic personal interest, challenge and stimulation, personal involvement, and significance are less obvious.

Some multilevel marketing schemes are legitimate, but nearly all are set up so that it is difficult to prosper through sales of the product alone. The real action is in recruiting people to work under you; it is from their sales—and those of *their* recruits—that you gain a percentage. The touted freedom is erroneous; most people grind away to eke out a living.

Multilevel marketing means running your own business. When you own a business, you are, in some sense, always working, and the business tends to spill over into the rest of your life. Running any business successfully requires time, systematic disciplined effort and tenacity, and patience while playing the multiple roles of secretary, president, vice president, and sales manager.

Independent contracting and freelancing, including the building trades, consulting, counseling, photography, and journalism, can provide, in varying degrees, the first nine of the dozen work benefits and sometimes the others on the list. Since no one besides the government takes a piece of the fees you charge, it is possible to earn more than you could by working for someone else while enjoying independence. You arrive on the scene, dispense a skill or knowledge, and then leave. And in the case of consulting, you only advise and leave others to carry out your recommendations.

Independent contracting, however, requires promoting yourself and your business. It takes consistent effort over time to develop a reputation for your services, referrals, and a steady clientele. Moreover, controlling your time and work flow is an art. Those in the building trades, for example, having already been paid most of the bill for their work by the time the job nears a close, are often eager to get a fresh start and a new infusion of cash by beginning a job somewhere else. Because they want to get that new job off to a good start without delay, they are tempted to have work going in two places and consequently lose time and efficiency running between jobs and explaining themselves to dissatisfied clients whose jobs go unfinished.

Building contractors often meet a promised start date by dropping off some tools, delivering materials, and setting stakes a few days later before disappearing for a while. You may find that finishing the details of a nearly completed project can stretch on for weeks or months, causing you to lose interest, even in something you designed. Moreover, you also have to deal with clients' individual styles and occasionally demanding personalities, particularly when you have kept them waiting for a long period of time.

Underpricing services and overestimating financial revenues are common self-defeating traps for independent contractors. Making yourself available in the beginning at virtually any time of the day or evening can be an interim strategy that often becomes permanent because people come to expect your perpetual availability. The freelancer often has difficulty starting and stopping work and separating work and personal time and can spend great energy keeping the employee—himself or herself—in line.

The creative arts, from music to literature to the plastic arts, also present a strong appeal to SLHPPs. Potentially, these areas offer many of the twelve work benefits, with the notable exceptions of dependable income and job security, although occasionally artists achieve even those, particularly if they take a teaching position. Creating something new is a staggering challenge, however, requiring devotion that nearly amounts to sacrifice.

SLHPPs falter here for reasons associated with all creative work and with work in general: creating something is not easy, and persisting without success is wearing. Writers face repeated rejections of their manuscripts and screenplays, and stop-short writers remain on the margins of success, where they battle writer's block, self-doubts, and inconsistent work habits. Plastic artists sometimes *do* experience a variety of legitimate difficulties associated with fulfilling their visions, but misunderstood geniuses abound in the plastic and performing arts. Though most who stick with creative work come to accept and deal with its challenges, commercial success is often unrelated to excellence and is obtained usually either by good self-promoters or by those who pander to mass tastes. Some SLHPPs, most notably rebels, charmers, and extreme risk-takers, join that particular segment of the artistic garment industry that purveys new clothes to gullible emperors.

Fortunately, for people with creativity, sufficient ambition, imagination, and a willingness to take calculated risks, there are other opportunities, some of which may provide many of the twelve benefits on the wish list. Everyone has heard stories of the person who began to implement a great idea in his kitchen or garage and then turned it into an amazingly successful venture. But such schemes involve risk and require tenacity, drive, and hard work as you use trial and error, keep learning, and endure setbacks. And these schemes also put you up against the unfinished business of your own process of self-mastery.

▶ Zack reaches over, hits the snooze button, and groans. When he set the alarm, he told himself that he could not be late to work again. Now, at 10:15 A.M., that thought cannot compete with his wish for a little more sleep.

At 28, Zack still does computer consulting but quit his programming job three years ago to work at a small video store devoted exclusively to foreign films. Eventually he wants to start his own business renting windsurfing equipment, but he has had difficulty putting together enough capital. He decided that today, between customers if necessary, he would at least finish the rough draft of a business proposal to present to some of his father's friends—potential investors.

Once at the store, between going across the street for coffee and a newspaper and visiting with Cecil, the postman, two hours pass, and he has not yet restocked the shelves with the overnight video returns. Behind on his schedule anyway, Zack punches into the Web and takes a look at his frequent flyer mileage account, then visits his favorite Costa Rica websites because they offer inspiration. "This is where to run the business," he sighs.

He takes out his laptop and begins to write but decides first to get a sandwich and finish the newspaper. He will restock the shelves after lunch and be able to tackle the business plan well nourished.

But after lunch he takes a look at the help-wanted ads for programmers—just to keep up with current salaries—before restocking the video returns. By the time he finishes restocking he notices it is four-thirty. The afternoon is now too far gone to tackle the business plan. He tells himself that he needs a long stretch without interruptions to really dig in and get it finished, and the usual late afternoon rush of customers will soon be descending.

He thinks about doing it at home tonight, but since he never works well at night, he calls his friend, Al, and they decide to go to a little club in the Mission to hear a saxophonist play his first San Francisco gig. They will get home late, but since Zack will be working an evening shift the next day, he promises himself that he will work on the business plan before he goes to the store.

Zack hesitates because of a profound, hidden ambivalence—a haunting mixture of submerged feelings about his future. The windsurfing business is an interim step—something to do during what he calls his "entrepreneurial phase." It is the larger decision of what he will do when he really grows up that gnaws. He wants it to be something special.

Zack is not alone in his struggles. If you are talented and seeking out an unconventional path, nothing is laid out for you. By comparison, formal education and professional training follow definite paths. They take time, but you know the exact period of time required when you begin. You clear the hurdles, and you get your ticket punched.

When you begin to chart your own course, however, seductions, distractions, frustrations, and blind alleys abound. The absence of formal structure can lure you into the usually mistaken belief that you can achieve success quickly. You're a good writer. You should be able to sit down and write that screenplay in no time. How hard could it be? It could be harder than you think, but not because you aren't a good writer. That killer software application should be easy? Not necessarily.

Two intertwined difficulties lie in wait for you if you choose to go your own way. First, creating a path where none exists requires skill and self-discipline. You may have developed these already, but you must still battle doubts, self-defeating habits, and self-limiting beliefs and be extremely attentive to stay on course. And second, none of this effort *guarantees* success.

In Zack's case and many others, getting launched is often the most difficult part. For others, the difficulty is in pursuing an idea despite the setbacks. Having to hustle for investors or clients, encountering the toils of running a business, and dealing with the lag before seeing a return on their time causes many to stop prematurely. Others keep their vision small and their success marginal, or they never start at all.

Given all the trade-offs we have examined, many SLHPPs operate from a shorter wish list and fall back on seeking a job that primarily promises that other compensation I mentioned—namely, a lack of demands. Settling for far less than the twelve desirable qualities of a job already a move in a certain direction. The fewer ideal qualities a job has, the less rewarding it is and the fewer opportunities it provides for gratifying accomplishments.

## Work Styles

Ideally, adult life *should* finally bring you the freedom to set your course and aspire to what you want. SLHPPs who have maintained a pattern of success with minimum effort often plunge into adult life expecting to do well with no more effort than before. If you had talent but didn't fully engage, this transition can prove to be as unexpectedly complicated for you as it was for Derek. If you suffer a major setback, you may re-create your school experience by taking a job for which you have little respect and then develop a work style that expresses your disengagement.

The following styles of selecting and performing work reflect mediocre commitment and effort and bring about mediocre results. If you approach work with little enthusiasm, you may recognize elements of more than one of the following types in your style:

**Job Coasters:** Job coasters stint on effort and take shortcuts whenever and wherever they can, making it their central goal to expend minimum effort. Though coasting in some way underlies all of the self-limiting styles described here, coasters specifically seek to dodge work itself. Job coasters leave work unfinished, leave unpleasant tasks to others, and fail to update their skills or stay abreast of developments in their field. On the job they do the bare minimum and often perform poorly.

There are job coasters in every profession and at every level. Some adopt this style from the beginning of their work lives, while others do so later as they go through the motions, kill time, and wait to retire.

In organizational settings coasters don't prepare for presentations or meetings with colleagues and cursorily scan the agenda after arriving. Job coasters consciously reduce the expectations of others through spotty work performance and procrastination, and by appearing just unreliable enough to ensure that they won't be given demanding responsibilities.

SLHPPS who job-coast work to survive rather than to meet other needs or to express themselves creatively. A few make slacking a lifestyle choice.

**Demand Avoiders:** Demand avoiders deliberately seek work for which they are overqualified. Because they value freedom more than any of the other dozen work benefits, they must avoid anyone or anything that would place demands on them. Unlike job coasters, demand avoiders perform their jobs well and do not take shortcuts. Some may even make good money, but they avoid taxing, worrisome positions. Tapping into their talents or expressing their passions is not a part of the picture. Demand avoiders are often delayers, checkmates, or best-or-nothings.

**Hiders:** Hiders stay below the radar in large organizations by finding a seam or black hole in the organizational chart into which they disappear for months to work on some obscure project.

> ► For years, Marvin, 38, has deliberately sought and found work assignments in areas other than those considered "hot," high-profile, or attention-grabbing by those wishing to further their careers. Marvin's ability to work away from the spotlight has resulted in less pressure and scrutiny because he always reports to supervisors who are consumed with more pressing concerns.

Hiders arrange to be overlooked and usually postpone putting out finished products as long as possible, since by definition their work is not pressing. Hiders are often stop-shorts, extreme low-risk-takers, or sleepers, but they may be checkmates or covert, low-profile rebels.

**Niche Builders:** Similar to hiders but operating in small organizations, professional practices, or college faculties, niche builders perform mundane or unpleasant but necessary duties that are uninteresting to others to avoid more threatening or demanding duties. Those tasks may include nonprofessional or ancillary activities, like committee work, that they originally took on temporarily but then never relinquished.

> ► When expected work failed to come through, Lorna took over some office chores in her two-person law office while her partner, Stan, continued to make court appearances. Six years later she continues to do office chores, confines her legal work to research, and has not been back inside a courtroom.

Niche builders are usually extreme non-risk-takers or stop-shorts, but they can be checkmates.

**Flashers:** Flashers demonstrate their exceptional talent in tantalizing but inconsistent "now-you-see-it-now-you-don't" bursts. Flashers work on their own terms rather than in response to the needs of a team or organization, but in an emergency they may be the one who does something dramatic to save the day. They are rarely interested in rigor or the day-to-day normal activities that keep a team or enterprise going. In fact, they never really seem to join a team. They are independent commandos who, though never producing dependably, demonstrate sufficient potential to be kept around.

Flashers neither address their weaknesses nor round out their skills and therefore do not develop their full potential. Instead, they repeat what they already do well. Like a playwright who keeps rewriting the same play, or a guitarist who keeps repeating the same brilliant riff, they are incomplete and their abilities remain fallow.

Advertising agencies, marketing departments, the creative arts, and athletic teams tend to attract flashers—left-handed pitchers and seven-foot basketball players in particular make millions playing this role.

Flashers most often are best-or-nothings, extreme risk-takers, misunderstood geniuses, rebels, and, occasionally, charmers.

**Hopscotchers:** Hopscotchers launch one career initiative after another, staying with one only long enough for the novelty to wear off before moving to the next. Hopscotching is most associated with sales work, forays into multilevel marketing, and various other entrepreneurial, freelancing, or self-employment situations. Hopscotchers routinely bungle these attempts because they do not patiently build the networks of contacts and client lists they need to succeed.

Those who hopscotch often have a naively rosy view of what they can do or an inadequate understanding of the time required to accomplish something. They are impatient with anything short of immediate success, and they often leave a potentially good situation for the promise of quicker returns or higher future earnings elsewhere, even when the other opportunity involves a similar timeline for bearing fruit. Feeling that the last delay was due to the product, the support, or the situation, they are confident that this time things will be better.

Ironically, some hopscotchers manifest a complementary opposite pattern: they are curiously reluctant to abandon clearly mistaken ventures. They perversely linger, as if wishing to prove that their latest move was not haphazard or incorrect. Thus, hopscotchers alternate between leaving too soon and staying too long.

Hopscotchers most often are best-or-nothings or extreme risk-takers, but occasionally they are delayers, charmers, rebels, or misunderstood geniuses.

**Job Surfers:** The job surfer drops out of a conventional career path to take an entry-level job at a bookstore after another at a bar, staying with any one job only until bored, then going to the next. Though job surfers share some characteristics with demand avoiders, demand avoiders do not make as many moves and do not necessarily hold entry-level jobs. By comparison, job-surfers usually lack the training and experience to qualify for more demanding positions.

Job surfing often arises as a default choice for those whose early decisions and choices eliminated other possibilities. They may have abandoned a talent or failed to act on opportunities they could have easily pursued. Job surfers are most often floater/coasters, sleepers, delayers, extreme non-risk-takers, or rebels.

**Temp Surfers:** Temp surfing is a version of job surfing that involves gaining work through temporary job placement agencies. This strategy provides steady work and eliminates job searches, since the temp agency finds the job for you. Temping, basically an employer-employee dating service in which neither side makes a long-term commitment, allows temp surfers to avoid remaining in unpleasant situations. Rising to the top of a temp agency list involves being available and dependable in reporting to assignments. Played well, temp surfing allows flexibility between periods of work and downtime. Temp surfers are often sleepers, floater/coasters, delayers, misunderstood geniuses, or occasionally extreme low-risk-takers or rebels.

Many SLHPPs, especially those who have been slack in their commitments and have only toyed with their talents, consciously dread committing to a career. Committing means showing your hand and giving up other possibilities to stake your future to a specific choice. The chilling quality of finality makes those SLHPPs who are unprepared for such a serious choice feel hemmed in. Tom, 32, discussing his struggle to decide on a career, says, "I felt when I opened one door, I would hear a thousand other doors closing behind me. I just did not feel ready to do something so permanent."

Many SLHPPs delay facing up to the need to choose a career for as long as possible. They want to wade into adult life a little more slowly and get used to the water. Maybe you wanted to catch your breath and wait a little longer too. To the relief of many SLHPPs, it is possible to delay career involvement, and most other aspects of adult life, for quite some time.

## Wiggle Room

There is no single moment when the apprenticeship of childhood ends and adulthood officially begins. There is in fact no single, practical definition of adulthood. Are you an adult upon finishing formal education and getting a first serious job, or upon marrying and starting a family? Each of these steps alone suggests an increase in adult responsibility, but none is definitive, and they do not follow a prescribed order.

With each step expectations for excellence and seriousness of purpose increase, but it is well known that people can complete all of them and still fail to manifest qualities of adult maturity. Moreover, graduate and professional training extend well past the age associated with adulthood, preventing those students from truly beginning their careers until later in life.

This ambiguity about the onset of adulthood provides room to maneuver. Every step can be postponed for practical reasons, or at least ones that sound good. Some SLHPPs slide into a kind of limbo at this frontier and create lives marked by postponements and false starts. These SLHPPs are delayers, and their struggles deserve closer examination.

► April, at 40, still has not reached firm decisions about career, relationships, or having children. A repeated college dropout, she avoided choices that would have give her "that claustrophobic feeling of settling in." Instead, she traveled to India and Tibet, found house-sitting jobs in exotic locations, did temporary work on special events, and worked other jobs here and there, like helping a friend design and open a small boutique.

► Bryan, 46, has held a variety of jobs while freelancing sporadically as a journalist, but his frequent changes of direction and location have limited his progress in that field. After a recent move to the West Coast, he thinks it's finally time to get more serious.

Although April and Bryan appear to struggle with indecision much like Ronald, the would-be professor, and Stacy, the would-be choreographer you formerly met, each of them at times has taken solace in it. Not ready for finality, each has extended the period when life, like a dress rehearsal, allows for many retakes. For each, the first line of defense against adult responsibilities has been to put them off.

Delaying tactics begin even before the netherworld between adolescence and adulthood sets in. Poor school performance, discussed in chapter 2, is often the earliest indication of ambivalence about leaving home; poor grades can postpone departure to a four-year college. No matter what you professed, if you had really wanted to leave home and had felt ready to do it, you would have seen to it that your grades allowed it. Poor grades buy time and can lead to a minimum of two years or more of community college or a fifth year of high school, or both. Moving out is often not final either. Some young people move back home more than once, a few move back permanently, and a few never leave.

College is also a safe haven from which to delay entry into the adult world. As a way station for intellectual and social experimentation in the midst of vibrant, intelligent, attractive people, it is easy to grow accustomed to its womblike atmosphere of pleasant activities, self-selected hours, and not quite adult expectations. Why have it end in just four short years?

Since support for college education is nearly universal, extending this interlude usually meets little resistance as long as you make at least some progress. This is all the more true for parents who previously battled with their child over school performance. Such parents are often content to see even a mild interest in completing a college education and readily put their blessing on slower than normal progress.

Heavy enrollments often make it difficult for even earnest students to complete course requirements within a four-year period, but if you drop out, wait to declare a major, change majors repeatedly, or transfer from one school to another, you engineer further delays. Changing majors requires that you start new upper-division classes, and to transfer you must meet different general education requirements. Individualized study programs and double majors also add semesters of work.

This is not to dispute the value or necessity of these choices per se. They can be important, even vital, in transforming a generic college education into something richly rewarding. But done for the wrong reasons, extending the time you spend getting an undergraduate college degree can have damaging effects.

▶ When he came to the Maximum Potential Project, Ben, 38, was considering going to graduate school for a degree in art history, a late-developing interest. He had dropped out of college, returned for a year, and dropped out again. For the next four years he spent time working in Alaska on a fishing boat, in the San Joaquin Valley doing farm labor, and then in San Francisco as an apprentice carpenter, before moving to Los Angeles, where he enrolled in the L.A. State film program. Waiting tables and attending school part-time, he graduated seven years later.

Ben eventually decided against going to graduate school, which can be a lengthy stopover. With less structure and less formal coursework than they had as undergraduates, graduate students can work for years on vague projects, encounter difficulties, scrap them, and begin again. SLHPP graduate students may never complete a degree but hang on for years by working as research assistants to professors while postponing completion of their own theses. Other promising SLHPPs begin and quit one graduate or professional school after another.

> ▸ At age 34, Luke had dropped out of a Ph.D. program in psychology to work in behavioral biology. When he left psychology, he was convinced that it was more important to make the right choice than to be in a hurry to finish. But he now questions the value of academia and wonders about applying to law school.

Whether they have previously delayed or not, many college graduates take a breather before settling into a permanent career. Some kick back, while others travel abroad, live in diverse cultures, learn a foreign language in a native setting, or soak up some other kind of life experience. As goals, these pursuits are meritorious and hard to fault. Many students who do not take a break after graduation later wish they had. And after a fixed break many come back and get down to work. For some, however, the break expresses a more profound ambivalence about choices and is a first step toward avoiding adult life.

SLHPPs who drift into an extended form of delay stretch this break indefinitely in a variety of ways. Some go back to their university town to sort things out and associate with other graduates who have also stayed nestled in an environment where important choices remain down the line, yet to be made. All decisions set precedents. Delays at this stage can be elaborations of the strategies they learned previously within their family system or at school.

Some continue to remain unwilling to leave behind the loose structure, comforting familiarity, and open-endedness of the journeys of discovery of this postcollege period. They stay rootless and uncommitted, gliding from one adventure to another, continuing an extended time-out, and considering next steps, while keeping the pressure low and avoiding seriousness.

Frequent moves become part of this way of life, and SLHPPs set up their lives to accommodate them. For example, a much greater number of project participants give a post office box, instead of a home address, as their mailing address than any other group in my psychotherapy practice combined. A PO box saves the hassle of completing post office change-of-address forms. Project participants have confided that while packing the boxes for the latest move, they fantasize about doing the next move differently or better.

You may have moved from place to place, apartment to apartment, living group to living group, city to city, or coast to coast trying possibilities on for size. Some moves may have been stopgaps, some may have been made on a whim without adequate reflection, while others may have been the fallout of other decisions. In the beginning the advantages of a new situation loom in the foreground, appearing to solve the drawbacks of the old situation with the freshness of a new start.

When you are young, the future extends indefinitely before you. Tomorrow, it seems, will never come. Searching for the right thing and not quite finding it, delayers settle for positions they consider at first merely stopgaps. But their early choices often limit their later ones, and they develop characteristic attitudes toward work as a consequence of their delay. Delayers mostly work only for pay, and only because they have to work. They arrange their lives to avoid as much as possible the invasion of job demands.

## Working for Pay

Most jobs are structured, a fact that weighs heavily on those SLHPPs whose main wish has been to extend the freedom of the period before adulthood. Structure is precisely what they have sought to avoid.

▶ Anna, 36, feels that she is not cut out for the absurd and barbarous requirements of the standard forty-hour workweek. She views herself as constitutionally different from those who rise day after day at 6:00 A.M. and come home sometime after 7:00 P.M.

She has taken jobs at boutiques solely because she could arrive for work after 11:00 A.M. She has also taken telemarketing jobs with odd hours just to avoid working a straight eight-hour shift. Anna says she would prefer to have lived in another era, when her life could have been attuned only to her own natural rhythms.

People like Anna have no wish to enter standard careers or hold conventional jobs. Positions involving flexible, nontraditional hours, few demands, and little structure are the only ones they will consider.

► Damien, 29, feels that he is not—and should not be—defined by any job. This attitude may be partially defensive because he does not hold a high-status job in the conventional sense, but he says that status concerns destroy life and send people chasing phantoms.

He is hardly immune, however, to considerations of status: while making a root beer float at the trendy spot where he works, he slips into the conversation that he almost completed his doctorate in sociology and that he could have taken a job as a rock critic but turned it down.

Damien has complicated feelings about having been in the doctoral program. He left hastily when he thought he was not cut out for a career as a professor, but he has had ongoing twinges of regret for having cheated himself. His awkward solution has been to attempt to work both sides of the street in defending his image. He lays public claim to the intelligence and ambition of having entered a doctoral program ("Though I am working here at this soda fountain, don't be mistaken. I am intelligent. I was smart enough to be in a doctoral program") but subtly disavows its importance at the same time ("I was not the kind for that and dropped out"), as if to build some redeeming notion around having left school. In truth, Damien has come to realize that his regret runs deeper than he thought. He has covered his regret with Tara-style rationalizations, but he wishes he had completed the program first and then reached a decision about his career.

Coasting, job surfing, and demand-avoiding SLHPPs may hold entry-level jobs, but like Damien, they gravitate toward workplaces that are special in some way. Work at an unusual café or trendy boutique makes mundane work more palatable to an SLHHP and allows him or her to escape from feelings of ordinariness.

▶ Darla, 39, claims she has a greater loyalty to herself than to any job or employer. At best, she remains ambivalent about working for a living and often dislikes it. As a result, she switches jobs if she sees an opportunity elsewhere.

She says only half-jokingly that she is philosophically opposed to striving for material gain, but then quickly points out that this is different from being opposed to material gain. Darla notes that despite the absurdity of it, she busily churns out fantasies of winning the lottery or becoming the benefactor of some other largesse that would rescue her from having to work.

Many SLHPPs claim that they are not driven by money, arguing that they prefer to live on less rather than accumulate empty affluence or work stressful jobs. They want money for travel and other pursuits, however, so they work at a dull job for a while if the pay is exceptionally good. Inevitably, even the money is not enough to hold their interest.

▶ Tamara, a 46-year-old waitress at an upscale restaurant, does not like work to intrude upon her personal life. Her work is demanding while she is on shift, but when she leaves, the job is done. She also earns more money than her housemate, a middle school English teacher who gets up at god-awful hours and then brings home papers to correct at night.

Work, as Tamara sees it, steals time. She would therefore rather do something simple that she can leave behind when she goes home than carry work considerations back and forth with her. As a waitress, she enjoys her free time during the day.

▶ Rod, a 31-year-old parking lot attendant, has never expected his work to be enjoyable. To him, work is purely a means to an end. On weekends he does valet parking at a San Francisco restaurant for the tips. From time to time he works on a screenplay, though with less enthusiasm than when he began it. He finds many interesting, inexpensive things to do in the Bay Area, including hiking and riding his bike in the regional parks.

In terms of trade-offs, a job such as Zack's at the video store or Rod's at the parking lot has few qualities from the wish list but is attractive for its completely mindless requirements. Rod's simple duties and after-rush-hour shift ensure that he works virtually stress-free, when he works at all. With no supervision, he sometimes has time to doze, read a book, pay bills, or write correspondence that would otherwise have to be done at home. The net result is a job that allows him to handle mundane chores on the job and have more free time off it.

Having a job that does not satisfy subtler needs is not necessarily a problem. Career is not the only path to fulfillment. I have a hard time imagining Einstein being enthralled by his work at the patent office. If he did quality work while there, it is much to his credit. What he did on the side, however, was his passion, fascination, and contribution.

▶ Tanya, 44, says that no matter how compliant she appears on the surface, she chafes at being told what to do. She prefers not to be closely supervised, evaluated, or scrutinized at work, since such oversight would impinge on her sense of autonomy; further, she says without boasting, she is more intelligent than most of her employers or supervisors. She considers herself a professional no matter what her position is and prefers to be treated as one.

SLHPPs bridle at being treated as ordinary. No matter how ordinary their work is, they themselves are *not* ordinary, never have been, never will be, and no one should forget that. It is easy to see that this perspective leads to the endless quest for freedom that characterizes the lives of those committed to delaying the inimical aspects of adult life. So what is the underlying source of the delay, and what purpose does it serve?

## Fear of Failure

It should be clear by now that if there is one factor around which self-limiting behavior and consequent underachieving revolve, it is fear of failure. Fear of failure prompts you to step away from risks—to escape—but as soon as you do you limit your life.

Escape has more downside risks than does failure. For one, escape invites others to step in and take over. There are, however, other aspects to escape. First, it does work in the short run, in the sense that it provides immediate relief from anxiety. As a result, the escaper is highly likely to do it again. Second, escape stops a flow and interrupts momentum. Remember Pete, whom I saw at his brother Mark's wedding? His break from being the perfect student became terminal.

To understand the costs of escape, consider the following rudimentary example. A piece of mail arrives—not a personal letter, but it is long and you feel busy. You start to toss it but decide you should take a look at it before just throwing it away. Since this will take more time than you feel you have now, you set it aside for when you will have more time.

Whether you realize it or not, in this moment you have created a monster: a piece of unfinished business. When you next touch that same piece of mail, you push it away more quickly. It is something you did not have time for before, and this moment is no better. You know what you will think the third time: *Anything I have set aside twice must be something awful that will require much more time than I have now.*

Unfinished business registers in the brain in this way, gathering compound interest.

Theorem: anything you leave uncompleted is harder to complete the next time you come to it. Corollaries: (a) if you avoid anything once, you are more likely to avoid it again; and (b) when you avoid one major life issue, you make the next one harder to face.

This is the heart of the problem for any kind of delay or other escape. You raise the threshold for completion of the task you set aside. Paula, 34, says that each time a pile of mail begins to collect, she feels herself encircled by a web of nearly imperceptible threads tugging at her attention, and like Gulliver tied down by the Lilliputians, she is eventually imprisoned by it.

Avoiding mail is one thing. The stakes are higher when the issue is a life choice or a dream, although each instance of avoidance plays out in a similar way. The tendency to avoid can generalize from an isolated instance to a pattern, and from a pattern to your view of the tendency as a personal trait. Seeing that you do not persist, you conclude that you lack persistence. Seeing that you avoid, you conclude that you are an avoider. Furthermore, a classic, sometimes unrecognized way of justifying a self-defeating, self-limiting choice is to repeat it, as if to say: "That was not a bad decision. I'll prove it. I'll do the same thing again."

Remember Denise, the keyboardist who made the self-defeating choice to avoid learning the music theory that people with lesser talent studied? Originally, she only postponed studying the theory because it was boring and required a lot of extra effort. For what reason, she thought, should she engage herself in such boring little details?

For everything. The filmmakers, choreographers, playwrights, finish carpenters, sculptors, athletes, and body and fender repairmen who produce memorable work that is deeply satisfying to them are relentlessly attentive and realize their vision down to the smallest detail. They put themselves in the position of continually failing and continually correcting for their failures.

Avoiding details backfires. If you stifle your attention to small details, you pull away before you reach the good part. Satisfying achievements and deeper understandings take time. If you sign on only for what is immediately fun and easy, you shrink your life down to a limited range of shallow activities and interests.

I have often given SLHPPs the exercise of accurately describing how they spend their time each day by writing it up as if it were a job posting to appear in a newspaper. "Must work x hours per day on the same repetitive activities, without stimulating goals and time devoted to reflection or to profound pleasure, etcetera, etcetera." Would they or anyone else want to apply for the life they live? Typically the answer is no.

This is the unhappy payoff of succumbing to fear of failure and starting down the path of avoidance. Other problems also arise from paying limited attention to and avoiding details.

## Going for Broke

► Kevin, 45, is in debt, and not for the first time. He has always gotten out of debt before, but he doesn't know how he will pull the rabbit out of the hat this time. He leans back awkwardly in his chair, hands clasped behind his head, as if lying in a hammock, and stares at the ceiling. He smiles. He was going to have plenty of money to make it through the winter. He had figured in "everything." His spreadsheet showed that, with any luck, he would have reserves available to pay down his credit card debt. He even told his girlfriend that this was the year they would finally go on the vacation he had been promising.

Kevin assures me that he has made good money in the past, especially after he graduated from Stanford and went to work for a pharmaceutical start-up firm. But he took what he considered a well-calculated risk and put all the money he had, along with some he borrowed, into extra stock options. When the stock went public and the price rose, he chose not to sell, confident that it would rise further and he would eventually make "a real killing." When the stock began to decline, he remained optimistic and held on. Eventually it was worth less than he had paid for it, and he found himself in serious financial trouble.

Little by little he worked himself out of that hole. But for the last fifteen years he has not saved a penny. When he starts to get ahead, "something always happens." He currently has no medical or disability insurance but feels confident of his good health and stamina.

He works as a ski instructor in the winter and as a whitewater rafting leader in the summer. Because this year's winter snowmelt was low, he had to cancel his entire schedule of September and October outings. Before the season began he developed a brochure and an elaborate web page to advertise his trips by using money he owed to the IRS and by maxing out his credit cards as well. He says that if he can sell business executives on his expeditions as team-building experiences, he will be home free.

Many SLHPPs, like Kevin, maintain a kind of fuzziness about their financial lives. Although they complain of bad luck or insuperable obstacles, their real problem is that they often prevent themselves from seeing the whole picture. A realistic appraisal might dampen their enthusiasm or impinge on their cherished feelings of freedom.

With finances, SLHPPs, especially extreme risk-takers like Kevin, can be enthusiastic, creative, impatient, and impractical. They are also often broke. If you, like Kevin, have made unrealistically rosy financial projections, even if you are capable of making money you may still squeak along on just enough money to survive.

Income is related to career choice, but finances are not. Poor career choices and poor work performance often lead to a poor financial situation, but making a lot of money is no guarantee of a sound financial position. As you fall further and further behind with your finances, the harder it is to convince yourself that a methodical, tortoiselike strategy is the way to go for a hare like you. This can lead to playing catch-up through wilder and wilder schemes.

Once behind, SLHPPs can be attracted to shortcut schemes for acquiring wealth and tempted by high-risk investments. Only rarely do these ventures pay off, however, and usually they just bring greater problems. Moreover, when SLHPPs hit it big, they often spend money as if they are uncomfortable having it and fall into a cavalier "easy-come-easy-go" attitude that mirrors their stance toward their talent.

Low-risk-takers rationalize that other things are "more important than earning a living," but they often owe money to relatives or are swamped by credit card debt, late payments, and poor credit ratings. A striking number of SLHPPs with whom I have worked receive part of their income from a trust or count on an inheritance to bail them out someday. Others live spartan lives devoid of extras, then splurge on cameras or fancy additions to their computers.

Without some money, you are restricted. Many SLHPPs, like Kevin, remain short of money because they handle it recklessly. Others, like Greg, simply make the amount they think is possible, which is usually very little. Greg compounded the problem by being self-employed.

▶ Greg, 49, has never worked for any employer for longer than eleven months. Extremely bright, a math major with an English minor, he had always performed well academically. An only child, he had been the center of his parents' life; they made it clear that they adored him.

Neither parent graduated from college. His father began working on televisions when they first gained popularity in the 1950s, opened a repair shop, and managed to support the family reasonably well when Greg was a child. His mother did not work outside the home but cooked, sewed, and gardened. His parents never emphasized career.

Greg planned to marry after his college graduation, but when the relationship fell apart, he responded to an advertisement in the campus newspaper and began editing dissertations and manuscripts on a freelance basis. Immediately, he preferred the freedom of choosing his own hours to working for someone else. In the beginning he undercharged for his work as a way to develop referrals and meet immediate expenses, but soon underpricing his work became a pattern.

He has lived in three different university towns, taking advantage of the libraries, relatively cheap housing, and good cafés and theaters. Financial success has been a low priority: Greg's aspirations have never extended beyond being able to cover much more than the next month's rent. As a consequence, he has had to borrow small amounts of money from friends and his parents to cover expenses when work was slack.

Greg, a passive floater/coaster and extreme low-risk-taker, eventually reached a point at which he always felt overwhelmed by his finances.

## Downtime

You might expect that an effort-avoiding SLHPP would be expert at exploiting leisure time for relaxation, recreation, profound rest, and physical, emotional, and aesthetic pleasure. You would be wrong. Instead, SLHPPs often alternate between two extremes when it comes to their free time: they are either rushing, late, and exhausted, or immobile, allowing their time to just dribble away. They never get around to lying in the sun, relaxing with a good book, or doing some other activity they promised themselves they would do.

Because SLHPPs often feel exhausted, their attempts to catch up steal their free time. Consequently, their lives are full of painfully repetitive drudgery and lack pace, elegance, or the simplicity Thoreau sought. SLHPPs, in short, spend precious little time doing things they really enjoy, and they long for rest. Instead of being free, they are unable to escape a prison of their own making.

Greg, for example, often felt that all he did was work. Every space in his house reminded him of some unfinished assignment, and he rarely went out, because something always needed attention. When he rebelled occasionally and went out anyway, ignoring unfinished jobs, his misery was only compounded, since once again he would have to spend a weekend gloomily toiling away.

SLHPPs are curious hedonists. Their pleasure is often reduced to the amorphous and nearly meaningless goal of "kicking back." Real pleasure seems to escape them, much as other accomplishments elude their grasp. Enjoying leisure requires setting time aside and protecting it. Protecting leisure time involves completing other tasks so that they do not intrude on and detract from it. Completing other tasks requires initiative, good planning, scheduling, and making very good use of the time you have. And exploiting and enjoying leisure time takes reflection and consideration. What would you really like to do? How much and when? Preceded by what and followed by what? Making these decisions is hardly drudgery—even a small amount of time spent thinking about what you want sets the stage for that sort of downtime—but amazingly, since SLHHPs do not expend this effort, they often wind up settling for less.

> ▶ Nancy, 39, single and working in sales, is frustrated and weary of feeling dull and unproductive when she is not doing work-related travel. She says that she looks forward to relaxing after a long sales trip, but by her fourth or fifth day of watching video rentals and eating snack food at home, she notices that this time is not enjoyable. When asked what she is doing about it, she responds with slight irritation but a spark of curiosity, "Well, I suppose I could get a group together and discuss films or something."

Nancy does not take her precious leisure time seriously enough to give it the attention it deserves. She needs pleasure and relaxation, and they deserve careful attention to prevent them from becoming habitual and mechanical. You may want to examine your own use of leisure time. You may be following decisions you made long ago and never reexamined.

If you feel you do not deserve pleasure because you are not caught up in other things, you are mistaken. Making your life pleasurable requires the same skills you would use to achieve any other goal, so seeking satisfying leisure is a good starting point for learning these skills. But beyond that, you need pleasure for its own sake. How can

you presume that you will successfully tackle stiff, aversive, complicated challenges if you do not carefully seek out pleasure? Plan the perfect Sunday for this weekend, and then enjoy it whether or not you are
caught up on every chore. Then use the same care you used in planning
that Sunday to take care of your ongoing obligations so that you can
have another perfect Sunday the following week. Seeking this kind of
perfection is great practice for living better.

Perhaps you know the other patterns: feeling too rushed to take the
time to do anything differently, resisting doing even simple things that
would improve your situation, feeling less joy, feeling barely in control,
meandering in circles without a plan, staring blankly, sighing, eating
things in which you have zero interest, grinding endlessly away without
making any headway.

Is this a way to live? I think not.

There is more to adult life than work, finances, and downtime.
There are also relationships. They likewise require nurturing, care and
attention, and perfecting.

## Relationship

For those accustomed to sailing through life effortlessly, real relationships present unaccustomed demands. It takes more than social contact,
good times, clever conversations, interesting stories, and lively exchanges
to make a friendship. Profound relationships develop over years and
involve all that it means to be human.

To be profoundly satisfying, relationships require wisdom, sincerity, honesty, reflection, forbearance, self-control, patience, and time.
This in itself is a tall order. But they also involve risks. SLPPs are often
at the center of a lively discussion at a party and are, as we have seen,
likeable and often well-liked. But they often have few truly profound
friendships because they prefer to avoid hassles and exposure to rejection. Some SLHPPs reduce risks of rejection by never inviting and
always waiting to be invited. Eventually, people drop away. Intimate
relationships require even more work, and if you skip over learning the

skills that relationships demand, the complexities can overwhelm you. As with any other achievement, investing energy produces rewards.

▶ Cindy, the woman you met earlier who was startled to find herself in a relationship with real substance, discovered she was was a charter member of the Society for the Prevention of Vulnerable Feelings in Relationships. Her solution to the potential humiliation of the naked and vulnerable stage was to just not let herself get that involved. She needed to feel in control of herself. Cindy wanted to avoid feeling the emotional equivalent of being a pill bug stuck on its back, legs kicking furiously, trying feverishly to right itself. Rather than learn to express herself clearly, set and respect limits, and reach compromises, she had chosen to keep things light and stay disengaged, by claiming to search for an unreachable ideal. When her new boyfriend proved capable of, and interested in, knowing her deeply, she unconsciously felt exposed and defenseless, and began to look for ways to reject him before he could reject her.

With regard to lightness a genuinely lighthearted approach is not necessarily a bad idea. Always keeping things light, however, requires making some things light that are not. Relationships then become "lite," like the dietary trend toward tasteless pretend food with no nourishment or flavor. As with Doug's wish to keep things light with his daughter Amy, "lite" relationships shut out closeness and connectedness.

It's fine not to want to struggle and have heavy discussions. If every discussion is a struggle, the relationship is pointless. But the sign of a good relationship is not merely the absence of complications. By keeping things "lite" and largely staying indifferent, Cindy never developed skills she needed to really have or be a soul mate. If your idea of a good relationship is one in which you do not have to lift a finger, you are ignoring complexity. Being intimate, for example, occasionally involves saying and listening to difficult things. By this, I am *not* referring to the "getting-things-off-my-chest" style of confrontation that is usually just a low-skill exercise in ventilating aggression. Tact may be harder to develop, but genuine friendship requires it. Skipping over unpleasant situations because you want to keep things pleasant, though, is inevitably self-defeating. Each time you suffer in silence or are unwilling to listen to the other person, you hasten the demise of the relationship because you become impatient with the other person, alienate your affection for him or her, and drive a wedge between you. You poison the water, then complain about the dead fish and wildlife.

There are instances when it is best to withhold comments because making them serves no constructive purpose. To achieve genuine intimacy, make these fine distinctions and refine your skills. If you want a good outcome with a client or a supervisor about a delicate matter, it pays to think in advance about what to say. When it comes to an intimate relationship, do not hope things will work out owing to the sheer force of passive friendship or mutual attraction. The extension of this losing line of thinking is deciding that if you eventually have to work at things, it means that affection has fallen short or the flame has died. Do not unnecessarily tax the attraction you have. Passion and attraction are strong but also delicate. You can wear them out if you do not use care.

In matters of the heart, SLHPPs are prone to take one of two self-protective, fundamentally self-limiting stances: tough-minded and "realistic" or excessively romantic, and often one is a mask for the other. Realists pooh-pooh romance and view relationships in pragmatic, functional terms. Romantics search for ecstatic, meaningful connections but set up tests that others cannot pass. Each type is frightened of being trapped and of being hurt, and both erect walls that prevent them from appreciating their partners as real human beings and friends. In addition to realists and romantics, all of the following subtypes diminish their involvement with another person by avoiding the work necessary to achieve a truly satisfying relationship. You will see obvious similarities to styles of approaching career-related work.

■ *Relationship Coasters:* Relationship coasters avoid not only needless struggles but also necessary ones, like talking about difficult subjects and communicating clearly what they mean. Relationship coasters pretend nothing is wrong and thereby undermine relationships before they develop. Then they focus on every thing that is wrong and decide it is time to move on. They get involved in relationships out of convenience or passion only.

■ *One-Track Lovers:* One-track lovers reduce personal involvement and ease eventual separations by exclusively seeking intense sexual involvements that involve little personal attraction and little personal involvement.

■ *Hiders:* Hiders avoid intimate relationships with a pretext such as a dependent child, an existing relationship, or some other responsibility that prevents them from becoming fully involved.

■ *Role Players:* Role players develop mildly unpleasant personas, such as sexual athlete, unbearable macho, radical angry woman, or victim, to deter others from coming too close.

■ *Relationship Hopscotchers:* Relationship hopscotchers leap from one relationship to another, in each case making a commitment—often marital—to the person they think is finally right. When they inevitably become disappointed, they once more imagine that the solution is someone new and once more imagine that they have made the right choice and are signing on for the long term.

■ *Relationship Surfers:* Relationship surfers prefer brief, intense involvements to long-term entanglements. They adore the stage of falling in love but cannot seem to successfully take relationships beyond that point. They despise the mediocrity that usually follows romance, and they tend not to marry.

■ *Sheets Surfers:* Sheets surfers conduct sexual conquests for sport and adventure, engaging in one-night stands more for the pleasure of the seduction than for the sex. Sheets surfing is practiced by those who seek validation of their sexual attractiveness and enjoy high-risk thrills.

■ *Plungers:* Plungers impulsively take on high-risk involvements, like sudden marriages, elopements, or other dramatic moves, within a few hours of knowing the other person.

■ *Perfect-or-Nothings:* Perfect-or-nothings discard otherwise promising relationships in favor of the never-ending search for Prince Charming or the ideal woman.

As adult life moves on, SLHPPs keep accumulating the consequences that stem from their limited tools. Unprepared for an ordinary life, they ultimately face questions, self-doubt, and the corrosive effects of regret.

# Regret

His mental sufferings were due to the fact that that night, as he looked at Gerasim's sleepy, good-natured face with its prominent cheekbones, the question suddenly occurred to him: "What if my whole life has been wrong?" It occurred to him that what had appeared perfectly impossible before, namely that he had not spent his life as he should have done, might after all be true. It occurred to him that his scarcely perceptible attempts to struggle against what was considered good by the most highly placed people, those scarcely noticeable impulses which he had immediately suppressed, might have been the real thing, and all the rest false. And his professional duties and the whole arrangement of his life and of his family, and all his social and official interests, might all have been false. He tried to defend all those things to himself and suddenly felt the weakness of what he was defending. There was nothing to defend. "But if that is so," he said to himself, "and I am leaving this life with the consciousness that I have lost all that was given me and it is impossible to rectify—what then?"

Tolstoy, in this passage toward the end of *The Death of Ivan Illich,* captures the moment of coming face to face with the realization that one has wasted time not living the life one should have lived. Regret is perhaps too soft a word for the feelings that accompany this recognition. To feel that your life has been in vain, that you have nothing to show for the time, that you fell asleep, made false moves, or settled for something far less than you could have—that is painful. And if you know that you saw what was happening, were capable of turning it around, but did not act, that is something else again.

Be careful with regret. It is tricky territory. Learn from it, but avoid indulging in it. If you are not careful, regret can lead to wildly mistaken attempts to make up for lost time. You begin tossing beanbags from the oddest angles and farthest reaches. Or on reviewing what you consider irremediable mistakes, you collapse in on yourself and become immobilized. Self-doubters/self-attackers usually land here with a hard thud.

> ► Derek, who forsook his position with the consulting firm when asked to take on a new challenge, contracted slowly from life and eventually came to a complete halt. Though he had not begun as some blithely self-indulgent, reckless prodigal son, he felt he had descended to the level of slopping hogs. No fatted-calf return to his father's mansion was in the offing. He began to have the dark feeling that all that remained for him was the power to oversee his own demise.
>
> He succumbed to inactivity. His belly was soft from lack of exercise. He stopped dating, deciding that women sensed his dissatisfaction and did not find it sexy. It had been several months since he had read a book or listened to a serious piece of music, and he had begun watching late-night get-rich-quick infomercials.

When you stop blaming circumstances, bad luck, and other people for where you are, you can make progress. It is important to recognize your own hand in having arrived where you are. But attacking yourself is different from taking responsibility for your mistakes. Attacking yourself is actually a way to avoid deeply reflecting on, and soberly acknowledging, what you have done to get to this point. When you attack yourself for your errors, you leave that kind of rational self-appraisal behind. If you accuse yourself of being inherently defective and having no redeeming qualities, you can indulge the notions that change is impossible and you are off the hook. These are false conclusions, and bogus escape routes.

Though you might have liked to have learned from your mistakes before you made them, you couldn't. Do not use self-punishment as a way to avoid examining them and changing your approach. Besides, if you lack compassion for yourself, you will only turn past mistakes into a worse present day and future. You must counter regret, or it will destroy you. If you do not succumb to regret, recognizing your errors can provoke a positive crisis.

> ► Jennifer, 42, says: "It got to where I started hating to see myself in the mirror. I hated the clutter and my maddening disorganization, hated my car, hated my apartment, hated my clothes, my unread books, and my pretending that I did not care, and hated all the promises to change that I never kept. Most of all, I hated being too big a coward to do anything about it."

Some SLHPPs insulate and accommodate and enduringly settle for less. Be happy for your crisis if you have it, and make good use of it. Jennifer used this moment as an impetus for change. Touching bottom has a way of either bringing clarity and a riveting sense of purpose or self-absorption, self-pity, and frozenness. I suggest you opt for the former.

Do not wait until the moment of death to have as your last conscious thought: "Oh, my God, I was alive." You are the gatekeeper. Each day you do or do not decide to live differently.

# PART II

## Essential Tasks

# All About Change

We must stand firm between two kinds of madness: the belief that we can do anything; and the belief that we can do nothing.

—Alain, *Alain on Happiness*, Translated by Robert D. and Jane E. Cottrell, 1989

If change were easy, there would be no need for this book. If change were impossible, there would be no point in writing it. Devoting yourself fully to something you want—something truly worth doing—is the basic part of the formula for reaping the extraordinary pleasure of directing your life and thus becoming progressively more accomplished. But how do you get there from here?

You may feel that you have wandered down your share of blind alleys. You may want to change direction permanently without further delay, but in your previous attempts you have encountered repeated frustration. No one changes habits, particularly not long-standing, intricately connected ones, with a flick of the wrist. Replacing them requires focused effort, and therein lies one rub. If "flick-of-the-wrist" efforts are all you have in your bag of tricks, you will come up short. What originally stopped you from realizing your potential effectively stops you from changing. Is the situation hopeless? Not at all. You lack only familiarity with certain knowledge and skills. Gaining that familiarity is the subject of the second part of this book.

Far more difficult than the actual steps and tasks associated with change, however, is the abstract conception of changing. If you resist the *idea* of change, believing that old dogs don't learn new tricks and that people fundamentally do not really change, you will defend those beliefs and either resist change or not change at all.

If you want to change but are skeptical that change actually occurs and can be intentionally and consciously directed, read on. You may simply be unclear about what is possible and not know what is required. There are methods for proceeding that are simple and effective. Misconceptions abound, however, about the process of change and what is necessary to bring it about. Some people believe that change requires some form of illumination or enlightenment and, if not the guidance of a guru, at least psychotherapy. Some propose that change can be accomplished simply by visualizing it. In this chapter, I give you a definitive, unambiguous portrait of the change process, what you can and cannot expect from it, and what you can gain from changing.

To make the effort to change, you must accept the proposition that change is possible. To help you accept that proposition I will start by cutting through the questions, myths, and misinformation about change.

## Making It Difficult

When I moved to Paris, I left the comfort of a million seamless, mindless, intricately interwoven habits for an extended period of irritating unfamiliarity. Once there, I felt awkward and frequently out of sync, and I did not welcome these kinds of irritations and looked for ways around them. In the process I often slowed the process of adaptation and made it more difficult.

This is true of all change. Whether we initially perceive it as positive or not, necessary or not, welcome or not, we easily, and often unintentionally, resist it. Psychiatrist Milton Erickson said that people come to psychotherapy because they want to change, but they want to change on their own terms—the very terms that have prevented change.

In Danish author Karl Gjellerup's Nobel Prize–winning novel *The Pilgrim Kamanita*, the title character, wanting to change his life, is certain that he will attain enlightenment and the life for which he longs by setting out on a pilgrimage to find the Buddha. One night on his journey Kamanita is forced to share a room at an inn with a monk, who, upon learning of his quest, tells him many disturbing and mistaken things about the Buddha's teachings. Incensed by such ignorance and unpleasantness, Kamanita resumes his journey the next morning, glad to be free of this troublesome wretch—and unaware that the man he passed the night with was the Buddha himself.

On the way to new understandings you inevitably drag along preconceptions. When you face new information, you are like one accustomed to darkness who squints to avoid the discomfort of intense light or closes his eyes and turns away to resume the comfort of familiar, dimmer light. Or you plunge ahead without thoughtful preparation and, while pouring new wine into your existing wineskins, encounter troublesome leaks.

If you do not prepare well for change, are not open and pliable, and do not pay close attention, you undermine your attempts to change even as you are making those efforts. If you do not prepare properly and get bad results, you are like the carpenter who blames his tools when the problem is that he has measured poorly.

For change to occur, you must take action. Holding external forces responsible for what has gone wrong only keeps you stuck. Your personal involvement in making change is inevitable and required. If you decide that change demands that you assume too much responsibility for your own behavior and that you don't want or need to behave so responsibly, you will not change.

We can be particularly resistant to change when it threatens to alter what we believe about ourselves. In his 1948 book *The Theory of Self-consistency*, Prescott Lecky argues that people prefer retaining a consistent view of who they are to changing that view, even if the change would be positive.[1] As we have seen, the idea of who you are resides at the center of your sense of reality. It is part of the glue that holds your reality together. You believe that if you know anything, you know yourself. And you feel that you know how you behave and what is possible for you.

What you *actually* know is what you have habitually believed and how you have consistently behaved. Police investigators have long relied on the consistency and continuity of human behavior to solve crimes. You have a modus operandi. It seldom varies in significant ways. You tie your shoes the same way, use the same foot to enter the bathtub or shower, have the same habitual thoughts and feelings, and repeat the same crimes.[2]

When you come to the brink of change, you are weary of your malady but unaware of how it influences the cure you seek. Like Kaminita, you see the solution to your problem through the prism of your pre-existing ideas and biases. This leaves you predisposed to pursuing some convenient advantage, like Nasrudin, who, in the Sufi story, searches for his lost keys under a lamppost, not because he dropped them there but because the light is so excellent. To change you have to set aside preconceptions and open to new, sometimes surprising possibilities.

> ► Carly, back for a follow-up visit six months after finishing the project, remarks that the most significant change she has made is one she had not anticipated. She is a creative freelance photographer, but her work had been sorely limited by her intolerance for the details of running her business. She frequently researched promising ideas but either avoided doing all the work of a written cost proposal or submitted it late. Learning to stay with what she thought of as dreary details has made the difference between doing ordinary and fascinating projects.

If you have wanted to change but have rejected the facile answers that fuel late-night infomercials, you were right to do so. If change were that easy, you would have already changed. You know that change requires more.

# Secrets of Change Revealed

Here is the secret truth about change. Once you understand what I am about to tell you and heed it, you will make the changes you seek, and much more efficiently.[3]

If you choose to change, the guidance that follows will prevent you from wasting time going down blind alleys or aborting a potentially successful change effort. To increase your efficiency and make the likelihood of success close to inevitable, absorb these ideas and allow them to inform you.

■ *Change is easier when you selectively focus your efforts.* Trying to pull off multiple changes simultaneously is the kiss of death. Do not overreach. You cannot change everything in one fell swoop, if for no other reason than that your attention is limited. I will provide you with a basic template for how to proceed and tell you where to put your effort to gain the greatest effect. Be modest and methodical. Setting too many simultaneous goals is tossing beanbags from the back of the room: it is classic self-defeating behavior.

■ *To change you must adopt an appropriate long-range perspective.* Speed seems important, but it is not always the point. Disappointing early results do not mean you are on the wrong path any more than exciting early results mean you are on the right one. An appropriate long-range perspective involves persistence and utter devotion to making permanent changes. Instead of planning a quick fix, the emotional equivalent of a crash diet, think in terms of permanently revising the specific, decisive aspects of your life that will make a difference. Such revision takes time and diligence, though not as much as you might suppose, and certainly not more than you are capable of. Diets fail when they amount to brief, drastic measures from which you return to former habits. If your previous eating habits made you gain weight and you did not change them, it should come as no surprise when they make you gain weight again.

When you emphasize speed, you are prone to leave out vital steps, or you fail to sustain them for as long as necessary. People who lose weight and keep it off permanently change the way they eat and change other things as well, such as increasing their activity level. To change is to permanently alter what you do.

■ *Change requires that you persist even when your efforts are having no apparent effect other than making you feel disrupted, inconvenienced, and bothered.* Change takes time, and early results are often unpleasant. Many attempts to change end because this is not understood or accepted. Change involves making adjustments to the existing system of thoughts and habits operating in the background of your consciousness, and you will have some temporary hell to pay for tampering with it.

■ *Chaos and setbacks are proof that you are changing.* It is essential that you fully understand this point. By luck, advice, or reasoning, many people begin on a path that would eventually lead them to successful change but misunderstand that the initially chaotic results are actually evidence that progress is under way. Unaware that the chaos will attenuate over time, they become disenchanted. Change involves altering routines, and the new routines may feel disturbing until you grow accustomed to them. If you understand this, you will persist in the face of challenges that otherwise might discourage you.

■ *You cannot change the past.* If your life has had a mediocre plot so far, you cannot go back and revise it. Fortunately, you do not have to. You can learn or do now anything you did not learn or do at some point in the past. You can change the direction of your story from this minute forward.

■ *The problem is not, has never been, and never will be who you are. The problem is always what you choose to do.* Certain habitual actions have short-circuited your success. Change begins with noticing your ability to choose new ways to act and then doing it.

■ *Change requires that you become fully engaged for a period of contemplation, preparation, and decisive action, followed by continuing maintenance.* Change makes demands on you until you lock in new habits, but it is an investment worth making, because staying where you are has a steep price that you have only begun to know.

■ *Change is not something that happens to you; it is something you do.* Change stems from making effort. If you wait for change to come along or for circumstances to change, you will keep waiting. Waiting for fortune to smile on you is not a method for change. Fortune has already smiled. You are gifted. Waiting only postpones change.

■ *Change is a learning process: you learn to do some things differently.* You have learned and changed all your life. This is not new, complicated, or overwhelming. Besides, you have always learned quickly.

■ *Failure is necessary for learning.* When you learn, you make attempts, learn from your mistakes, and gradually refine your skills.

▶ When Clarice, 40, was 8 years old, she desperately wanted a pair of ice skates so that she could join her friends on a pond near her rural Massachusetts home. At first her parents refused to buy the skates, saying that skating was too dangerous. She persisted, however, and she got the skates as a Christmas gift.

After Clarice had the skates on for the first time to try them out, her parents insisted that they accompany her, and they did, each supporting her by one arm so that she would not fall. For the next three weeks, each time she went out they accompanied her in the same fashion. After three weeks, having made no progress, she lost interest and permanently put away the skates.

Clarice didn't fall, but she didn't learn to skate either.

Experiment. Take aim in the right direction, see where you missed and by how much, and then take aim again. You must submit to feeling clumsy and to failing if you want to learn. When it comes to change, the wheel has been invented, and you can build on existing knowledge. But you will make mistakes anyway, so welcome them.

■ *Change occurs unevenly.* Change takes an irregular course. The pace is not the same all the time. Sometimes you progress quickly, sometimes more slowly. And like the life cycle of the butterfly, some things do not show for a while.

■ *Change involves repeated setbacks.* Not only are setbacks a part of the process of change, but they are often evidence that you are changing. When you leave familiar grooves and carve new pathways, you encounter hindrances. Even when change goes well, you may briefly revert to older, more familiar behaviors, or you may hit plateaus, drift off course, momentarily slide back, and then have to right yourself again. Avoid worrying and don't wring your hands. Setbacks are as ordinary as falling while learning to skate. If you turn them into a big deal, they become a big deal—a justification for quitting.

Of course, since setbacks are unpleasant and steal time, you should do everything in your power to avoid them. You do not have control over everything, but you do have control over your responses. If anticipated help does not materialize or unexpected obstacles arise, take an attitude of acceptance (Oh, a setback—that's interesting) and keep moving. Learn about it, investigate ways to prevent its recurrence, but do not lose unnecessary time.

■ *You hinder change when you attempt to make too many separate changes simultaneously.* The problem, as mentioned, is limited attention. When you focus on too many changes at the same time, you spread yourself thin. Better to concentrate your attention and efforts on one or a few specific changes than to attempt greedily to change everything the same week. If you attempt multiple simultaneous changes, you will be exhausted and you will surely fail.

■ *You make change best in small, manageable increments.* Change made gradually and incrementally allows you to accommodate new skills.

Change begins best as a series of small adjustments in your routines, on a scale you can manage so that you can begin making solid progress you can observe. Some steps, by their nature, have a greater impact than others—they create leverage because they influence everything else. These steps make efficient use of your time and effort. Selecting simple changes that nevertheless have a sweeping impact is a key part of the Fifteen Tasks, which I introduce in chapter 6.

■ *Change proceeds best from a considered plan.* What you select to do and when you choose to do it are of prime importance. A random, scattershot approach is inefficient and ineffective. Be thoughtful about your change effort and choose carefully what to do. Time spent on planning pays off well in your rate of progress. What you choose to change first has a great impact on what is possible for you to change next. If you take a considered approach rather than a hasty one, you will reach your goal more quickly. Proceed from a plan.

■ *Change builds on itself.* By making one well-selected change, you make another one more likely. When you make an initial change, you cross a threshold not only for that area of change but also for change in general. When you cross any threshold, you lower it and it is easier to cross the next time. If you acquire essential basic skills, you can go on to develop more complex skills much more easily.

Positive change thus creates two effects: along with a tangible improvement of some kind, you learn something about *how* to change. And as you build up a store of successful experiences, you build the confidence to create more change.

The following are the most frequently asked questions about change:

■ *Are important changes really possible?* Many people change very little. They resolutely cling to routines and prefer the ease that consistency confers. On the other hand, many other people do make important changes. They lose weight, quit smoking, change careers, take up the clarinet, or learn salsa dancing when they never danced before in their lives. The difference between these people is a difference in outlook. People who change do not question whether change is possible or look for reasons why they cannot change. Instead, they decide to change and do whatever is necessary to accomplish it. Changing, which always involves a resolute decision, becomes their priority. When people do not change, it is not because change is not possible but because they put limits on their possibilities. Self-defeating habits are no different from other habits people successfully change.

■ *Doesn't change require personal qualities that you either have or you don't have?* As human beings, we have all the qualities we need to change or our species would not have survived. Humans adapt. Moreover, SLHPPs are often far more adaptable than most people. People adapt their schedules to changing events, make appointments, set dates, keep engagements, and remember to do things. These are the skills required to change, but you have to employ them consistently and properly. You have the capacities and the strength you need; you have only to *decide* to use them.

■ *Won't changing self-limiting patterns require special insight or some fundamental change in my personality?* Changing self-limiting patterns requires nothing fancy. It does not depend on a burst of insight or a personality change but proceeds instead from something less glamorous and extremely commonplace. It comes from observing and developing new skills, the same tools you have already used to construct your world and move toward independence. To change, you observe the habits that have blocked your success and then replace them with new skills and habits. You make progress by changing what you *do,* not by trying to change who you are.

■ *Doesn't change require getting yourself motivated and in a positive mood?* People waiting to be in the mood to change can postpone change indefinitely. If you wait to be in the right mood to change, you will wait longer than necessary. The kick of motivational workshops fades in hours. You need skills more than you need a mood. Besides, moods shift as a consequence of actions you take. Regardless of your mood beforehand, doing something that makes you happy is the quickest way to be happy: waiting for a better mood is just a way to postpone pleasure. Many things affect mood. Participate in shifting your mood and learn to take control over it. If you count on change to put you permanently in a positive mood, you will be disappointed. Nevertheless, living optimally is a solid basis for being happier more of the time.

■ *Do I have to be in psychotherapy to change?* Psychotherapy is a good thing, and self-awareness is highly beneficial. You can change self-limiting habits, however, without profound self-knowledge, and certainly without psychoanalysis or psychotherapy. Nevertheless, you absolutely must keenly discern and carefully observe your self-defeating, self-limiting habits. If you need help to see the patterns that block you, psychotherapy can assist and be a useful tool for you.

On the other hand, I have seen people use psychotherapy as a reason to postpone making helpful changes by claiming, "I have to work through a lot of stuff before I can change." Being in therapy should not be the reason you don't change your self-limiting habits.

■ *Won't my negative habits keep me from changing?* Negative habits have blocked your success. They can get in the way of progress if you let them. To change, you often use the characteristics that have held you back, but in a new way. If you have been stubborn, for example, note that stubbornness in one situation is tenacity in another. Deploy stubbornness on behalf of a new cause. If you have had low tolerance for frustration, become intolerant of low frustration tolerance. If you hopscotch, realize that sometimes the very best thing you can do is to start over instead of staying locked in a strategy that is not working. Leave behind the things that are not working instead of repeating them over and over again while hoping to get different results. Turn your attributes around in this manner and you will see more clearly the possibilities that exist within your liabilities.

Think long enough and deeply enough, and you will discover

advantages and disadvantages in all of your characteristics. Finding the positives within your negative habits gives you more with which to work and will help you be kinder in your judgment of yourself. As you think more flexibly, you free yourself from restrictive conventions. You are more than the sum of your characteristics, and you need not be the victim of your personal history to date. Channel the tendency to want only the advantages into an effort to find advantages in what seem to be disadvantages.

■ *Isn't change just too much work for someone who does not like work?* Change involves serious effort. Paradoxically, it takes more time and effort to skip steps, apply half-assed effort, and live in a mediocre fashion because you have to undo thoughtless errors and explain your listless efforts and feeble results. Save a lot of effort over the long term by putting in a little concentrated effort now. The serious effort necessary to put new habits in place results in far less work and wasted effort and far easier living, and you spend the precious time you have living life in a different register.

■ *Aren't there some things that some people just cannot change?* This question is related to the earlier question about having what it takes to make changes. Undoubtedly, there are things you cannot change, like the problem of being unable to fly by flapping your arms furiously, but more typically, what you think you *cannot* do is something you simply have never done before. When you encounter situations that ask you to do what you've never done before, you use your history as evidence that you cannot do what is being asked of you.

This is fallacious reasoning. There are countless things you do now that at some point in your past you had never done before and thought you could not do. Talent and familiarity make some things easier to do than others. But change can be broken down into discrete, manageable steps that you repeat to the point of mastery.

■ *What if I passed on some opportunities, missed my chance, and now it just seems too late to start over?* All of us have passed on important opportunities. If you decide that it is too late, you compare yourself only to others who made a choice at some earlier time. Then you get trapped in regret and ignore the opportunities that exist now. You cannot relive or undo the past, but you have this moment. You have to decide what to do with it.

You discover opportunities by seeking them out or by creating them through your initiative. You need not conclude that you missed your *only* chance because you did not take some particular path at some certain time. There is no one single moment in a person's life, no one single choice. Believing that you missed your chance is a way to justify current inaction.

■ *What if I am too lazy to change or do not have enough willpower?* You are only as lazy or lacking in willpower as you think you are. Henry Ford said, "Whether you believe you can or believe you can't, either way you are right." He was right. Laziness is a set of habits, something you practice. It operates like an inherent quality when you decide that it is one. Willpower is also a set of skills that can be learned.

What if even with all this new information you try to change and still fail? Let's take another look at fear of failure—the cause of so much unnecessary failure, and so many lost opportunities.

## Fear of Failure Revisited

If we make avoiding risks our only concern, we fail dreadfully.

Jesus' parable of the three stewards left in charge of varying portions of their master's assets (Matthew 25) illustrates this problem. Before traveling, the master of the estate entrusted one steward with ten talents (a sum of money, but the other meaning suits our purposes too), another steward with five, and yet another with one. The first two stewards invested their master's funds, and upon his return each had doubled the amount left to him to oversee. The master lauded their efforts and rewarded them handsomely.

The third steward, fearful of making an investment mistake, had buried the talent given to him in the ground. The master's response was swift. He rebuked the third steward for cowardice and unfaithfulness and fired him on the spot.

Failing to try is already failing yourself. We can only succeed by trying. Talent in itself means nothing. It is a vehicle that leads to something only if it is expressed. To hoard and never use the vehicle is an act of unfaithfulness. By refusing to face up to the risks and make reasoned responses to them, the unfaithful steward betrayed his master's trust. His shortsighted attempt to alleviate his own discomfort stole the expected returns from his master's purse, and he betrayed not only his master but himself as well.

Apparently, Jesus took a dim view of sitting on talents and of nonproductivity. He is reported to have cursed a fig tree to its death for failing to bear fruit. If you have been sitting on your talent, perhaps you too have been unfaithful to yourself.

The poet Rainer Maria Rilke, who struggled with productivity throughout his career, had this to say to those who seek an easy way out: "People have (with the help of conventions) oriented all their solutions toward the easy and toward the easiest side of the easy; but it is clear that we must hold to what is difficult; everything alive holds to it, everything in Nature grows and defends itself in its own way and is characteristically and spontaneously itself, seeks at all cost to be so and against all opposition."

Many SLHPPs spend their youth saying they wish they could take charge of their lives, then spend their adult lives trying to avoid responsibility. It is often at the very brink of some breakthrough that they flee, fearing a Derek-style big mistake from which they will not be able to extricate themselves.

In truth, a life lived well is marked by one failure after another. This is nothing to mourn or evade. To begin the journey toward a real life you must embrace this reality. It is only by taking risks and experiencing failures that you gain sufficient knowledge to learn how to live. Learning and changing involve failure. If you always accomplish things with ease and without failure, either your ambitions are modest or you have confined yourself to familiar territory. If your primary objective is to avoid failure, you put an immediate lid on how far you can go.

You write your autobiography daily, moment to moment. If you do not take risks into account, you will not survive. If you make evading risks your only concern, you miss opportunities.

Remember Clarice, whose parents insisted that they hold her arms when she was trying out her new ice skates? She needed to fall—needed to fail. If what you wish to do is new and complex enough to be worth doing, you will not get it right on the first try. Without a steady diet of failures and falls, Clarice could not progress. Neither can you. SLHPPs would usually agree intellectually that every situation in life involves risk of failure and that failure is a normal part of life—but only for other people. They do not perceive their own consuming wish to avoid failures. When you attempt to avoid failure, you withdraw effort and do not exercise your talent. Given enough time, you doubt your abilities. Your self-image changes, and despite your evasions and excuses, the image other people have of you inevitably changes as well.

In response to fear of failure, SLHPPS seek badly flawed solutions. All choices involve trade-offs, some mixture of gains and losses, but the ones SLHPPs choose make big losses after only paltry immediate gains.

Failures, in fact, are exactly the opportunities you need. You need as many as it takes to grow accustomed to thinking in this way. Edison systematically tried over sixteen thousand different materials in search of a filament in what he hoped would be an electrical source of light. Only after sixteen thousand failures did he find success. Learn to consider failures the ore from which you extract success, for failure is a richer source of information than quick success.

The remarkably brave Katherine Butler Hathaway,[4] whose book *The Little Locksmith* is well worth reading, wrote this shortly before she died at age 52: "I can't deny it or pretend it's not so, mine was a life of failure—one thing after another—like most lives . . . but that is all right, it is universal, it is the great human experience to fail."

We cannot read this as the self-pitying remark of one filled with regret if we consider what else she said about her life: "Oh, lucky beyond most human beings is the refined and well-brought-up person . . . who is bold and crazy enough to defy the almost overwhelming chorus of complacency and inertia and other people's ideas and to follow the single, fresh, living voice of his own destiny, which at the crucial moment speaks aloud to him and tells him to come on."

Hathaway's life was a voyage filled with risks, enchantment, and pain. Stricken with tuberculosis and bedridden from ages 5 to 15, she was permanently disfigured after the disease lodged in her spine. She had the height of a ten-year-old child. She decided, however, to fashion a life worth living and then did just that, becoming an artist, writer, and passionate participant in life and in love relationships.

She did not arrive at her understanding by an easy path. She used the failures she encountered as fuel for her growth. Your own obstacles might be less difficult, but problems are predictable in the life of any person.

The only way to deal with fear of failure is to face it head on. When your ideas of what constitutes success and failure change, your fear of failure dissipates. SLHPPs often define success as being the best at something and failure as being anything less than that. The only real failure you will ever experience is to not begin; not being the best at something is only a progress report. Pursuing your heart's desire with unquenchable effort is worth doing whether or not you succeed. The real achievement in life is to participate instead of hanging back.

When you shift your ideas about failure, you interpret mistakes differently. Mistakes are vital signs that you are pushing away from the familiar to learn new skills. Falling is a part of learning to ride a bike—part of the process of learning. If you do not experience failures, you have set the bar too low. You are making a life of tossing beanbags from a position directly in front of the clown, ensuring that you will make no mistakes but having no adventures either.

Knowing this abstractly is not the same as digging in and making mistakes. You will find out only by committing mistakes that this idea is a reliable principle. Instead of hanging back—not risking anything and criticizing others while remaining above it all—muck around and make mistakes. It will give you a solid knowledge of real life and what works best for you.

Knowing what works for you allows you to form a framework to govern your choices so that they are no longer random and improvised. This provides a context for your actions—your own personal map. It frees you.

By accumulating successes, you build a track record of managing fear-inducing challenges, which in turn brings you a quiet confidence. The practices and skills you develop now, paired with your natural gifts and talents, provide you with a basis for real achievement.

Katherine Butler Hathaway had this to say about making decisions: "I would sort out all the arguments and see which belonged to fear and which to creativeness, and other things being equal I would make the decision which had the larger number of creative reasons on its side. I think it must be a rule something like this that makes jonquils and crocuses come pushing through cold mud."

Experience teaches you how to back up, reevaluate, and restart. You need to know how to recognize a dead end and an opportunity in order to operate with confidence and efficiency rather than overreact to the simple inevitability of frustrations and setbacks.

"I believed that everybody should pursue his own kind of happiness boldly and positively," Hathaway offered. "Because I happened to have been deprived of what is generally considered necessary for a happy life, I had used all my wits to circumvent my fate, to make something out of nothing."

## The Case for Change

It is never easy to go through awkward new beginnings, even when you are prepared or when it is in the service of a dream. How you think about the unpleasant sides of change, however, is one aspect of making your way through them.

Consider my experience in Paris. Not only did I not know French when I arrived, but I had never lived in France. My adventure in Paris thus began as an endless series of small upsets and jarring daily encounters that required me to negotiate the most ordinary sorts of transactions. At the grocery I was unaware that I was supposed to weigh the vegetables and affix a gummy label to the plastic bag before taking them to the checkout. When I went to pay for them, those in line behind me shifted their feet and cleared their throats while I had to take the unweighed, unlabeled vegetables back to the vegetable section and start over, receiving shouted instructions in hastily spoken French from the front of the store.

For days after the vegetables episode I noticed the effect of this incident as I sought out street markets where I did not have to weigh vegetables or label them. (Of course, the street markets had their own rules. You do not simply start selecting produce and popping it into your bag. Someone selects it for you, and you are to trust his skill and goodwill to give you the best.) It was only when I forced myself to return to the grocery and repeated the exotic new practice of putting vegetables on the scale, pressing the button with the picture of the vegetable and its name (in you know what language), tearing off the gummy label that was ejected from the little slot on the side of the scale with much whirring and clicking, and attaching it to the plastic bag that I began to feel a sense of accomplishment—a tiny fragment of competency that earned me one more entry into the life of Paris. So I absorbed the many jolts that accompany change in the service of a personal dream. It was taxing, unpleasant, and tiring. Did I feel incompetent? Yes. Was it worth it? Yes. Because finally, after paying the necessary price, I experienced a sense of mastery.

Those who fail to appreciate that change comes with a price and who want the process of change itself to be as good as the change they seek soon find themselves checking the shade of green in the grass that disappears in their rearview mirror. It is true that if you stay put and stay the same, you avoid the hassle of changing. Avoiding this hassle is the case for *not* changing.

In deciding whether to pay the price for change, you must consider what you will get in return. Many do not get this far; others take a passing look and decide that the price is not worth it. They pay a hidden price, however, for standing pat with choices made long ago and not reexamined—choices they made perhaps by default or without adequate reflection, yet ones they adhere to nonetheless. When they remain in their familiar groove, they pay a price in lost opportunities and experiences.

Moses, finally nearing the Promised Land after forty years, sent spies in to do some reconnaissance about problems and payoffs. Some returned to praise the new land for its riches and produce. They were enthusiastic about going in immediately and asking questions later. Others were concerned, however, about giants in the land and other possibly insurmountable problems. They were ready to call a halt and conduct extended feasibility studies. Both points of view were valid, but both were partially mistaken.

As one who has always wanted to be everywhere, see everything, and miss out on nothing, I accept the following reality, though not without a twinge of disappointment: you cannot be in two places at the same time. You cannot stay where you are in the desert and not miss out on what you might have experienced across the river. You cannot live in the Promised Land and enjoy its advantages while escaping its drawbacks. You cannot change without experiencing some passing unpleasantness—even serious unpleasantness.

You must, as I did with the vegetable scale, override negative first reactions to unpleasant experiences and persist on behalf of your dream. I had to stay in Paris through that first cold, endlessly drizzly, non-California winter to experience that first glorious, sun-drenched day in May, sitting in the Tuileries, the happy prisoner of flowers, sunlight, and murmuring voices.

Some months later I emerged on a late summer afternoon, after being holed up writing intensively for a few days, to walk out onto a street that had in some way changed. Something had happened. It no longer looked foreign—it was *my* street. I could even chat a little in French with the man at the copy shop. I was in Paris, and it felt like home.

This is the case for persistence; this is the case for change.

To reach that day in May and the summer day that followed, I set things in motion much earlier. Change follows a familiar path and begins before you recognize that it is even under way or can discern the shape that it will take.

# The Change Process

Psychologists studying how people change have come up with a five-stage model of the process.[5] Models are summaries of reality and somewhat arbitrarily suggest clean breaks in the usually messy flow of human affairs. In my experience people oscillate between these stages and can manifest aspects of more than one stage at any particular moment. Still, I think you will find this model a useful tool for understanding change, and a guide to help you appraise where you are in terms of changing. I have adapted the model to the kinds of change you may anticipate.

## 1. Precontemplation

Precontemplation is a period of growing unrest—a time of increasing discomfort and first glimmerings that precedes changing. During this stage change is not necessarily your conscious concern, and you have set no timetable for change.

In this period you are aware that something is not right, but you are not necessarily sure you know what's wrong. You have not yet considered solutions to what nags you or thought through any actions you might take. Instead, you consider what you are going through to be perhaps a blue period or a time of nonspecific agitation and frustration. You are uncomfortable, knowing something gnaws at you, but that is where your understanding ends.

During precontemplation, change is hypothetical, distant, vague, and unlikely, and the way you speak of something "bugging" you and your wish that things were different convey that.

> ► Diane, 41, has begun to notice that despite her apparently successful life, she is often experiencing boredom and a sense of pervading emptiness. It has no name and no face but continues to grow over a period of weeks and months. She considers it a stage she is going through, maybe a midlife crisis, or just some

flat spot. Finally, she can no longer continue to ignore it. She begins to write in a journal, something she did long ago but set aside. In a few weeks she notices that her entries are telling her some things.

Diane's lag between noticing her discomfort and doing anything about it is typical of the precontemplation period. If you ignore this discomfort or find sufficient distractions, precontemplation can last indefinitely and not necessarily lead to any change.

## 2. Contemplation

In the contemplation stage you acknowledge that you have a problem and begin to consider what it is and whether you can change it. During contemplation you would still prefer not to have to change but begin to weigh the trade-offs of standing pat versus acting. You may alternate frequently between wanting to take action and resisting it, question your ability to change, and feel moody and irritable. You have not yet made a commitment to change.

The way you talk to yourself expresses your feeling that change is necessary but demonstrates your lack of commitment to taking action. In this stage people say things such as, "I've got to do something about this, I can't go on this way, I hate it that I keep . . . ," and, "I should. . . ." Embedded within these statements are the uncertainties and indecisiveness characteristic of the contemplation period, uncertainties such as: "It's going to be a lot of work, and I'm not sure I'm ready," "I'm not sure if I tried I would be successful; maybe I can ride this out without having to change," "I'm not sure I wouldn't give up in the middle, so why go to all that trouble then quit," and, "Maybe I'll do it someday."

## 3. Preparation

Preparation is the stage when change becomes a concrete reality, beginning with small, important, necessary steps. This is an active stage, even if your actions are provisional or if you hold something back in reserve. You gather information, make phone calls, check class schedules, or enroll in a class to get a feel for what it is like to be back in school. You examine your schedule to create time for activities that support your change. You begin to think and act with change specifically in mind.

Part of preparation is getting internally accustomed to change. This takes the form of fantasy, the mental rehearsal in which you let yourself imagine what life will be like when you change. Mentally trying things on for size helps you ready yourself to deal with higher expectations and new demands. In this phase you face your fears openly.

You now say, "I am going to do this," and set a date, such as, "I will be ready to begin changing on New Year's Day." At this stage people are certain about their commitment to change but may measure what they say to others about their goal to change. Though well under way internally, their change may not yet be fully evident to others.

## 4. Action

The action phase is the stage at which your change yields signs that become obvious to others.

> ▶ Randall has become a man possessed since he decided, at age 35, to go to medical school. He has moved, changed jobs so he can complete missing coursework and study for entrance exams, and taken up running again. His wife calls him single-minded, and he feels a kind of inspiration that has been lacking.

In the action stage change spreads throughout all aspects of your life. Things you mulled and incubated for years now unfold quickly. As you change you develop affiliations with people who support your change efforts.

## 5. Maintenance

The maintenance stage follows the flurry of specific actions taken in the previous stage but is in itself a very active period. Maintenance, despite its dull name, is an absolutely vital phase of the change process, for it is at this time that you bring the rest of what you do into line with the change. In this way you support, fortify, and enhance your gains and extend their effects. This stage is thus a stabilizing period but can also provide a potent catalytic boost to trimming and reshaping your life. The more attention you devote to nurturing and solidifying your new habits, the faster they fall into place. In only a short time you acquire a comfortable level of ease and facility with the change in your life.

At this or any other stage, guard against the self-justifying urge to go missionary and attempt to get others to join you. Be content to know that your path is right for you and learn to validate it from the inside. People who are not ready to change can be threatened by the idea that change is possible. If you seek their validation and do not receive it, you could become needlessly discouraged. Be careful in trying to change others. You may see the light, but not everyone may want your message, and very few people will respond positively to a mission designed for your own reassurance.

If begun with good intentions alone, efforts to change are soon overmatched by the enormous inertia of daily life. If you assume that good intentions will get you there, you will undercut the specific actions necessary for change. Good intentions alone are a Stone Age tool, colored a little too sky-blue and cotton-candy-pink for reality.

You cannot change for other people or for some distant or personally trivial cause you do not connect with in your own heart. Changing requires heart, not a fairy godmother or genie waiting in some bottle. There are a thousand false leads and ten thousand dead ends. You must sustain your effort over time, and you cannot afford to lose time spinning your wheels. If you focus on the right things, the process becomes much easier.

Your life is what you do with your time. You need to make specific adjustments, at first very small ones, in how you spend your time. Focus on your habits of spending time and viewing your possibilities.

Here is one final thing to know about change. Occasionally when people become serious about changing, they experience a surge in fear. And paradoxically and perversely, it can occur precisely when you finally begin to accomplish something, because then you can attack yourself for not having done it earlier. *Why should this be the day I change? What makes me believe this day can be any different from the rest of my life?* And upon taking action you can accusingly ask, *Why didn't I do this sooner?*

These thoughts are simply the death rattle of the old self-limiting habit patterns.

# 5

# Prerequisites

From a certain point onward there is no longer any turning back. That is the point that must be reached.—Franz Kafka, *The Great Wall of China: Stories and Reflections* (1946)

Until one is committed, there is hesitancy, the chance to draw back, always ineffectiveness. Concerning all acts of initiative (and creation), there is one elementary truth—the ignorance of which kill countless ideas and splendid plans: that the moment one definitely commits oneself, then providence moves, too. All sorts of things occur to help one that would never otherwise have occurred. A whole stream of events issues from the decision, raising in one's favor all manner of unforeseen incidents and material assistance which no man could have dreamed would have come his way.—W. H. Murray, *The Scottish Himalaya Expedition* (1951)

Whatever you can do, or dream you can, begin it. Boldness has genius, power, and magic in it. Begin it now.
—Goethe, *Faust*

▶ The first thing Max does is to buy an alarm clock. At age 39, he has never owned one. He has hated the idea of a mechanical device disrupting a natural process. He finds the mechanized life of others appalling and dislikes structure, priding himself on never doing anything the same way two days in a row.

His checkbook is unbalanced, his paperwork chaotic, his house stacked with piles of magazines and correspondence. He is late for his first appointment with me and apologizes for not having showered. He says that "things have been building" for some time, but a conversation about family and career with a former college roommate was the catalyst for coming to see me.

Married at 22, Max left his wife after ten years of feeling completely stifled and writhing from the boredom of a superficial relationship. He worked at a variety of jobs over the years and succeeded at most, but he never sustained an interest in one thing for long.

Without formal training, he has hung drywall, done concrete work, and designed furniture, and although he occasionally makes good money, he tires of "chasing business." He doesn't like having to put himself out there to others and "beg." Besides, entering fields through the back door makes him feel like a fake, so he undercharges for his services because he is learning on the job. As a result, he never makes quite enough money. He is interested in writing but feels he can never match the talents of his father, who wrote television scripts.

Max was on his way to change by the time he came to therapy. Tired of his life, he already had taken the action to contact me. When you even vaguely recognize that something is wrong, you have already entered the initial stage of change.

By now, you may be considerably further along yourself and may have begun to understand how you stifle your potential. If so, you have moved not only beyond precontemplation but also through the second stage of change—contemplation—as well. This is no small accomplishment, since the first two stages are by far the longest ones in the process of change. You are now ready to begin the third stage of the change process—preparation—in which you begin to take concrete steps toward your goal. To fully realize change you need only complete the phase of preparation, take necessary actions, then lock in and solidify your gains.

The necessary first step is to definitively cross an internal line and make an intentional commitment to beginning a new life. In this chapter, we take a broad look at this and other essential prerequisites for moving from a self-stifling, self-limiting style to an engaged, healthy, and achieving one. We focus first on the crucial decision to go forward, and I provide tools to help you accelerate that process. Next, I detail a series of specific imperatives that set the stage for, and ensure the success of, the series of tasks I introduce in the following two chapters. These include recruiting appropriate support, talking to others about your plans, learning the basic principles from which to operate, developing master skills, creating order, developing a work space, and finding aesthetic and sensual pleasure in ordinary tasks. By following these prescriptions, you greatly improve your chances of success.

This entire chapter has to do with preparing within yourself a sound foundation upon which to base future efforts. It's no longer about smoke and mirrors, about phoning it in, improvising, taking unnecessary risks, or running away. But you need not worry that preparation and planning will strip away your sense of adventure and turn you into some well-polished cog. You raise the ante on adventure the moment you begin. If you want to leave blandness behind permanently, brace yourself. If you have stifled your ambitions, you soon will learn that there is a much more interesting way to live. Though you have a destination, you will pass through unexplored territory on the way, and you can count on the unexpected.

Sometimes the start, however, involves something surprisingly fundamental that was always the missing ingredient.

▶ Trevor, 29, originally came to the Maximum Potential Project at the suggestion of his girlfriend, who had tired of hearing him grumble about the boredom of his work. A floater/coaster, Trevor had made many other decisions in his life at the instigation of others. Making decisions on his own was new for him; his first decision was whether he actually wanted to participate in the project. As he began to grasp that he could choose the way he lived, his next steps were to decide how he wanted to live, prepare accordingly, and then carry through on his decision.

Beginning to live intentionally was a huge move for Trevor. The more sweeping the change or complex the goal, the greater the need for thoughtful, purposeful preparation, and clear intention.

The first step on the way to revising your life is to commit quietly but fully to change things and vow that you will not stop before reaching your goal. At the moment you decide, you become formidable, like some hungry animal. Things become clear. Life becomes simpler because when you decide, you simplify it. One priority rises to the top.

Perhaps you have crossed the line already. You wanted to do things differently; when you knew you had to do it, you stopped equivocating. You stopped making excuses and looking for permission to act. You may not have known the details of how you would proceed. It is not necessary to know all that you will do, but you knew you would change, and so you began the process.

People *do* change, permanently and intentionally. If you have not yet crossed the line, you too can decide to change. It is never too late to begin—to go for your heart's desire or to take up something new. If you were to live but for one more day, your last day would be charged with meaning. No matter what you have done before, if something is worth doing, it is worth doing on your last day.

No one has the time to change. You must steal it. Start small if you must, but start. Do not fall into the "if-I-can't-meditate-for-an-hour-I-won't-meditate-at-all" trap. If something is worth doing, it is worth doing for whatever amount of time you can give it. If you can't read for two hours each evening, read for fifteen minutes. Fifteen minutes a night with Tolstoy's *War and Peace* will yield three months of pleasure and a sense of accomplishment to go with it.

## The Line in the Sand

At the Maximum Potential Project we have found it useful to be very concrete with our participants about crossing the line. We move furniture back and draw an imaginary line in the sand. One side of the imaginary line represents life as participants lived it in the past. The other side represents their new life. Crossing the line represents a complete, final, no-turning-back decision to create the life they want.

We begin by having everyone stand on the side representing the past. We then ask those who have already crossed the line internally, or are ready to do so at that moment, to cross; we ask those who are not ready to cross to position themselves accurately in relation to the line, depending on how ready they are.

This is not an exercise in coercion. This is an assessment, an appraisal done in external physical space as it relates to crossing an internal line. It allows each person to represent physically where he or she is internally at that moment. No one who is not ready is urged to cross. Though the stated purpose of the group is change, everyone understands that crossing the line is done on one's own terms. It is no different for you.

You must cross the line, however, at some point in order to change. Where are you in relation to crossing it? Though you might be tempted to skip this step or to do it only mentally, I urge you to do the actual physical exercise in the way I am about to suggest. Don't cheat yourself. Imagery can be powerful, but doing this exercise in space and time has a more potent effect.

☐ Stand in a room of your choosing and draw an imaginary line in the sand, with one side representing your past life and the other the life that is yours to make. If you have already crossed the line internally or are ready to in this moment, step across it physically. Note how you feel. If you have not yet crossed it, accurately position yourself in relation to this line and stand there, noting what it feels like to be where you are now.

In your notebook, write the date and an entry about where you are in relation to the line. If you have just crossed the line, draw a strong, dark, vertical line on the page and record your feelings before you crossed the line and your feelings after you crossed it.

If you have not yet crossed, answer the following: How far from the line are you? How far are you from crossing?

Now *visualize* yourself crossing the line at this moment, without feeling that it is yet time, and note your response. Record your feelings. Then answer the following questions:

- Is there something you recognize that remains in the way of your crossing?
- If so, are you ready to remove this barrier?
- If not, when might you be ready to remove it?
- Is there anything you need to do or find out before crossing?
- Does further delay bring you an advantage? If so, what is it?
- Is there some other reason to postpone crossing the line?
- Is there something more important to do first?
- Do you believe it is too late to begin? If so, could you imagine setting this belief aside? Are you prepared to set this belief aside?
- Do you believe that change is not possible? Are you afraid that you are not up to the task of going for what you want? If so, could you imagine setting these beliefs aside? Are you prepared to set these beliefs aside?
- Do you believe that you *could* reach your dream but if you tried and succeeded now you would have such regret for having postponed it that you would prefer not to reach it at all? If this self-defeating attitude holds true for you, could you imagine setting this belief aside? Are you prepared to set it aside?
- Do you believe that you *could* reach your dream but fear that you might be disappointed by it and would rather not expend the effort than be disappointed? If so, could you imagine setting this fear aside? Are you prepared to set this fear aside?

After years of study, I have concluded that there is seldom a real advantage to deferring change to some future time. Any apparent advantage usually turns out to be imaginary. By crossing the line, you go for your goals now. Whether or not you reach all of them, you head toward a life of greater depth and texture, one more interesting and worth living.

If you think it is too late to begin, take a closer look. It is never too late to begin. Does it make sense to spend the rest of your life in mediocrity because you waited to get started? In life, there are lines you cross and never recross. You have only the present moment. You can never recapture this moment later if you decide in retrospect that it was the best one. Postponing is not simply postponing; it is a failure to act. In any moment you either act or do not act.

You also need to watch out for the particular traps associated with your style; these can conspire to stop you before you get started. If you are a delayer, watch out for the self-defeating tendency to stall indefinitely as a way to avoid making a commitment. If you are a rebel, notice that you could resist what you know is a positive step because you think it is being forced on you. If you are a self-doubter/self-attacker, be aware that questions about your worthiness and capacity can creep in to undermine your resolve. If you are a sleeper, you need to know that crossing the line and all that follows is within your capabilities, and that you will be coached on what to do. If you are a stop-short, this action is the beginning of your liberation if you see it through. If you are a checkmate, this finally is the moment to break the logjam in your life, knowing that by trying to hang on to everything you really have nothing. If you are an extreme non-risk-taker, crossing the line puts you on the line and forces you to leave behind the bland safety of standing next to the clown's mouth. If you are a floater/coaster, you must move away from the principle that the least amount of effort is best. If you are an extreme risk-taker, consider your decision soberly before you move, then make all future steps methodically. If you are a misunderstood genius, crossing the line is a useful step toward harnessing your real genius and developing it with persistence and consistent effort. If you are a best-or-nothing, it may be time to think about pursuing excellence without concern for how you stack up against others or without sacrificing your ambition to do things exceptionally well. If you are a charmer, there is no audience and no one to sweet talk or convince. You are alone, and you must act.

Max, the man who had never owned an alarm clock, made one kind of first step by calling for an appointment. He had decided to act, but he could still change his mind. When he brought home the clock, he took another step that, given his history with alarm clocks, was both concrete and symbolic.

That action has reverberated through every aspect of his life. He has begun to decide ahead of time when he will awake and to plan his next day's activities. By planning, he can work around distractions when they arise. He has begun to accomplish more and to feel better. By using the clock, he has moved from *I'd like to change,* or, *I want to change,* or, *I've got to change,* or, *I'm going to change,* to, *I begin now. Let's do it.* Though he is far from having changed completely, he has begun the process. Regardless of how many additional steps there will be in the process, he has completed the critical first ones.

If you are still warming to the idea of a complete commitment, fine. Do not imagine that you are stuck or falling behind, or invent stories that something is wrong. And do *not* stop here, though, waiting for something to happen. Proceed to make preparations as if you already had crossed.

A few words of caution are once again in order. Waiting for illumination or anything similar is a dead end. Moods are unreliable, and motivational highs can be treacherous, because you must continue the process whether or not you continue to experience elation. Flashy sprints may be seductive, but you must know how to gut it out.

If you have not crossed the line because you do not yet *feel* the way you thought you would, ask yourself if not feeling ready is an isolated instance or if it is similar to previous delays that you later regretted. Some people *never* feel *quite* ready to take significant steps. If you are such a person, recognize that though it might be nice to *feel* ready, you may begin without having that comfortable feeling. At some moment you must take the concrete first step that signals that you are truly on your way to change. You must begin. You cannot pretend to cross. You have no one left to fool. When you are ready to change, cross the line and do not turn back or reconsider your decision.

When you cross, set aside a day to spend alone contemplating your new beginning. Arrange this day so that you view the rising and setting sun. Even if you crossed the line earlier, taking a day of reflection may still serve you well. On this day, do what you want, but be alone. You could walk by the sea or some other inspirational spot, or read poetry, or write in a journal. Be in deep contact with yourself so that you can achieve an appropriate recognition of your new beginning.

Milton Erickson, a master at helping people change,[1] regularly sent patients up on a mountain away from his Phoenix office to look out, down, and over the terrain as they contemplated making changes. He suggested that they would come down with an entirely new point of view, and they usually did. If you can arrange to go to a spot with a similarly panoramic view on this day, do it. It will help give you perspective on the entire panorama of your life.

The clear demarcation provided by such a day will offer you a reference point against which you can measure your change. We do this in life. We say, *"He was never the same again after he lost that job,"* or, *"I stopped being shy after finishing law school."* Use this day as a benchmark.

I suggest that you preserve something concrete from this day that you can keep in view—a seashell, a pebble or stone, a leaf from the forest. Perhaps you will want to keep it near the desk where you work or some other place where you can see it often and draw inspiration from it.

## Going for It

Habits weigh heavily on us, but making an unequivocal choice unleashes a nearly unstoppable force. To change you must decide completely and unequivocally to do so. If you don't decide to change, habits win out. If you like living casually, *unequivocal* may sound a little extreme, but it may not be. You have made your own share of unequivocal decisions and have doggedly pursued them to conclusion.

Who knows how many times you pulled yourself up in your crib, stood momentarily, and then abruptly landed on your bottom? And what did you do next? You hoisted yourself up, stayed balanced on your feet for a couple of seconds, then swayed and fell on your bottom again. You were calmly tenacious (without teeth-gritting or hysterics) and determined, and you stood up again and again. In fact, despite your own "casual" label, you might be passionately, fervently, and unequivocally casual. Observe yourself closely enough and you will find many things about which you are tenacious.

> ▶ Upon getting her second straight B on a calculus test, Bonnie, 34, recalls deciding that she had reached the end of the line in math. The evidence, though flimsy, was convincing, and the decision, made without reflection, was abiding. She had never studied for a math test before and had never gotten lower than an A. Math was something you either "got" or you didn't. How could you—and what would you—study? She stopped paying close attention in class and completing homework assignments, soon got proof that her conclusion was correct, and never looked back. Until she began the project, she had never reconsidered it.[2]

Stifling your potential requires tenacity. Whether or not your self-limitation stems from what looks like casualness, holding fast to the idea that you cannot change requires stubborn insistence. If you harness even part of your stubbornness for the purpose of change, you will have more than enough resolve to make fundamental shifts. All you need to do is to make small adjustments to put your tenacity to work for you.

A decision to move from where you are requires a concrete plan. That may sound daunting, but you already have a grasp of how to go about it. If you have ever plotted ahead of time about how to talk to your parents or how to get the attention of someone you were attracted to, you have experience in setting out a plan. Making a plan concrete simply requires taking that kind of strategizing and elaborating on it.

You need not remain frozen, looking over your shoulder, your gaze fixed on the past, always just about to make the choice that will change your life but never making it. You have only to turn, face the present moment, and begin to work from your current position. Until you do, you remain caught in the past, staying in the same place with what you already know and not moving ahead.

## Paving the Way

When you begin to change, people will notice. People who live, work, or otherwise spend time together develop a system of expectations and cues with each other. People have you pegged, just as you have them pegged. They know your routines, think of them as normal, and expect you to follow them. If you do not prepare them for changes, their reactions could create problems.

People you formerly joined on a moment's notice may feel slighted if you are suddenly busy, and they may attempt to nudge you back into your accustomed role: "What's the matter with you? Don't you have time for us anymore? I can't believe you're busy every night." Tell the people around you—particularly those with whom you live—to expect some changes.

As you change be sure not to abandon your responsibilities. Change does not require becoming self-absorbed and ignoring legitimate demands on your time. If adjustments are needed, talk them over openly to arrive at workable solutions. If you take these steps and do not receive support, simply address them once again. It is not uncommon to discuss repeatedly issues about expectations and responsibilities. If, despite your best efforts, no solution is forthcoming, bring in outside help if necessary. You might hold an open meeting with your housemates or have a session or two with a family therapist.

Be judicious, however, about *how* you talk about the specific changes you intend to make and be selective about whom you choose to speak to. Each time you tell someone you plan to change, you become vulnerable to his or her response. Pay especially close attention to any feeling you have that you must *explain* yourself. When you feel you must explain yourself, you implicitly ask for approval—of your plan and of your decision to follow it. People respond accordingly.

Some may automatically approve because they like you or want you to like them. Others may disapprove and dismiss anything that is out of the ordinary or threatening to them. Still others may not grant approval without knowing more than you may feel prepared to reveal. From your past experience with your friends, you may be able to predict which responses you will get from whom. The issue for you is to avoid seeking approval. Why put yourself or someone else in that position?

Be prepared also for another kind of response that can be much trickier. Some people may feel that you want them to tell you that you are wonderful the way you are and that such a plan is unnecessary. And they may mean it and say it *because* they genuinely care for you. Under ordinary circumstances, unconditional approval of this sort is nectar. If you have not yet crossed the line, however, any ambivalence you feel about the effort required can fuse with their suggestion and work to deter you. Even idle comments that seem only descriptive can have unexpected effects.

> ► Over lunch Chad mentioned to his close and supportive friend, Mike, that he had a new plan to study Spanish. Mike had a positive response to Chad's resolve but, having for years heard Chad complain that he did not have enough time, simply said that he was surprised to hear he had found the time to do it. Nearly six weeks later Chad realized that he had decided to cut himself some slack that very night and simply had not gotten back to his plan to study Spanish.

It is often better therefore to minimize talk. You might even get an overtly negative response. This does not necessarily mean that someone is not well disposed toward you. But you must still expend effort to defend your plan internally even if you do not externally defend it. Since people's reactions, even the most innocent ones, can have corrosive effects on your resolve—particularly before you have made an absolute decision to go forward—pay attention to your intentions and your need for approval.

This is not to say that you cannot benefit from having a sounding board. Remember, however, that your decision to change is yours. You should never put it in someone else's hands. Deciding whom you will talk to and how much you will choose to reveal is up to you, but for all these reasons I suggest proceeding cautiously.

## Someone to Check in With

The more serious the campaign or project, the more you benefit from personal support. Daunting things like change are easier to tackle when you know you have a support system. Having company on the journey is not an expression of dependency but a matter of having backing. Mature independence involves knowing when you can use assistance and being able to ask for it.

Involvement of the right sort helps you move further, faster. Athletes, for example, know they accomplish more when they train with others. It's up to you to choose how much and in what way someone will accompany you, but having a supportive person with you when you face discouragement or reach a lull in enthusiasm is a great benefit.

Truly complex missions are impossible without technical assistance as well. Astronauts have ground crews, Formula One drivers have pit crews, and government officials have aides and advisers. No climber would consider an assault on Everest alone. And although it is possible to learn a foreign language by getting a book and some tapes, taking a class or hiring a tutor usually significantly facilitates your progress. The traveling entourage of the great pianist Yevgeny Kissin still includes his piano teacher.

Therefore, begin now to weigh the issue of support and to consider enlisting someone to accompany you while you change. You decide on the role you want this person to play—witness, monitor, coach, personal trainer, cheerleader, confidant, or tyrant, whatever helps most. Depending on your needs and wishes and the abilities of this person, he or she might play any or all of these roles. The minimum objective is to have someone who can nudge you when you plateau, become distracted, discouraged, or otherwise tempted to throw in the towel.

Since changing is your decision, deciding *not* to talk to your support person about your specific goals is fine. You can just check in regularly about your progress toward your goals without revealing them in detail. If you start out this way, you can always talk more openly later if and when you feel more comfortable. If you prefer to begin even less directly, you might just have coffee with one or two people you find supportive and talk in general ways about goals and change to see how it feels to have such a discussion and to see where it might lead.

The person whom you eventually choose should be not only trustworthy and neutral but someone who does not have a stake in the outcome other than wanting what's best for you. This eliminates spouses, girlfriends or boyfriends, and family members, because they play other roles in your life that could create conflicts of interest or other complications. It is crucial that you respect your support person. Beware of rescuers and people who have a high need to control. This is *your* enterprise. The key issue is finding practical support for your effort.

Obviously it is of great importance that you choose a person only after considerable reflection. If you feel hesitant about asking a particular person, you may have good reason. But don't get bogged down in a hunt for the perfect person. This usually is a source of needless delay and an expression of avoidance. When you are reasonably sure you have the right person in mind, think about it before going to bed and literally sleep on it. If you still feel you have the right person, wait one more day to ask him or her.

Before that person accepts, the two of you need to reach an understanding about how you want him or her to play this role. Keep the relationship, and the demands on the other person, straightforward and simple. Do not request an open-ended or long-term commitment. Though beneficial, it is not necessary that you have the same person throughout your entire campaign. It will be helpful, however, for your support person to be familiar with this book.

Keep in mind that your success is *your* responsibility, not your support person's. If you ask this person to nudge you or be firm with you, do not be resentful when he or she does as instructed. If you foresee problems here, you might consider working briefly with a therapist to get around this sticking point.

Good therapy, either short- or long-term, is a beneficial investment, but since the goal at this point is to have someone neutral to monitor your progress and only secondarily to help you through emotional issues that could get in the way, it would be better to work with a therapist whose approach focused on practical, short-term, problem-solving approaches. A long-term approach to specific short-term objectives can delay you needlessly.

If the person you choose refuses your request, accept the refusal as the best outcome for the two of you. You would not do well with someone who does not want to take the role. You will find other support, so don't feel your success turns on one particular person.

An alternative is to partner or "buddy" with someone else making changes and to coach each other. This can be effective as long as you are both equally committed to change and you avoid competition. If you find someone with whom you wish to partner, make sure he or she is familiar with this book and arrange a trial "marriage" for about a month. Then you can review the arrangement and decide whether to continue.

So how do you finally use this support? Start simply and keep the situation limited. Meet to discuss your joint expectations, and go over your plan in as much detail as you feel comfortable with. After this, check in regularly (weekly is usually best), report your progress on specific goals and tasks, and set goals for the next check-in. If between check-ins you momentarily feel discouraged, call your support person. As your mutual comfort level increases, you can tailor and refine the process of receiving support. The goal is to keep you moving and on target. If you feel stuck, ask for suggestions.

▶ Tony, 37, turned to an old friend, Phil, to serve as what he called his "tyrant." Tony asked Phil to insist mercilessly that he keep to his plan and reach his goals, to goad him, and not to let him off the hook. Their years of familiarity allowed Phil to play the role both seriously and humorously, and the experience added something new to their relationship while deepening their friendship.

## Acquire Knowledge and Develop a Constituency

As you adjust the way you live, there are plenty of things to learn. Be a sponge. Soak up knowledge. The more information you have, the more confidently you will move forward.

You are happiest when you are learning. You feel most alive when you stretch yourself. If you fear you cannot progress beyond some level, look again. You can do it. Besides, acquiring knowledge and polishing skills are immensely satisfying activities, while a lack of know-how and mastery is a source of chronic dissatisfaction.

The modern world has made adults far less knowledgeable about how to survive independently. Prior to the twentieth century, when life spans were shorter, a shepherd might have known hundreds of songs, poems, and stories and several languages, how to play several musical instruments, tan leather, make butter, dry and preserve meat, build a shelter, and prepare the dead for burial. By comparison, we know little.

▶ Charlie often regrets that he falls so far short of the shepherd's standard. His expertise with computers is suspect, and his dazzling success at sales is due, he complains, only to his ability to talk.

When he looks at it closely, his plunge into computers seems like an attempt to fix something with his own hands. He had once tried gardening. He worked feverishly at making a plot but found it hard to maintain, and by midsummer his garden had more weeds than vegetables. He tried repairing a fence but failed to measure the boards properly; as a result, the repair had what he calls "a rustic irregularity not altogether lacking in charm." He then retired from such efforts.

Charlie could survive without playing the cello or blowing the sax, and you can get a fork to your mouth without knowing history or epic poems, but why accept limits? Though no one skill or subject matter makes for a satisfying life, eliminating the possibility of acquiring skills that require effort restricts you and leaves you with no sense of being accomplished. To feel alive you need to learn. And to learn, be it flower arranging, aikido, archery, sculpting, or writing, you need to do repetitive practice.

Obviously there are many sources of information and instruction. Classes are available through community centers, university extension programs, and electronic media. In looking to acquire certain skills, you will find people who have passed that way before you. Begin now to identify those people who know things you have not yet mastered. Then begin to think in terms of a sort of constituency of people, beyond your support person, who can provide you with various kinds of information.

Tennis player Andre Agassi transformed a languishing career by teaming up with a physical trainer and a tennis coach to jointly develop a plan. With his physical trainer, he followed a strenuous conditioning regimen; with his tennis coach, he learned to think strategy and tactics. Both supported him emotionally by accompanying him to nearly every match. The results: Agassi came back from an unranked position to capture major championships.[3]

Concrete practical support can be as beneficial to your change effort as it was to Agassi's. With Agassi, the roles of support person and constituency were mingled, and they could be for you as well. Simply by providing direct information and assistance your constituency will offer significant emotional support, while your support person may offer technical expertise.

Develop a constituency that suits you and your needs. You may not need the structured formality of Agassi's team. Think of people from whom you can learn, however, and when the time is right, sound them out about sharing their information or skills. You do not have to inform these people of your overall plan or tell them they are a part of your constituency. You decide how much you want to reveal, and for your purposes a sketch may be enough.

On the other hand, you may find someone able to mentor you or arrange for you to shadow him or her. Shadowing—actually observing someone working and taking notes on what you observe—allows you to see firsthand how that person reacts and thinks; it also permits you to absorb subtle intangibles such as attitude, pace, and the "feel" of the activity as that person carries it out. Before someone agrees to do this, however, he or she may need more information about what you hope to accomplish.

Through this process you may discover someone who provides unexpected assistance, or you may move in unanticipated directions. If gathering information requires talking to unfamiliar people, ask members of your constituency or friends for names of people who are willing to talk. You will usually have a series of leads quickly. If you get only one name out of this process, however, the person you interview may give you additional names. Interviewing a friend of a friend can be an easier first step than trying to go it alone. You have resources at your fingertips that you may have overlooked. Open yourself to these possibilities.

## Two Principles

Use what you've got—take advantage of your opportunities. When Robinson Crusoe is shipwrecked, the course of his life changes and progress toward his earlier goals is interrupted. His prior destination no longer matters. How he responds to his new situation is all-important. He does not mourn what he has lost. He uses the island (and the wreck) to provide him with what he needs to survive. Crusoe exploits his possibilities by playing the hand he is dealt to its maximum advantage. Had he chosen differently, and bemoaned his circumstances, he could have spent his time grieving for what should or might have been, and perished.

A contrasting rationalization adopted by many SLHPPs is to think that if only they could get their hands on something they lack (a better guitar, a trip to Hawaii) and were not plagued by handicaps (lack of funds, too small an apartment, insufficient time, weak résumé), then they could realize their potential. Or they feel that they have messed up so badly that they don't have a prayer. Realizing your potential requires something different: using what you *do* have.

In a notable Sufi story, Fatima is tossed by fate from one seemingly disastrous and apparently unrelated situation to another. The only continuity in her life is an unwavering attitude: in each new situation she masters patiently what she must learn in order to survive. In one situation she learns to sew, in another she makes canvas sails, and in each instance she devotes herself to doing her craft well. As fate would have it, she, like Crusoe, is finally cast up on land after a shipwreck. But she has arrived in China, and in this new land she combines all the disparate skills she has learned to create amazing tents for the emperor and become an honored dignitary in his court.

Become the master of what you have and what is available. Exploit the advantages of what seem to be your disadvantages. A person with a small apartment, for example, does not have to worry about mortgage payments and can get rid of nonessentials and distractions. If you don't own a place, you have greater freedom to move if you need to do so.

If you feel you lack funds, become expert at stretching your resources. Go to museums on the days when admission is free. If you want to travel cheaply, find out about being a courier. Use public libraries; discover what your community has to offer. This is the "if-you-have-a-lemon-make-lemonade" idea. Just because you are part of a throwaway society, you do not have to throw away opportunities—or talent, for that matter. Throwing away opportunities in such a self-limiting way shows a distinct lack of gratitude and humility.

People of great accomplishment learn the secret of turning every-thing to their advantage. In the later years of his life psychiatrist and hypnotherapist Milton Erickson used his multiple infirmities to teach. He told students, for example, that he used the concentric rainbows in his vision caused by glaucoma to go to sleep at night; he would imagine walking through them. His personal story instilled an idea: use what you are given to further your purposes.

The key element of Erickson's effectiveness was his use of his patients' individual characteristics. Erickson would observe some small thing about a patient's way of speaking or personal history and use it as a way to help that person make significant changes. Erickson, of course, had used to his advantage what others would have considered liabilities. Afflicted with polio at a young age, he used his immobility to become a keen observer of the smallest details of human relationships. He used these same powers of observation as the basis for highly skilled hypnotic interventions with patients.

Erickson suggested that people volunteer to work for free at some job to gain experience. Erickson would then coach them in becoming very useful to their employer. At some point, he would suggest that they tell the boss they had to quit because they needed a paying job. Usually by then a salary was immediately forthcoming, but if not, they were still far ahead because of what they had learned.[4]

This example demonstrates that by being resourceful and tactical you can make use of opportunities—or even create them. Do not fall victim to conventional thinking, your own or someone else's, about what is required for you to achieve or on what timetable. Act on what you *have* now and from where you *are* now.

After all, underachieving is simply not using what you have. If you are gifted, you have a lot going for you regardless of how many opportunities you may have squandered. If you married at 18 and had to bypass college to support a family, the question at age 38 is, what do you do now? Whether you blew a scholarship, fellowship, grant, or relationship, approach your life now from the point of view of taking advantage of current opportunities. Look for them, and notice them.

Robert Bresson's film *A Man Escaped,* the true story of a man imprisoned by the Nazis in France, demonstrates the idea of using every available resource and squandering nothing. It also illustrates a second crucial principle: being flexible and learning from mistakes. From the beginning of the film one thing stays the same: the man refuses to accept the certain death sentence that awaits him. On being taken into custody, however, he impulsively tries to escape by leaping from the car that is transporting him when it is stopped at an intersection. He is severely beaten and placed in solitary confinement. But he is adaptable enough to learn from his mistaken impulsivity. If he is to escape, he must use caution and control and patiently develop a plan.

Unfamiliar with the prison and potential paths of escape, he begins by learning the comings and goings of the guards. When they are out of earshot, he sharpens a spoon and begins to carve through a place on his cell door. When he is finally able to open it, he climbs a ladder to the roof of the building, surveys the possibilities, and develops a plan. He seeks an ally, but his fellow prisoners are too fearful or too resigned to join him. All consider his plan impossible, including one who rejects such meticulous preparation, makes an impulsive dash to escape, and is shot.

Bresson's character uses everything at his disposal: scraps of metal, sheets, bedding, pieces of twine, and keen powers of observation. Nevertheless, in the end he also needs luck and a little unexpected help.

The man accomplishes what he does because he decides to act and then begins with the actions he *can* take. He refuses to accept that escape is impossible and his execution inevitable. He refuses to surrender to the idea that it is futile to try. He assumes the maximum control possible in a seemingly impossible situation through keen observation of patterns and simple, intelligent acts. He is flexible when necessary, but he neither acts carelessly nor improvises. He is courageous but does not indulge in bravado. He takes risks, but not unnecessary ones. His unequivocal decision to escape and his focus on his mission are at the heart of his success. He allows the desperateness of his situation to heighten his powers. He does things of which he would not have considered himself capable.

In a Sufi story titled "The Increasing of Necessity," an impoverished man, looking to receive a reward of gold to support his wife, lies to the king and says he can make a magical figure from Middle Eastern lore, Khidr, materialize in the palace. The man receives the reward, gives it to his wife, and then prepares for his death, the penalty the king has invoked if he cannot deliver on his promise. While he prepares for certain death, the man develops new abilities and understandings. On the day he finally faces his execution in the king's court, Khidr suddenly appears.

In a story from the Old Testament, four lepers, banned from the city, are starving and near death. One of them suggests that they make their way to the city gates on the off chance that someone will have mercy and give them something to eat. The others resist initially, but eventually he wins them over. When they arrive at the city gates, they discover that the city has been abandoned because of a threatened invasion by an opposing army. The lepers eat their fill.

Make it a priority to search for and exploit your opportunities, and be unwilling to throw away any opportunity. Do not be a victim of your own ingratitude. Do not discard what you have.

As you move forward with preparation, you reckon seriously with what you must change.

## A Point of Order

Ignore your notion that people who write phone numbers down in a book instead of on smalls scraps of paper come from another galaxy. Set aside your prejudice that people who carry calendars don't have any fun in bed. If you want to take control of your future, the first thing you're going to have to do is get your life in order.

Open yourself, as Max did, to the possibility that people who create order may be on to something of which you are unaware. If you know someone who keeps his or her space well organized and affairs in order—files up to date, paperwork caught up—take another look at him or her. Staying on top of petty details may provide that person with an edge you could use. Make an appointment with him or her (and be on time) to learn what you can about this mystery known as order. You may make this person the first member of your constituency.

If order has not been your specialty, the first thing to find out from this person is what the payoffs are for generating order. Ask questions, observe how this person orders his or her life, and keep an eye out for what it is about order that he or she enjoys. Be curious. You may see pleasure in ordering your life that you may previously have missed.

Undoubtedly, you *do* know that order has advantages, but you may have at some point decided that it was something you were simply not cut out for—or concluded, like Auguste, that the steps involved were not worth the bother. If so, hear this: if you decide to replace haphazard patterns with order, you are going to save time and avoid frustration. Skipping steps to save time *always* wastes time. And if you have been long convinced that the gene for keeping order was mysteriously left out of your DNA package, you need to know that organization *is* something you can learn.

You will discover that orderly people are not just goody two-shoes who do it for gold stars. Of course, there are neatniks who fall into a different kind of disorder by avoiding real action. Don't let them mislead you. Seek the counsel of those who keep order because they find power and aesthetic pleasure in devoting immediate attention to things. They may tell you that order is not only utilitarian but conducive to tranquility and control, thus allowing everything else to be done with ease.

As Max has discovered, disorder is actually not cool. He continuously lost time chasing his tail in search of a phone number, a crucial document, or an address. Disorder disrupted his flow a hundred times a day. It can also make the change you want harder to complete.

As you know, when you do not take concrete steps toward your wishes, you and they can float indefinitely. Order is a huge asset when taking action. Clear a path now for what is to come. If you truly hate spending time on meaningless tasks, begin now to create a little order here and a little order there in every part of your life. Wherever you go in your house, work space, or car, take a moment to leave it a little more orderly than you found it. This guarantees progress by putting an emphasis on order as an *ongoing* task.

The ongoing part is essential. Otherwise, instead of maintaining order, you create disorder through inattention and must later attack the accumulated disarray. You can come away from this effort exhausted, and for that reason slide immediately back into the old approach. So make it a point every time you enter a room to find one thing you can do to make it more orderly before you leave it.

Pay attention to your own internal order as well. If you spend even just a little time reviewing your wishes and following up on them, you achieve more internal order and better external results. If you feel that you need help to create internal order, seek out the help from a trusted friend or your support person. The next chapters model an orderly internal approach to external tasks. In the meantime, find someone with well-developed organizational skills and meet with that person until you are able to adapt these skills for your situation.

## Out of Order

Skills that support order—organization, attention to detail, consistency, breaking complicated tasks down into steps—become helpful as soon as your aims exceed your immediate concerns. Without order, you can run quickly into chaos. Instead of dismissing your desires as not worth the trouble, fashion new skills. SLHPPs, for example, often wind up with multiple interests pitted against each other because they do not focus on how they use their time.

Max resisted carrying a schedule book until well into his adult life. He thought that if he ever needed one it would be a sign that he was too busy. With his preference for spontaneity and reliance on memory, he often missed concerts, films, and exhibitions for want of having jotted down a note.

Will you miss out on fun if you become more orderly? It depends on your definition of fun. You might not make as many trips across Paris in pre-Christmas traffic without map or directions, but then . . . Unfortunately, spontaneity is too often a nice word for a knee-jerk adherence to past conditioning—a grade B version of automatic pilot. You will not lose real spontaneity or fun by becoming orderly or knowing what you want to do before a day begins. Rather, you'll provide a structure within which true spontaneity can flourish.

From the time of Freud's observations concerning anal fixations, obsessions, and compulsions, orderly people have been the subject of unwarranted smirking. When Freud talked of anal fixations, he was not talking about order; he was talking about an inflexible, obsessive fixation on order and *compulsively* orderly behavior. True order is the product of an orderly mind and forms the basis of all interior and exterior accomplishments. Freud himself was an orderly person and an orderly thinker.

If you feel you have sunk into mediocrity, see if disorder accompanies you or if disorder is in itself a prime cause of your slide. Take a little field trip. Go to your garage or wherever you keep household tools. How do your tools look? Can you put your hand on a Phillips-head screwdriver or that set of vice grips? Where is the black electrical tape? If you cannot find these items, it's hard to say this is some kind of plus. Every second you hunt for your tools is time that could be spent having fun. Do you know where your tax papers are? Okay, you've heard enough.

There are many other forms of disorder.

Besides losing time searching for items you need, you may also waste time correcting things you overlooked or did not handle correctly the first time. You may find yourself spending unsatisfying amounts of time on the phone trying to get that late charge or parking ticket waived. Having to go to court to plead your case is a time-wasting inconvenience. A lack of order in these matters frequently has you in crisis mode, putting out fires; you end up spending the precious little downtime you have catching up on things left undone or done haphazardly. To a truly striking degree, many SLHPPs spend weekends and even holidays digging out from under accumulated tasks long postponed.

Compare that kind of disorder to the following characterization of order:

What comfort, what strength, what economy there is in order—material order, intellectual order, moral order. To know where one is going and what one wishes—this is order; to keep one's word and one's engagements—again order; to have everything ready under one's hand, to be able to dispose of all one's forces, and to have all one's means of whatever kind under command—still order; to discipline one's habits, one's efforts, one's wishes; to organize one's life, to distribute one's time, to take the measure of one's duties and make one's rights respected; to employ one's capital and resources, one's talent and one's chances profitably—all this belongs to and is included in the word order.

This excerpt from *The Private Journal of Henri Frederic Amiel*, written in 1853 before personal digital assistants, still holds up today. Order is a luxury. Order is a necessity. Order is an art and a key to internal and external mastery.

## Sources of Disorder

Disorder arises from many sources but comes perhaps most often from simply not completing something you are doing. It accumulates from avoidance and postponement. We have looked at avoidance—the recipe for quickly multiplying the unpleasantness of anything. In a matter of days you face a formidable pile, but in a month you face an avalanche of routine things you let accumulate. There are, however, other sources of disorder.

You may have dismissed a strong unmet need for order because you feared you would not be able to maintain it.

▶ Thirty-four-year-old Ray's needs and aspirations for order are so high that he cannot envision fulfilling them. Consequently, when he tries to put his affairs in order on three-day weekends, he feels acutely disappointed for failing to complete the task. He then does not come back to the task for weeks, falls back into extreme disorder, and claims he is not the type to keep order.

Ray understood that taking a perverse pride in disorder and connecting it somehow to general feelings of superiority is a self-limiting solution. But at some point he concluded that he would never be able to stay on top of his paperwork or keep his belongings organized; he is only able to make headway when he sees that that decision was a dead end.

If you still do not know where to begin, I have good news for you. Even fifteen minutes per day devoted to organization and order will eventually cut through any disarray. You must persist, however, in putting in the time. Instead of waiting for any more disorder to accumulate and telling yourself that there is no point in starting until you can get it all done at once, set aside those fifteen minutes per day and make whatever headway you can. Then on weekends try setting a timer; work on order for ten minutes every hour and spend the other fifty as you choose. Before long you will be caught up. If you keep up the same routine, you will maintain order.

You do not have to be *bound* by such a schedule. But a schedule can keep you focused so that you can enjoy your other interests. With a good schedule, you can prevent the frustration that Max suffered from a lack of proper planning.

Disorder is neither a positive aesthetic experience nor a source of pleasure. The next time you are fuming because you cannot find your keys, stop and create a solution: an orderly habit for dealing with your keys that you will always follow. If your goal is to do more than just get by, focus on order.

Disorder can even stem from a strength such as adaptability. Shifting your attention and becoming involved in a new activity rapidly can keep you from dwelling long enough on mistakes to learn from them. When frustrations roll off too easily, you squander opportunities to solve problems. You may remember that, as disturbed as my friend Auguste was the afternoon we spent in traffic, within half an hour he was fine again. His habit of quickly setting aside turmoil kept him from focusing a little intelligent attention on how to always be sure he had a map in his car. Don't allow adaptability, low emotional intensity, and a predominantly good mood to void good common sense.

Adaptability, like any other temperamental quality, is not something that sets final limits. On the contrary, it is at the heart of using what is available to you. You are the one who sets final limits or frees yourself from them. Work *with* the positive side of adaptability and *around* its shortcomings. It is a manifestly positive quality that creates disorder only when it is relied on too much. Take decisive steps to deal with the problem of disorder. You will not regret it.

If you work with apparently negative qualities, you can convert them into positive ones. If you are five-foot-three and wish to play professional basketball in the NBA, you are poorly suited physically to the task. First, you would have to endure the criticism of those who would say the task was impossible. And second, you would have to work the height disadvantage to turn it into an advantage. But Mugsy Bogues, five-foot-three-inches tall, did not just make the league but also went on to have a lengthy and successful career. He turned quickness into an asset and learned to shoot the ball with a higher arc to clear opposing defenders. He had to be tenacious. He had to use what he had. And he had to think in an orderly way. It is the way we think that creates disorder from strengths or order from weaknesses.

If you are adaptable, you have to pay greater attention. When you lose the keys, you have to make a note to come up with a real, permanent solution. Never forget that you are resourceful and creative. If you decide to focus on something, you will come up with solutions that work for you. If you have not yet developed solutions, you have in all likelihood simply skipped that step.

Being orderly is a decision. There are many tools to help you get there. If you think your problem is laziness, realize that laziness resides in all of us, side by side with ambition, energy, and any number of other qualities. If you give laziness sway, it will be influential. Most achievers I have known have told me that in the beginning they had to learn how to work around laziness and prevent it from stopping them. Remember: laziness is not the single trait that characterizes your existence. It can be there when you need it, however, such as when you decide you want a day of profound relaxation.

Begin to think that, like the director of a film, you run the show and will tell your cast of traits what you want of them and when you want it. If at times you have behaved lazily to your detriment, you have also worked energetically. All processes are reversible. All scripts can be written differently from any moment forward. One of the best ways of dealing with laziness is to create order and follow a plan, thereby defeating the tendency for laziness to rise up and fill the vacuum. You are accustomed to thinking in a certain way about yourself. The limits are of your own invention.

# Order and the Art of Working

For several years before I developed the Maximum Potential Project, I offered workshops in which I introduced a range of voluntary physical tasks designed to focus on the process of work as an adjunct to verbal group psychotherapy.

People arriving for these workshops were given a list of possible tasks from which to choose and the chance to work on them alone or with others, but the tasks were to be done according to unusual instructions: participants were to move, walk, and work at half speed—literally in slow motion. They were asked to notice bodily sensations, observe the path of their thoughts, and abstain from conversation unless maintaining safety or doing the work required it. Designed to pull people out of habitual modes, these instructions promoted a different kind of attention to work.

The tasks themselves included such things as hand-weeding a flower bed a single blade of grass at a time, moving a pile of firewood from one location to another one piece of wood at a time, and painting a wall with a tiny trim brush, using exactly the amount of energy necessary to apply the paint to the wall, no more, no less. The periods of time devoted to tasks were irregular and interrupted at unexpected intervals in order to keep the focus of conscious attention applied to the process of work and away from task completion.

In response to anonymous questionnaires, participants reported a variety of changes during the time they attended these workshops. The instructions to work slowly and be silent baffled many at the outset. Participants had a variety of typical first responses to these instructions, including feeling frustrated and ignoring or forgetting them. Slowly, as they grew more accustomed to them, they shifted their focus from completing tasks to experiencing the moment-to-moment process of working at them.

Most reported developing a kind of quieting of the mind in which they became more aware of themselves and their surroundings and experienced inner stillness and tranquillity and an absence of urgency.

Many reported a fundamental shift in their approach to routine tasks outside of sessions, and most reported that these workshops accelerated the benefits of ongoing therapy or provided breakthroughs they could not have envisioned.

Whatever the explanation for these impressive results, when concrete physical activity accompanies learning, new understandings are more fully assimilated, and not just among so-called kinesthetic learners. Just as music helps you memorize long pieces of information (like the alphabet song you learned as a child), physical movement also enhances learning.

You can experiment with this way of working on your own with simple household chores such as washing dishes. Work slowly and in silence for short periods of time, which you can increase as you like. You need not increase the total time by much. The key is in the amount of attention you pay to the process.

When you observe your body and thoughts as you do things, your perceptions shift. Working while focusing on the *process* of working is an aesthetic experience.

The key to this way of working is attention. The Zen saying, "Chop wood, carry water" means doing what you do with simple detached attention. Instead of withdrawing attention from simple chores, infuse them, even flood them, with minute attention. Then notice every sensation. You will make the simplest chores sensual.

Also, pay attention to the quality of the light in your surroundings, listen to sounds, feel and examine textures, experience sensations of warmth and cold, wet and dry, sense the feeling of your clothing on your body and, if outside, the caress of the sun or breeze on your skin or hair. Feel your body, the kinesthetic sense of your body. This kind of attention is the master antidote to boredom. It is an art you can develop easily.

Boredom stems from a withdrawal of attention. By doing anything you have previously considered monotonous with exaggerated attention, you transform it. Make it a habit to drench with attention activities you consider boring. For example, the next time you attend a meeting with a boring speaker, pay greater attention instead of less. Focus on exactly what it is that makes what he or she says so boring.

Think of ways each thing could be made even more boring and more interesting.

Attention keeps you engaged. Boredom starts by stifling attention; it is usually an intolerant reaction to frustration. Decide not to allow external things to control your inner state. All work provides an opportunity to create order. You already do these chores; why not gain from them? You gain the most from each opportunity by applying attention. In fact, if you view all work as an opportunity to work on yourself, you will advance rapidly in terms of setting an internal order. External work is exactly that: an opportunity to work internally.

When you withdraw attention from work, you miss opportunities for learning task mastery and self-mastery and pass up possibilities for learning the skills you need to reach a different level of personal fulfillment and accomplishment. To move mountains, begin by engaging yourself in your work. If you infuse work with attention and thereby transform it into a form of moving meditation, you infuse it simultaneously with meaning.

## True Efficiency

There is something profoundly nourishing about working with attention. All work touched by attention becomes something richer. If you fear that you do not have time for such a leisurely approach, you will soon learn a paradox. True efficiency involves the investment of time in the right activities at the right time.

Listen again to what Amiel has to say in another excerpt from his journal:

> To know how to be ready is a great thing! A precious faculty, and one that implies calculation, clear-sightedness, decision. For this one has to be able to cut the knots, for not all knots can be untied; one has to be able to disengage the essential, the important from the endless minutiae; in a word, to simplify one's life, one's duties, one's affairs, one's impediments, etcetera.

> It is astonishing how entangled and wound up as a rule we are
> in a thousand and one obstacles and duties, which are not real
> duties and which yet shackle us in our movements.

How do you separate the essential from the nonessential? How do
you increase your speed without rushing? Develop a method that provides a basis for making the decisions about what to cut and what to
retain. Katherine Butler Hathaway always chose what looked like the
most creative alternative. Being able to shift is a good thing. Responding to circumstances only because you have no plan and are ill prepared
is something else. Directed by forces outside your control, you can find
only occasional crumbs of time that are truly yours.

If you work from a methodical plan not only will you feel an enormous liberation, but you will also see and experience firsthand the benefits of true efficiency. Rushing and improvising bring disorder. Order
is the path to true efficiency.

More Amiel:

> To know how to finish is at bottom the same thing as knowing
> how to die; it means distinguishing the truly necessary things and
> putting the others back in their place. To be as free as possible at
> every moment, one must have a great deal of order. It is disorder
> that makes slaves of us. The disorder of today takes its toll from the
> freedom of tomorrow.
>
> The things we allow to trail along behind us rise up in front of us
> later and obstruct our road. When each of our days regulates that
> which concerns it, liquidates its affairs, respects the day that is to fol-
> low, we are always ready. Whatever encumbers us destroys all ease, all
> liberty, all clarity; and encumbrance is the fruit of procrastination.
>
> Do not put off to the morrow what can be done at once. Noth-
> ing is done while something remains to be done. To finish is the
> mark of the master.

If you want a simple principle from which to begin to inject order
and efficiency into your life, the last paragraph of this excerpt from

Amiel is particularly noteworthy. He invokes a fundamental principle that summarizes the basic task of creating order. You would be hard put to find a simpler, more powerful principle than this: complete the affairs of each day. A master skill, finishing offers a great sense of mastery.

If you are like most of those whom you have met on these pages, freedom is near the top of your wish list for your life. Amiel again underscores the freedom that awaits one who achieves order. Moreover, Amiel makes it clear that by successfully pursuing and finishing one objective, you accomplish other objectives at the same time. Such leverage is important to change. Seek changes that bring other positive changes along with them.

On the other hand, procrastinating, quitting, and not finishing have powerful leverage too. Each brings additional disorder along with it. Eliminate these habits and replace them with completion, and it will make a revolutionary impact on your life.

"To know where one is going and what one wishes" is another of Amiel's definitions of order. Having goals is like having a rudder on a boat. Goals help you steer yourself instead of allowing winds or currents to push you along. If you spend only a few minutes each morning considering what you plan to accomplish that day, and then tell yourself to keep that plan in mind, you will be far ahead. If you don't have an idea of where you are going, you are much more vulnerable to distractions and what Emerson called "idle curiosities." These cause you to lose time when you come back to earth and try to remember what you were going to do.

Saint Paul said in one of his letters, "A double-minded man is unstable in all his ways." One of the things I learned quickly by running groups for SLHPPs was that most participants did not make their final decision to take part until the very last moment. Even if they expressed serious interest, they postponed the final commitment. I also learned that a certain number would come for a first consultation and then not return for a second appointment. Given my experience with SLHPPs, I began to appreciate what it was like for them to run their lives without much planning. It is tiring to live in this way. The apparent freedom becomes a prison.

Part of this pattern stems from a hesitancy to commit yourself to anything that could lead to disappointment. You do not want to be fooled. But ultimately it is a lack of clarity about where one is going and what one wishes that lies at the heart of the problem. Finding that clarity requires reflection, a reordering of priorities, and the choice to pursue some things and let go of others. If you have preferred to leave things fuzzy and have a habit of alternating your feelings about some things, this double-mindedness can easily make you unreliable, even to yourself.

The following telephone message, left on the Maximum Potential Project voice mail by someone considering signing up, came three days before the group was to begin:

> Hi, Dr. Shaw, it's Garth calling back. I'm sorry I haven't called or written sooner. It's because I've been really ambivalent. I got the forms in the mail, and there are a couple of things that were bothering me. One is the use of so much written material, and the whole idea of committing to fourteen sessions is just really problematic for me. And also the complete financial commitment and not knowing if it's like a thing that's going to work out or not. I just was really ambivalent about that. So I don't know what to say. I tend to say if someone else is waiting in line, go ahead and give him the space, and then again, I'm not sure, 'cause I'm still considering it. Anyway, I wish I weren't this ambivalent and more sure, but I am, so anyway, if you want to call me, my number is . . .

If ambivalence paralyzes you, reflect on what you want and you will naturally discover the goals you want to set.

## Create a Workspace

A rich vein of psychological research supports what hoteliers, bar and restaurant owners, architects and interior designers, and feng shui masters have long known: the physical arrangement of space, including the type and arrangement of the seating, the location and orientation of furnishings, and the type and intensity of lighting, fosters or inhibits different activities.[5]

Physical environments are a different kind of structure and provide a different kind of order. Replete with signals that are processed outside your conscious awareness, they dictate more than you commonly notice. If a space is designed so that it supports your efforts, it beckons you and makes everything you do there easier.

Be sure to reap the benefits of creating a pleasant and well-designed workspace. Do not presume that you will work as efficiently with interference from conflicting activities or without supplies you need available and within easy reach. "To have everything ready under one's hand" is another of Amiel's definitions of order. Do not pretend that you will be just as effective with inadequate lighting or by working from your bed in your underwear (or without your underwear for that matter). Notwithstanding Marcel Proust and Anna des Noailles, who wrote from their beds, bed is best left for sleeping and making love. Those are its fundamental associations. If you work from bed, both your sleep and your work efficiency usually suffer. Let's hope your sex life doesn't suffer too. Why take the chance? Work works better elsewhere.

You are most efficient when you dedicate spaces for certain activities. It is ideal to set aside a space or a room for your exclusive use. It is even better if that room can be under lock and key, a sanctuary others do not enter. But if you cannot afford this luxury, you can approximate it by having a workspace set up exclusively for your own use. Ask people you live with to respect this space and to not touch or move the things you leave there.

If you are pursuing more than one activity—say, studying trigonometry and learning about lapidary—it is beneficial to use one space for one activity and another space for another activity. And if you can, set both places completely apart from the place where you pay bills or do correspondence. In this way, each workspace has only one set of mental associations; when you approach that space, you will experience unambiguous signals to work on only that activity. The lack of ambiguity will help you focus.

Depending on your living situation, these arrangements may or may not be easy to create fully. Be active in approximating them. Organize your space or spaces with one main objective in mind: to increase your ability to study, read, write, practice a musical instrument, reflect, or plan. By doing so, you will immensely support your efforts.

Start by considering each activity you will pursue. For example, the activities related to changing your self-limiting approach will involve completing written exercises, making some timelines, and reflecting and planning. For some of these activities, you will need a good-sized flat surface upon which to work. You will also need a space where you can either post the timelines or place them for easy retrieval. If you cannot leave the timelines and other reminders in view at all times, you might want to purchase an inexpensive portfolio, the type artists use to store and carry around drawings. These are readily available at art supply stores. In a pinch, you can approximate one by creating a large folder with firm enough sides to protect your work.

Next, consider what additional minimum requirements you may need to carry out your activities. Think of it this way: everything in your space should be working *for* you and supporting you; nothing should be working against you. Therefore, remove anything from these spaces that might distract you—telephones, stereos, and perhaps even pictures of your lover. In general, strive to eliminate all obstacles that could test unnecessarily your frustration tolerance.

Arrange to have good natural and artificial light. You must be able to work in this space without straining your eyes and adding unnecessary fatigue. Use a good-quality computer screen to keep glare and eyestrain to a minimum. Choose a spot that is isolated enough from other activities. To work in maximum comfort and with minimum strain, make sure you have a good supportive chair and a desk or table of the proper height.

Also, be sure that the supplies you need are within easy reach. And be certain that your paper and writing instruments are of good quality, feel good in your hands, and are pleasing aesthetically. The idea is to make your workspace as practical and efficient as possible. Then arrange the entire environment so that it communicates the same message: this is a great, comfortable workspace. Beyond these minimum requirements, your workspace works even better if it appeals to your senses and is aesthetically pleasing. Make your office space a seductive pleasure. Make it literally beckon you.

Choose your favorite colors as a decorating scheme. Choose a chair and desk or table that appeal to your eye and sense of touch. Over time make your workspace approximate as closely as possible the most ideal workspace you could imagine.

Of course, maintain order in this workspace. Treat it with respect. Keep things where you want them. Always include a few minutes of scheduled time to reorder the space before you leave it. Time spent reordering your workspace will reap many benefits, not the least of which is creating an inviting space to which to return. You will be more efficient, working with greater inner harmony and tranquillity.

## Master Skills

It is one thing to eliminate ways in which you have blocked yourself, but another to develop the skills necessary to complete things you begin. These are skills that may have been left undeveloped when you were not challenged, or you may have found ways to avoid developing them. They need to become master habits.

Even if you disdained some of these skills, they are likely to be the basis for the habits you need to do something really worthwhile. So now it's catch-up time. In Amiel's words, to be effective one needs "to discipline one's habits, one's efforts, one's wishes."

Master skills provide that discipline. They are habits you bring to the performance of *any* activity. They are the qualities of effort you bring to bear as you approach tasks of all kinds. For example, you have a set of discrete skills and habits related to, say, blow-drying your hair. You take out the dryer, turn it on high or low, and perhaps use a brush. Your actions are habitual and do not require great thought or attention. Blow-drying your hair is not in itself a master skill. Master skills govern the care and attention with which you approach blow-drying your hair or polishing your shoes or filleting a salmon. Master skills are habits related to the *quality* of the effort and attention you expend on all that you do. They certainly do affect the outcome.

To succeed at a high level, you need to learn to employ the following skills habitually:

- The skill of order
- The skill of patience (related to tolerating frustration)
- The skill of deploying attention, as discussed in relation to work and boredom
- The skill of persistence or tenacity
- The skill of consistency
- The skill of thoroughness and follow-through
- The skill of finishing
- The skill of repetition

All goals contain some tasks that are less pleasant than others. If you have avoided these tasks, you are unaccustomed to their requirements; you are out of shape to deal with their demands. You must now get in shape and increase your capacities in each of these areas. Target the areas in which you need work and proceed from there. To extend any capacity, physical or emotional, you need regular exercise, progressively increasing demands, and rest.

To begin running, for example, it's best to start by going a short distance at a slow speed. If you push yourself mercilessly, you are likely to injure yourself or simply quit. It is the same with any new habit or skill.

To build emotional stamina and resilience, start appropriately. Choose to begin with one thing and do not attempt too big a step. If you have quit previously at the first sign of difficulty, you must build up your ability to endure frustration by choosing to do something you abhor. What?!!! Yes. Stay with me. This is not some perverse exercise in crawling over cut glass or wearing a hair shirt; it is not masochism.

▶ Miller, 44, who needed to increase his emotional control, had difficulty listening to what he considered his wife's unwarranted complaints without going ballistic. His first goal was to maintain his composure by simply listening for three minutes without responding in any way. At first, this seemed an impossible goal since he found her exasperating. But soon he was able to look surreptitiously at the sweep second hand on his watch and listen quietly for three minutes. It was a beginning.

What you choose can be something practical but to you, unpleasant, like organizing the paperwork in your office, or impractical, like packing spools of thread in a shoe box and then unpacking them. The purpose is *not* to increase your pain tolerance or to teach you to sort widgets. The goal is to learn how to work when the work is not flashy. What I am prescribing is what Roberto Assagioli called "will training."[6]

To start, experiment once a week with a ten-minute session of doing something mildly unpleasant. Set a timer for that amount of time, and stop when it sounds. Record your thoughts and observations in a new section in your notebook. What you do doesn't matter, as long as it is simple and mundane. You could organize your underwear, software, or flatware. You could take your socks out of your drawer, sort them by color, and put them back, or alphabetize your CDs.

Apply the kind of nearly loving care and attention that I asked of the people who participated in my workshops on work. You can work on every master skill by doing what I have just described. The best tasks for teaching persistence and tenacity are the ones to which you return again and again without seeing much discernible progress. For example, you could sand an old chest by hand to prepare it for refinishing. Instead of using those nasty chemicals to remove the old layers of paint or stain, sand the chest methodically over a long period of time. The best tasks for teaching consistency are those that require patience, such as keeping a garden weed-free. As you work on these things, the work you do works on you.

*Kung fu.* I am told that those words actually mean "consistent practice over time." So a brush stroke in calligraphy can be kung fu—something a painter has practiced over and over until he can freely make the stroke with his whole being. Playing the piano, tying your shoe, making a soufflé, sanding a chest—all can be kung fu.

Practice repetition so you *can* apply it as a skill whenever you need to learn something new. You will eventually forget the discomfort and begin executing the broad, big strokes. You need repetition to perfect all the master skills and to have them ready to use.

While you perform exercises, do not focus on whether you are developing new qualities. Don't dig up the corn seeds to see if they are sprouting. Remain empty. Just do the repetition, and then do it again. This alone is an exercise in patience. Put in the time, and shifts will occur internally whether or not you notice them on the outside. Allow your attention to remain on the process, on the actions you take and the movements you make. Leave the soufflé in the oven.

Repetition is the key to developing the skill of patience. When you surrender to lengthy repetitive processes, you increase your ability to persist, tolerate frustration and monotony, and continue to work despite setbacks. Repetition is not a matter of forcing yourself. It involves tuning in to the process rather than focusing on its outcome. You do not go to a concert to hear the encore. Devoting attention to the sensual aspects of what you do helps you learn to engage yourself in the process and develop your capacity for persistence.

Since learning new skills requires repetition, learn to love it. Although it is wonderful to grasp things quickly and be able to do remarkable things effortlessly, the skills that demand repetition yield a different kind of pleasure. Do not miss out on this pleasure. If you quit music lessons or dance lessons, or skipped more practices than you completed, you lost opportunities to master repetition and patience. By taking pleasure in it, you can more easily make the gains associated with repetition. If that challenges your existing beliefs, I say, try it and experience it for yourself.

Master skills are the accumulated outcome of repeated, discrete acts. Developing patience through repetition is the master skill equivalent of doing physical reps in the weight room. Do not ignore the cumulative power of small repeated actions. If you consider small acts trifles not worthy of the bother, you will remain unable to do large things. You must get in shape and build emotional endurance. Repetition builds internal muscle—basic emotional and task-oriented muscle.

One more point about repetition and persistence: in many situations purposeful delay is a source of pleasure. Sex is more than orgasms. Anticipation and delay are a part of the pleasure. An emphasis on immediate outcomes goes hand in hand with an extrinsic focus that strips away pleasure. Many things develop only with the passage of time. The cobblestone streets of Paris have taken centuries to look the way they do, and the best balsamic vinegars are aged a lifetime. If quick is your definition of pleasure, you are sorely limiting yourself.

Many worthwhile ventures are lost because of lack of persistence and patience. If you had only given them more time, they would have borne fruit. You do not go from photography student to Pulitzer Prize winner in a year; you do not go from sketching a skirt to having your own line of clothing in eighteen months. Especially, new and creative ideas must be nurtured long enough to take root.

Persistence means continuing to work and continuing to keep your feet moving, no matter what. If you pay attention to the process rather than the goal, you nurture persistence. Much impatience derives from focusing on end points and outcomes rather than on doing things well. When things are worth doing, all of the parts are worth doing.

Rainer Maria Rilke, a man who persisted through numerous difficulties to create lovely poetry, said,

> . . . Ah! but verses amount to so little when one writes them young. One ought to wait and gather sense and sweetness a whole life long, and a long life if possible, and then, quite at the end, one might perhaps be able to write ten lines that were good. For verses are not, as people imagine, simply feelings (those one has early enough),— they are experiences. For the sake of a single verse, one must see many cities, men, and things, one must know the animals, one must feel how the birds fly and know the gesture with which the little flowers open in the morning. One must be able to think back

to roads in unknown regions, to unexpected meetings and to partings one had long seen coming; to days of childhood that are still unexplained, to parents one had to hurt when they brought some joy and one did not grasp it (it was a joy for someone else); to childhood illnesses that so strangely begin with such a number of profound and grave transformations, to days in rooms withdrawn and quiet and to mornings by the sea, to the sea itself, to seas, to nights of travel that rushed along on high and flew with the stars—and it is not yet enough if one may think of all this. One must have memories of many screams of women in labor, and of light, white, sleeping women in childbed, closing again. But one must also have been beside the dying, must have sat beside the dead in the room with the open window and the fitful noises. And still it is not yet enough to have memories. One must be able to forget them when they are many and one must have the great patience to wait until they come again. For it is not yet the memories themselves. Not till they have turned to blood within us, to glance and gesture, nameless and no longer to be distinguished from ourselves—not till then can it happen that in a most rare hour the first word of a verse arises in their midst and goes forth from them.[7]

If you are a best-or-nothing, realize that being best requires you to develop and not simply hang on to what you can do already. It requires persistence. If you are a hopscotcher, realize that you have left many unfinished things behind because you lacked persistence.

## Time and the Five-Minute Rule

Amiel says that "to organize one's life, to distribute one's time" is a fundamental element of order. Does this mean that you can never be free or spontaneous again? Not at all. But some aspects of order require drastic measures. Time is one. There is no form of order more significant than being in control of your own time. Begin now to exercise what may seem to be stringent controls over your time. If you do not, random events or other people will control your time for you. Develop and keep a firm schedule of appointments with yourself for the crucial activities that make your life full—the ones you do not wish to leave out.

Does this mean that you are rigidly bound to follow this schedule and do the same thing every day in every year? Not at all. You can alter your schedule. The schedule exists for *you*. It is a tool to serve *your* needs so that when you develop a habit of including something in your life and you wish to retain it, you do not let it drop.

For example, if reading Balzac is a major goal, you may decide to devote ninety minutes each evening to reading his work. But then you discover that Jane Siberry, Yevgeny Kissin, or someone else whose artistry you enjoy is going to be performing at the time you read. Weigh the value of seeing this artist perform. Since some artists perform flawlessly on CD, you might decide that attending a live performance is not worth the disruption, travel time, and cost. Or you might decide that the chance to see this artist perform live is not to be missed.

To attend the concert, you must make space for reading somewhere else in your day. Through whatever creative means possible, devote as close to the full ninety minutes to reading as you possibly can, including skipping lunch that day. Be purposefully compulsive about the reading in order to keep it wedged into your life; consider it nonnegotiable.

On the other hand, as Jesus reminded his followers, the Sabbath is made for man—man is not made for the Sabbath. If you are unable to shift things around completely, do not skip your devotion to your new commitment completely. Instead, invoke the five-minute rule: if faced with a truly rare opportunity or an emergency, do a minimum of five minutes of each activity in your usual schedule rather than leave it out entirely, then resume your schedule the next day.

A writer friend of mine has, for the past twenty-five years, written in her journal every day without fail, no matter what. She has never dropped that thread. On a day when she underwent ten hours of surgery, she wrote in her notebook at dawn before going to the hospital; the following morning she had her daughter bring her notebook to her recovery room, where she determinedly scratched out at least one line though still groggy from morphine and anesthetics.

Upon hearing a story like this, it is easy to dismiss such consistency as some kind of mysterious, aberrant willpower known only to otherworldly beings. But you would not have called two or twenty days of journal-writing an example of great willpower. Had she stopped at either of those points, you would have been right. The difference was that she simply continued to do what she did on the second and twentieth days. Perhaps on the six-hundredth day of writing someone might have commented that she had great willpower. It would have made more sense then, but in truth, other than having continued to write all those days, how was she different from who she was on the second or the twentieth day of writing? She was different only in that she had continued. She practiced consistency and turned it into an art.

Of course, you have other priorities and responsibilities. Shift your emphasis. You will discover that things drop out naturally when you pit them consciously against what you most desire. *Consciously* is the operative word. If you operate strictly from habit and without conscious attention, you will continue to do things in a suboptimal way.

If you feel exhausted, for example, and continually in search of a little pleasure to inject into the madness, you probably lack experience in controlling time realistically. This leaves you tired of hassles, seeking to escape, and *reacting* to circumstances. Step back, let the dust settle, and then quietly impose small amounts of order. Even if you decide to spend just five minutes a day writing in a journal before you go to sleep, do it. Otherwise, someone or something else forever calls the shots, and instead of being the director, you are just one more cast member in your own movie.

Even when you become the director of your own film, however, life still intrudes. To be unable to react to changing circumstances or new information is to suffer a crippling form of rigidity. At the very least, you could miss out on the unique pleasure of seeing Ms. Siberry perform. But leaving your schedule unplanned means you will continue to suffer from an equally crippling form of inflexibility, one based on improvisation and knee-jerk reactions. You need control. Maintain activities that you will not drop, no matter what.

Amiel again:

Order means light and peace, inward liberty and free command over one's self; order is power. Aesthetic and moral beauty consist, the first in a true perception of order, and the second in submission to it, and in the realization of it, by, in, and around one's self. Order is man's greatest need and his true well-being.

# 6

# Preparation

Where there is no vision, the people perish.
—Proverbs 29:18

Failure to prepare is preparation for failure.
—Johnny Wooden

A life without a serious objective is a moral failure.
—W. W. Comfort, *French Romantic Prose* (1928)

Preparation"—the chapter title alone might have once sent shivers through your "fly-by-the-seat-of-your-pants" heart, but as you now know well, preparation is the crucial step preceding action. Peace Corps volunteers do not just show up in the host country. They prepare meticulously. To do anything well you must prepare well. Remember Auguste, the man who tried to help me buy the paint for my new apartment? He left out the crucial step of having a map in his car. Preparation does not waste time or delay beginning. It *is* the beginning.

This chapter and the next detail a master plan for changing. It is not a permanent program for conducting your affairs. It is a plan for breaking out of self-defeating patterns and establishing measures for dealing with roadblocks.

A good master plan tells you what to do and when to do it. This master plan, the Fifteen Tasks, provides a sequence of steps to revise self-limiting patterns. The tasks are arranged so that each follows logically from the one before. Though you may find good reason to alter the order—for example, you can begin the first three tasks concurrently or in any order—beware of the temptation to skip tasks or to get ahead of the game. Most tasks lay groundwork for the tasks that follow. Skipping around too much can slow you down and compromise your progress. Think of it as constructing a kind of cathedral. Drafting the blueprint and putting the first shovel into the ground are both necessary and important steps to building it.

You are talented and creative. You may feel that you have learned the essential lesson of a task without performing it. As seductive as this feeling is, resist it. Getting the idea is not sufficient and will result in time lost rather than time saved. Skipping tasks is simply building in failure from the beginning. Make it taboo.

Almost all of the tasks require exercises (and a notebook to carry them out). This work is unavoidable, but I can assure you that none of the exercises is busywork. The exercises are lean and effective, and the repetition is purposeful and essential to success. You will find detailed instructions for completing the exercises.

There are many things in life that you cannot control. Control what you can—in this case, the quality of your effort. You will, as a result, make success inevitable.

### TASK 1: BEGIN POSITIVE PRACTICES

Positive practices are the place to start. This task is not a frill. Despite the many things required to be fully effective, you do *not* have to erase your emotional hard drive and reformat it. Pleasure is a more effective and efficient way to begin. Add at least one pleasurable thing to your daily life and make it permanent. You will immediately gain from this exercise, regardless of your self-defeating style.

You always need pleasure, particularly when beginning sustained, serious work. When you delete pleasure, you are less effective. You should spend a minimum of an hour a day on some combination of the following: reading literature, listening to music, contemplating or creating art, being in nature, engaging in physical exercise, or being alone.

If an hour sounds like too much, don't panic; *begin slowly.* Put in as much time as you can, then increase it. Better to apply some time than none at all. You can start even smaller; read a single page a day from a book you have always wanted to read.

If you have defined pleasure not as engagement but as *relief* from engagement, you may find that you have omitted from your daily life the very things that would give you the most pleasure. Don't save pleasure for the right time or put it off because it's too much trouble. Build positive practices into your life, and you will benefit.

▶ Ruth, 47, has a large collection of vinyl recordings. She has dreamed of listening to them in depth, replaying passages, reading scores while listening, hearing the complete oeuvre of this or that composer, and listening to different versions of the same works. Of this collection, she has listened to almost none, referring to it as her "retirement."

Ruth has begun by taking thirty minutes to listen to one side per night.

☒ **POSTPONEMENT ALERT:** *Of course you don't have time to add anything more to your busy schedule. You will start as soon as you get caught up.*

Do not wait. Make positive practices unequivocal and non-negotiable, especially if you feel you do not have the time. Time is amazingly elastic. You always make time for what you *must* do. When you have an emergency, you drop whatever else you are doing and take care of it. To make room for this new activity, think of it as a daily emergency that cannot be ignored. Consider yourself in crisis. It may not be so far from the truth.

▶ Kyle, 36, always physically active, moved from the East Coast six months before starting the project; during that time he had not opened a book or practiced tai chi. This left him depleted and inexplicably weary. On beginning the project he joined a health club and started reading nightly, despite feeling overwhelmed. Within two months he has found that instead of being further behind, he is better organized than at any time since his move.

What always makes you feel better when you do it? Find it and insert it into your life. Make it your start.

To begin positive practices, you have to find time, and to find time you have to examine your schedule and make decisions. Thus, you may have to smuggle pleasure into your life.

Nasrudin daily crossed the Afghani border with donkeys laden heavily with packages that border guards were sure carried contraband. For thirty years the guards demanded that Nasrudin unload the bags so they could search them, but they never found anything. Finally, on the day Nasrudin announced his retirement, the frustrated guards urged him to level with them. What had he been smuggling all those years?

"Donkeys," Nasrudin replied.

Shoehorning a new activity into your schedule is a painless way to increase your efficiency. Some starting places are better than others. Adding a positive practice is an extremely advantageous place to begin. The activity you want to add may already be obvious to you—perhaps it is something you have postponed. Do positive practices daily, increasing the time you spend on them until you reach a minimum of an hour.

## TASK 2: DEVELOP A VISION

To make your change worthwhile, it helps to have a big picture in mind. Link change to a personal aspiration—one you have toyed with or dreamed of secretly but dismissed and never acted on. In fact, it might be something you even judged a little foolish in the past and never quite let yourself pursue. Leaving self-limiting patterns behind is rewarding in and of itself, but directing all of your potential toward something that gets your juices flowing provides a focal point for your efforts. Having a dream or compelling vision becomes a key factor in engaging fully, because with it in mind irritations, obstacles, and inconveniences melt away. Give yourself this advantage. Begin to think in terms of a vision or dream. It will become the bedrock upon which you build.[1]

This vision could bring financial reward, but schemes designed to make money cannot match something you want to do for its own sake. Making more money may be sensible goal, but it's not a dream. Put your finger on something that has personal significance. Look for an aim of such importance that it is worth pursuing even if you fail.

Yes, failure. Having a dream includes the possibility of failing as you try to achieve it. For this reason you may have long shied away from thinking in terms of grand purposes. You may have relegated your dreams to the category of fantasy and congratulated yourself for being practical and tough-minded, or for having achieved some kind of Buddhist detachment. Jettisoning dreams, however, and ridiculing them as naive are standard defenses against a sense of loss or failure. To change from a mediocre status quo, allow yourself to reenter the realm of wishes, causes, purposes, and dreams.

A dream can take many forms. It could be a manner of living, relationships you wish to develop, skills you wish to master, knowledge or self-understanding you wish to cultivate, or travel or adventure you want to pursue. To serve you well a dream must be believable and specific and tangible enough that you can convert it into goals and subgoals. Simultaneously, it must be a bit of a stretch. World peace is worthy of everyone's practical effort, but beware of goals that are overly expansive. They can be hazy to implement, and you can stall out before you get started. Also avoid vague dreams such as, "I want to fulfill my potential." Yes, but how?

The exercises for this task ask you to lock in on a vision with sufficient concreteness and specificity. To begin, do the following:

☐ Take out your notebook and, as quickly as you can, freely write down a series of heart's desires, dreams, and fancies, no matter how far-fetched. Do not judge or edit—just write whatever comes to mind until you feel you have truly exhausted every possibility. Do this now, then read on.

If you have a clear and concrete dream that feels captivating, involves a larger purpose, and seems worthy of pursuing ardently whether or not you succeed, you are well on your way to completing this task. If not, you have not run into a roadblock. Don't worry if you feel bewildered. Many people get stumped during their first pass through the question. Having a vision, though, is not psychobabble advice; a vision gives purpose.

What follows are additional simple written exercises designed to help you contact a vision. Even if you are already able to state a dream, vaguely or clearly, I urge you to do the exercises for at least a week. If you have a dream, the exercises will deepen it or transform it into something new or unexpected, perhaps by making it bolder, more specific, and less tentative. Sometimes, however, a dream becomes simpler and more immediately relevant.

Don't worry if the first few times you come up blank and experience a sense of futility. This is *not* a sign that you failed. It is more likely a sign that you are entering previously closed-off territory. Do not worry about or judge any response you have. Take it on faith that it is *especially* worthwhile to continue the exercises if they leave you feeling frustrated.

The exercises do not take much time, and ultimately you will receive a lot of benefits for the time you invest. Do not be concerned if the exercises seem too simple or too complicated. Note your judgments in passing, then set them aside. Continue doing the exercises. I have repeatedly observed that, as a group, SLHPPs can be very judgmental, and having felt naturally superior to others from an early age, they turn that judgmental searchlight on themselves. This is especially true of self-doubters/self-attackers and best-or-nothings. By being judgmental you can thwart your efforts, however, since you fear being judged harshly if you are unable to reach the standards you associate with excellence.

I urge you to do these exercises when you first read them. You only have one chance to do these exercises a first time. Take advantage of it.

☐ In response to each question below, write down, as quickly as possible, as many things as come to mind, devoting a minimum of sixty seconds to a maximum of ninety seconds to each one. Set a timer if necessary. Write without stopping. If your mind goes blank, simply write the word *blocking* on the page. If a response you have written previously comes to mind, write it again.

Do not edit, judge, or evaluate your answers, either as you write or later. Do not worry about what your answers say about you or be concerned with whether they are original or repetitive, practical or consistent. Do not be concerned with whether you write a little or a lot. Just write. Do not plan to show your responses to anyone else, since this could inhibit what you write.

Do not seek epiphanies or even minor flashes of insight. If major revelations come, great, but if all you write on each page for a while is "blocking," do not be concerned. Do not worry if the alloted time does not seem enough, or seems too much. Just do each exercise each day, and accept what you write down. Each question opens to different possibilities. In the meantime, by being persistent you will at the very least increase your tolerance for frustration.

When you have finished answering one question, then and only then go on to the next question. Use a separate page (or pages) to answer each question.

Here are the questions:

- What would you do that you are not doing now, or have not done, if success were 100 percent guaranteed?
- What would you do that you are not doing now, or have not done, if you had twice as much self-esteem?
- As a child, what did you think you would like to do when

you grew up, or what did you see or hear that intrigued or fascinated you? (The source could have been a movie, book, newspaper article, or something you did at camp or on summer vacation. The interest does not have to be about work or career.)

■ As a child, what personal qualities or types of activities always inspired respect or awe in you, and later on as an adult, which qualities might you have cultivated in yourself if you had known how to develop them?

■ What activity would you undertake if you did not have to be concerned with making a living? In other words, what would you do if money were no object?

☐ From now on, start on a new page each day, date it, and simply write. Do not continue the next day on the same page you used the day before. In fact, it is preferable not to look back at your responses until the first week has passed. What came to you yesterday was what came to you yesterday. Do not let it influence what might come to you now. Be curious and interested in seeing what your mind offers you today.

☒ **QUITTING ALERT:** *If your first experiences with these exercises do not seem to yield much, do not judge the results and do not quit. Accept it on faith that you have neither wasted your time nor failed, and that the exercises will yield beneficial results if you continue them daily.*

*After one week,* and only after one week, examine your responses for themes. You may have an "ah-ha" experience, or you may not. If the same thing or same type of thing comes up repeatedly, however, you are beginning to zero in on a dream.

If you still have what you consider meager results, do not be concerned. You are putting things in motion whether you see visible results or not. Simply continue the exercises, and a dream will begin to emerge. If, on the other hand, you have remembered things you had long forgotten or arrived at entirely new thoughts but do not have a completely clear dream, nurse it along as you continue to do the exercises.

You will have completed these exercises when you conclude a minimum of a week's work and you feel you have gained a clear vision of a dream. Your dream should represent a stretch beyond your current position but *not* beyond your realm of belief. Your dream must be conceivable to you, even if it exceeds what you have previously thought to be realistic. If you are either an extreme low-risk-taker or an extreme high-risk-taker, heads up. Do not stand in front of the clown's mouth or shoot from the back of the room. Either position builds in failure from the start.

If after a month you have no dream, stop the exercise. The task is now to discover the meaning of the information you do have and to act on it. You do not have to have the perfect dream in order to move on. In the meantime, do not concern yourself with whether or not you are moving ahead. Not everyone arrives at the same place at the same time or in the same way. You're where you should be. The "talent-equals-speed" equation does not apply here. People are just different. If you feel after a month that you do not have a major dream, do not let that stop you.

► When she did the writing exercise for task 2 for the first time, Saundra, 29, became so outraged by her failure to write anything meaningful that she threw her notebook across the room, slammed several doors, and seriously considered quitting the group.

Fortunately, she didn't quit. After three days she went back to the exercise and did it repeatedly until she realized that expecting and demanding immediate perfection were extremely old self-limiting patterns. Saundra had to move past her initial reaction. In another ten days she had developed a clear, specific dream.

► Earl, 37, felt that after a month of slogging through the exercise he still had not arrived at any clear, overarching vision. He had a few goals—to get a short story published in a literary magazine and to climb Mount Shasta in northern California—but that was it. With a little more work, Earl's "couple of goals" actually served him quite well. It was the word *dream* and its overly grand sweep that had gotten in his way.

Don't trip up on terminology or preconceived notions. The recognized importance of a vision goes back at least to the Old Testament, where it is said, "Without a vision, the people perish." You do not have to have some monster dream that stops time in order to move on. Here is what Earl did and what you can do too:

☐ On a blank sheet of paper in your notebook write down a list of things you want to do, experience, or master before you die. These could be things you left languishing in the "Wouldn't-it-be-great-to-visit-Antarctica?" category. Get them down on paper. "See the Taj Mahal" might be on line 1, "learn to surf" on line 2, "learn to play the harmonica" on line 3, "learn acupressure massage" on line 4, "go back to medical school" on line 5, and so on. Do not judge the worthiness or practicality of what you write. This is in one way a repeat of the first exercise, but by now considerably more possibilities should occur to you. Be curious, and write down whatever comes to you.

Based on this exercise, Earl identified a number of travel destinations, including most of South America, the Pacific Islands, and Southeast Asia. He realized he had an interest in African masks and a desire to learn about wood carving. Now he was tapping into the realm of curiosity, passion, interest, and desire.

Identify the top five goals as your current dream, and use them in all future exercises that have to do with your dream. Many people flesh out their dream more fully when they do a visualization exercise. These days visualization is used successfully for everything from training Olympic athletes to treating cancer patients, to enhancing the benefits of psychotherapy. Visualization is easy, because it is nothing more than an extension of the child's game of make-believe. When you visualize, the clearer the images you create, and the more conviction and enthusiasm you bring to them, the better the outcome.

Do the following exercise in the morning upon rising and in the evening just before sleeping. Why then? At the moment of rising, before the day has begun and you have cued up your habitual modes of thought, your unconscious is more receptive. At night before you sleep, the last things you think about do not have to compete with further thoughts.

☐ Once in the morning and once in the evening, visualize yourself living your dream. Let yourself see what your life will be like in practical detail. Do this for a minute or so. Work gently. Picture in your mind's eye with as much clarity and specificity as possible scenes that summarize and encapsulate your dream. Picture what you are doing and notice what you are wearing, how you are feeling, the time of day, your bodily sensations, the temperature, and so on. Enjoy it.

▶ Litton, 33, an aspiring writer, was skeptical about this exercise. He simply did not see how picturing his receipt of a Pulitzer Prize was going to get him anywhere. He maintained his skepticism, but went forward with the visualization and over time began to savor it.

Lifton's skepticism is noteworthy. To simply visualize a glorious endpoint is not enough. Research demonstrates that the best results occur when you visualize yourself performing the actual activities involved in reaching a goal instead of merely visualizing the outcome you want.[2]

Professional golfer Jack Nicklaus said this about his use of visualization:

Before every shot I go to the movies inside my head. Here is what I see. First, I see the ball where I want it to finish, nice and white and sitting up high on the bright green grass. Then, I see the ball going there; its path and trajectory and even its behavior on landing. The next scene shows me making the kind of swing that will turn the previous image into reality. These home movies are a key to my concentration and to my positive approach to every shot.[3]

Research in athletics shows that when you combine visualization or mental practice with physical practice, you make more progress than when you do physical practice alone. Edwin Moses, an Olympic gold medal–winning hurdler and record holder, used to visualize a complete four-hundred-meter race, calculating the precise number of strides between each hurdle, visualizing crossing each hurdle, and seeing each stride until he crossed the finish line. Moses' visualization of the entire race was unquestionably more effective than a visualization of the victory alone.

On the other hand, visualizing an endpoint—like the victory stand or the golf ball on the green—serves a purpose. Keeping the ultimate destination in front of you helps you ready yourself mentally for reaching it. Research shows that if you imagine a hypothetical event, you are much more likely to consider it possible.[4] Make room for your dream. Children know the value of visualization; they mentally rehearse events and roles in their imaginative play. Your mental rehearsal creates a mental destination and prepares you to accept the idea of reaching your dream. It also helps you find creative solutions that you might not otherwise discover. Visualizing the steps of achieving your goal produces different additional benefits.[5]

If you decide to change your visualization of living your dream, whether daily or only from time to time, that is fine. Just make sure the scene remains pleasurable to experience and in some way represents or typifies the life you want to live.

The more you visualize and think about your dream the better. You do not have to confine thinking about it to two times a day. You may notice it creeping into the back of your mind while you munch a sandwich or start your car. It is in the service of fulfilling this dream that you will be willing to do the work of change. As you clarify your dream, increase its specificity. What do you really want to do and to be? The more specific you are, the more efficient you will be at achieving your heart's desire.

> ☐ After you do this exercise for a week, add the following step in the evening: upon completing this exercise each day, ask yourself, "What did I do today to fulfill my dream?" and note your answer. If you did nothing, ask yourself, "What did I make more important?" and note your answer. Add this version of the exercise to your daily routine, and *continue it indefinitely.*

### TASK 3: CULTIVATE RESOLVE

To be successful at changing you must develop a clear sense of mission and a calm, unwavering resolve to complete it. Whether or not you have been someone who begins and then abandons efforts, increasing your resolve is a no-lose proposition.

As I have noted, you, like most people, have made promises to yourself that you have kept. Even if you consider yourself lacking in willpower, start accepting the fact that you have resolve.

> ▶ Greg, the floater/coaster who had never held a job for longer than eleven months, was sure that he had never exercised resolve concerning any important goal. With some nudging, however, Greg came up with a list of forty-six accomplishments that demonstrated serious resolve, including learning to ride a bike, memorizing times tables, passing the behind-the-wheel part of his driver's test on the third try, and convincing his parents about his college choice.

No matter how foreign it may seem, you have demonstrated resolve countless times, if in no other way than by firmly adhering to self-limiting behavior. The exercises that follow are designed to increase your internal resolve and build more willpower muscle. *You will benefit from the exercises only by doing them repeatedly.* Don't simply read about them or try them once. Make them a part of your daily routine. Joining a health club is not the same as working out.

You can always find reasons to postpone doing these exercises, but that is the nub of the problem. Don't bore yourself by repeating patterns that keep you stuck. If you want to use an old pattern, go for the one you used as a child when you learned to pump yourself on a swing, roller skate, ride a skateboard, or skip rocks. You just did the same thing over and over again until you got it. Merely doing any exercise regularly increases your capacity for resolve, because doing something regularly is in itself an exercise in resolve. But what follows aims straight at the issue of developing resolve.

None of the exercises in this section require you to have a specific dream in order to be effective. Whether or not you now have a specific dream, you at least know that you want to stop limiting your own effectiveness. For that reason alone, do the exercises that follow.

☐ Once in the morning on rising and once in the evening before sleeping, visualize a scene in which you see yourself succeeding at something by doggedly overcoming obstacles. Develop the image fully, allowing it to involve the senses: see the sights, listen for sounds, smell odors, sense what you touch, and feel the temperature—even allow yourself to taste. If it is easier to remember a scene from the past, that's fine. See yourself persist because you have decided to persist, and accept nothing else. See yourself as resolute, even relentless. Then finish by telling yourself that you will use the kind of resolve you just visualized in completing each of the Fifteen Tasks.

▶ At first, Linda, 27, was stumped by this exercise. Then she developed an imaginary scene of rock climbing the face of El Capitan, a huge, sheer granite outcropping in Yosemite. She saw herself encounter problems and continue to try one path after another until she succeeded. Linda had never rock climbed in her life, but she had seen images of climbers on the face of El Capitan and used them effectively.

Do this exercise for one week, and then begin the next one. It aims at the heart of your campaign to change your self-limiting style.

☐ Remember Greg, who found he could list forty-six accomplishments that demonstrated his resolve? Search your memory archives and find instances when you were stubborn, determined, tenacious, even relentless, about something you wanted to complete.

Choose one such instance, preferably from the past six months. Now, instead of merely remembering the incident or mentally watching yourself, *relive* the situation as if it were happening right now. Note that reliving a memory is different from simply remembering it. You feel a distinct immediacy and vividness in your physical sensations when you relive an experience.

Retain those physical sensations, and bring them back with you to the present moment. Hold them in your body and allow them to build. Then, while retaining those sensations, take one task in which you are engaged at this moment and see yourself performing successfully each of the specified activities and exercises associated with it. Observe and enjoy what happens when you pair the physical sensations of being determined with a visualization of yourself doing the exercises. Develop clear mental pictures of completing these activities and of being pleased with the outcome. Every day throughout your change campaign visualize yourself completing the activities of each task on which you are currently working and each exercise associated with it.

Do these exercises in the morning on rising and in the evening before sleeping. Continue them throughout your entire campaign.

Many have come to feel that these visualizations were among the most important exercises they ever did, regardless of their self-limiting style.

As you accumulate these daily exercises, see to it that you set aside the time necessary to complete them. I urge you to consult your calendar, day-timer, or personal digital assistant. Adjust your alarm clock, put a reminder of the exercises on its face, put Post-it notes on your bathroom mirror, or drape a banner from your refrigerator to remind you to carry them out.

You must build these exercises into your *daily* life, since repetition is crucial to their effectiveness. It is also beneficial to choose a particular place for doing these exercises. Before you sleep, see to it that your notebook and writing instrument are waiting for you in the morning. In short, do everything in your power to facilitate follow-through. Make these arrangements without delay. Postponing is a danger, and good intentions are unreliable.

While bribes from others can produce negative side effects,[6] you *can* from time to time reward yourself for completing exercises. Make the rewards small but pleasurable. For some it may be an occasional piece of fine chocolate, and for others it may be a bracing walk in the fresh air. Celebrate your progress, and keep moving.

## TASK 4: MAKE A TIMELINE

You live in time. You need a clear sense of time in order to succeed. This task, the first of several having to do with developing your personal master plan, has you graphically place your change campaign and your dream within the context of your life.

For all SLHPPs, but particularly for self-doubter/self-attackers, this exercise can bring a surge of remorse when looking at what you have done with your life so far. Avoid grief and suffering. Nothing serious proceeds without deadlines, checkpoints, goals, subgoals—a planned sequence of events. A timeline is a way of depicting and recognizing the role of time in your life; it is one part blueprint and one part itinerary. Let yourself appreciate that you are now moving on.

If you are still specifying your dream, a timeline may seem premature. But while you may need to fill in some parts of your timeline later, it is not premature to do this task as well as you can now. Developing an overall master plan is an ongoing process, not something you finish in one sitting. Your timeline, a visual representation of your master plan, will be subject to revisions as you gather information.

If you travel through Manhattan or Paris and don't know which streets are one-way or didn't hear about the parade route blocking north-south traffic, you could catch a cab and still be hours late to your destination. The master plan you are going to construct will take into account your current situation and spell out the actions you must take to progress.

At this point the timeline is at best a rough draft. If making things concrete brings up a lifetime of accumulated fears about having to answer to others' expectations, do your time line in pencil, which will make it less scary, comprehensive, and binding. Remember that the timeline is a guide and not a judgment, and for your benefit alone.

☐ Get a large, mural-sized sheet of paper, and on the top half of the paper construct a timeline of your life with an arbitrary life span of ninety years. If you are older than 60 years, extend the timeline for your next thirty years. Mark the events of your life up to the present moment, noting major milestones. Do not get bogged down here. You can approximate dates, and you do not need to put down everything—fifteen or twenty major events will suffice. Construct your timeline in words, pictures, or whatever works best for you.

Mark the spot on the timeline that represents today. Based on your dream and the results of your self-appraisal, mark the date by which you think you will be ready to live your dream. This is not the same as making a deadline for reaching your dream. Instead, it is a measure of your current sense of when you will be ready to live that paradise.

Next, look at your timeline and pencil in the major steps you need to take each week, month, or year to reach your dream. You will make additional entries later, using the bottom half of the paper at that time.

If you have a completely private space for your exclusive use, post this timeline where you can see it daily. If you do not have such a space, put it someplace handy. Apart from your support person or someone in your constituency, keep your timeline away from the eyes of other people, who might offer comments and opinions that could derail your progress.

Secrets have a certain power, a certain motivating energy. Containing an idea keeps it yours, but turning it over to others can dissipate its energy. Your timeline is about *your* life and *your* dreams. Nascent dreams are fragile and easy to snuff out. If someone makes light of your life on mural paper, you could use their criticism as a reason to quit before you begin.

Review your timeline when you do other exercises.

▶ For seven years, Lifton, the aspiring writer, talked about beginning to write his novel in a "When-I-can-get-the-time-I-will-get-started" way. Obviously that had not worked. Only when he completed his timeline and began getting up at five-thirty every morning did he start to write.

## TASK 5: CONDUCT A CANDID SELF-APPRAISAL

To correct deficiencies and eliminate limits, you need to know where you stand. The questions that follow provide a basis for a thorough assessment of things in your life that require work.

Write answers to these questions in a new section of your notebook. Writing forces a different kind of reflection. You will use your written answers to target self-defeating behaviors and develop essential skills.

A word of caution: when you deal with negative patterns, vow ahead of time to resist being consumed by negative feelings. They are toxic and immobilizing. Self-limiting patterns are exactly that—patterns. You are more than the sum of your past patterns, and no matter how strong they are, you have at times managed to resist them. If it helps you to avoid hand-wringing, think of your patterns as those of someone else. View them analytically.

On the other hand, do not avoid identifying your negative patterns or you won't deal with them. Candidly survey them, and then move on to the next steps. Do not feel that the job is too overwhelming. One or two central things can usually hold together any self-limiting pattern. To make your efforts efficient target the following areas:

## Personal Characteristics

☐ Write down a number from 0 to 100 for how you usually feel about yourself, with 0 standing for the worst you could possibly imagine feeling about yourself and 100 standing for the best you could possibly imagine feeling about yourself. Circle this number. It stands for how you *usually* feel about yourself.

Write down a second number from 0 to 100 for how you feel about yourself *right now*. Put the current date beside this number.

List what you like about yourself, the qualities that make you feel good about yourself as a person.

Make a separate list of what you dislike about yourself, the qualities that make you feel badly about yourself as a person.

Write down any other major assets you haven't already listed. Write down any other major limitations you haven't yet listed.

Write down your answers to the following questions:

■ How and in what areas of your life have you typically settled for less?

- How and in what areas of your life have you typically achieved?
- Do you agree to appointments you do not want or cannot possibly keep because you do not want to disappoint or say no?
- Do you find a way to cancel such appointments at the last moment owing to some circumstance you claim is beyond your control?
- Do you regularly review your life and reflect on what and how you are doing?
- Do you think about what in your life is working and what is not?
- Do you think about what you want to do differently?
- Do you consider what specific changes you want to make in your life and how you will go about making them?
- Do you review your decisions and consider alternatives before acting?
- Do you translate your goals into specific, necessary steps?

## Master Skills

Consider where you stand in relation to the master skills:

- The skill of order
- The skill of patience (related to tolerating frustration)
- The skill of deploying attention, as discussed in relation to work and boredom
- The skill of repetition
- The skill of persistence and tenacity
- The skill of consistency
- The skill of thoroughness and follow-through
- The skill of finishing

## Other Skills

- What other necessary skills have you not yet mastered?
- Are you a good administrator of your time and your life?
- Are you orderly? When and when not?
- Are you thorough? When and when not?
- Are you appropriately meticulous?
- How well do you manage time?
- Are you realistic about time and what you can do with it?
- Do you plan your time in such a way that you are able to accomplish your goals?
- Do you take appointments seriously?
- Do you reflect before you make appointments or merely hope that you can fit everything in around them?
- Do you make and keep appointments with yourself for your activities?

## Self-defeating Habits

- How have you usually blocked yourself?
- What obstacles have you put in your way?
- When have you quit?
- What have you allowed to discourage you?
- What have you allowed to defeat you?
- What or who have you allowed to have power over you?
- When have you sidestepped taking reasonable risks?
- How, when, and why have you taken unnecessary risks?
- Do you make others responsible for your goals, your happiness, your choices?
- How and when do you make others responsible?
- When do you give in to others' wishes instead of staying with what you want?
- Whom have you blamed for your failures?
- What have you preferred to avoid?

- What have you not wanted to face, think about, look at, or learn?
- How and when have you avoided things when they got complicated or difficult?
- From what have you run?
- When have you coasted?
- What have been your escape routes?
- How do you delay?
- How do you make delaying okay?
- What have you usually postponed doing or taking care of?
- When have you procrastinated?
- Under what circumstances have you postponed going for what you really want?
- When and what do you take a stab at or simulate instead of really doing?
- What do you lie to yourself and others about?
- To what kinds of things have you usually given mediocre effort?
- Besides fooling yourself, whom else have you tried to fool, and about what?
- Who or what do you pretend to be?

## Rationalizations and Justifications

- How do you rationalize your lack of engagement, your lack of progress?
- What are the reasons you give for not living as you really desire?
- How do you rationalize your failures to act?
- Do you take responsibility for your choices?
- Do you say, "I cannot," when in truth you do not choose to act?
- How have you justified your inaction?
- Do you think that your personal characteristics limit what you can do?

- Do you believe you cannot change?
- What do you claim prevents you from reaching success?
- To whom or to what do you assign blame for your failures?

## Fears

- Do you fear involvement?
- Do you fear not living up to expectations?
- Do you fear failure?
- Do you fear being ordinary?
- What frightens you most about going for what you want?
- What do you fear about becoming accomplished?
- What do you fear about change?
- What do you fear about staying the same?
- How do you deal with fear?

## Goals and Work Style

- Do you think in terms of goals?
- What are your main goals?
- What has been your typical approach to setting goals?
- What do you do to support reaching them?
- Do you work in a consistent way or in occasional intense bursts of effort?
- Do you continue in the face of setbacks?
- What do you allow to distract you?
- Have you had sufficient resolve to deal with difficult issues?
- Do you have a positive attitude toward work?
- Are you self-directed? Do you get going without someone else's prodding?
- Do you take initiative, or are you passive? When do you take initiative, and when do you not?
- Are you realistic about what will be required to accomplish tasks?
- Do you sidestep the essential by getting lost in busywork?

■ Do you skip steps you consider unpleasant?

■ Do you complete things you begin?

## Features of Temperament

■ How adaptable are you? Does your adaptability lead to dropping things when they become difficult or less exciting in order to go on to something new?

■ How well do you tolerate frustration?

■ What is your prevailing mood?

■ Is your energy level high or low?

■ Do you move quickly or slowly toward new situations?

**TASK 6: CONSTRUCT MASTER LISTS**

To plan a cure, you need a diagnosis; to develop an antidote, you need to know the poison. In this step, you take the material from your self-appraisal and construct three master lists of targets for change.

■ Make a complete list of all the negative characteristics you stated in your self-appraisal.

■ Make a list of deficiencies in your basic master skills and other crucial skills.

■ Make a list of escapes and all other habitual self-defeating behaviors.

☒ **QUITTING ALERT:** *Yes, you can do all of this. Yes, it is worth the hassle. No, it is not busywork. And yes, you will survive it. You will feel surprisingly pleased with yourself, quietly proud, and perhaps even a little smug.*

Making lists, though indispensable, achieves little without accompanying action. In the next chapter, we focus on taking specific actions.

# Action

People have (with the help of conventions) oriented all
their solutions toward the easy and toward the easiest side
of the easy; but it is clear that we must hold to what is
difficult; everything alive holds to it, everything in Nature
grows and defends itself in its own way and is characteristically and spontaneously itself, seeks at all cost to be so and
against all opposition.
> —Rainer Maria Rilke, *Letters to a Young Poet* (1934, 1954)

Having once decided to achieve a certain task, achieve it at
all costs of tedium and distaste. The gain in self-confidence
of having accomplished a tiresome labor is immense.
> —Thomas A. Bennett

**Y**ou are continually perfecting behaviors that are either self-
defeating or self-enhancing. Ineffective behaviors sabotage success. Replacing habits requires that you initiate action, so let's
get down to a slightly different kind of work.

In this chapter, I present the remainder of the Fifteen Tasks.

## TASK 7: REPLACE SELF-LIMITING BELIEFS

A particular way of thinking keeps self-limiting behaviors in place.
The exercises that follow provide tools to alter that thinking. If you
prefer, do these exercises in short blocks of time rather than in one sitting. Don't leave out any of the parts, however. It is important that you
*complete each part of each exercise.*

To change self-defeating behaviors, first you have to become aware
of your power to choose.

☐ Go to the three master lists you compiled in task 6 and from each list choose the three most significant items you need to change or improve. At the top of nine separate pages in your notebook, write down one item, leaving the rest of the page blank. When you make changes in these nine target areas, you will experience sweeping alterations in how you live.[1]

On the page for each item, make a simple, self-descriptive statement using that item. For example, if the item is a negative characteristic, like "impatience," you might write, "I am impatient"; for the self-defeating habit of procrastination, perhaps "I am a procrastinator"; and for a lack of the master skill of consistency, "I am inconsistent." Do this for each item.

Next, below each statement write a sentence that gives an example or description of this behavior, such as, "When I think something isn't going to work right away, I become impatient." "When I have a deadline, I procrastinate until the last possible minute"; or, "I tend to work inconsistently."

Next, directly below each sentence, rewrite it inserting the word *choose*. For example, rewrite the sentence "When I think something isn't going to work right away, I become impatient" to become "When I think something isn't going to work right away, I *choose* to be impatient." "When I have a deadline, I procrastinate right up until the last minute" becomes "When I have a deadline, I *choose* to procrastinate right up until the last minute," and "I tend to work inconsistently" becomes "I *choose* to work inconsistently."

☒ **STEP-SKIPPING ALERT:** *You must actually rewrite each statement. You will miss out on several crucial benefits if you skip this step.*

☐ Now rewrite each sentence again making the following significant change: put the sentence in the past tense and modify it with an adverb, like *often,* that acknowledges that you have not always behaved in the same way. For example, rewrite "When I think something isn't going to work right away, I choose to become impatient" as "When I *have thought* something *wasn't working* out right away, I *have often chosen to* become impatient." Rewrite "When I have a deadline, I choose to procrastinate right up until the last minute" as "When I *have had* a deadline, I *have usually chosen* to procrastinate right up until the last minute." And rewrite the sentence "I choose to work inconsistently" as "I *have often chosen* to work inconsistently."

When you complete these steps, reread and review all forms of the sentences you have written, noticing the difference each simple change makes in the way you experience choice and possibility for change. Introducing a key word, a change in tense, or a simple modifier makes each sentence reflects a progressively less limiting idea of reality while more accurately acknowledging your freedom to choose. You are not bound by your past choices unless you decide to be bound. Most people understand and *feel* this difference upon reading each sentence.

To replace limiting conceptions and patterns, choose new, less limiting ones. Here is a step-by-step way to do this:

☐ On each page, in the space below the last sentence you wrote, write a sentence about a new positive behavior. For example, for the sentence "When I have thought something wasn't working out right away, I have often chosen to behave impatiently," write something such as, "When I think something is not working out right away, I *choose* to be *patient*." Below the sentence "When I have had a deadline, I have usually chosen to procrastinate right up until the last minute," you might write, "When I have a deadline, I *choose* to work *in a timely way*." Below the sentence "I have often chosen to work sporadically," you might write, "I *choose* to work *consistently*."

After you complete the new positive alternative sentence,

take another long look at each item and the sentences you have written below it, and let the progression sink in.

The next step is crucial. For two full weeks, repeat the new final sentences you have just written five times on rising and five times before sleeping. This is not the final step (that follows in the next task), but it is absolutely crucial to do this step fully. Do not try to speed up the pregnancy.

The last step lays down a new internal format, a new thought platform from which you can operate. You change your internal dialogue and create an association between yourself and this new quality.

During these two weeks you may also work on task 8, which uses the work of task 7 as the basis for replacing old habits with new ones.

### TASK 8: BUILD NEW HABITS

This task involves choosing a new behavior to replace each of the nine items you worked on in task 7, creating precise internal instructions for using it, and then practicing it until it becomes habitual. For each of the nine self-limiting behaviors, the first step is to find a typical situation in which you used the old behavior and find a new, *specific* behavior to replace it.

☐ To use impatience again as an example, recall a typical situation in which you have behaved impatiently. Perhaps when the post office line moved too slowly, you typically bolted suddenly and left in a huff, losing the time you spent in line *and* failing to complete your task.

Imagine this situation, see yourself in it, and then, at the point at which you formerly behaved impatiently, find a new behavior to substitute for leaving. Consider as many possibilities as you want before coming up with this new behavior. You might decide that you will pull out your well-worn copy of the Kama Sutra or a list of Spanish verbs you want to memorize.

This solution depends on carrying one or both items. If you do not regularly carry either one, you will first have to learn a new habit in addition to the new behavior. It's not that hard to learn the additional step, and it may still be worth doing if, for example, you spend a lot of time in lines. Whipping the Kama Sutra or Spanish verbs out of a pocket would certainly force you to rethink fuming and leaving.

On the other hand, a new behavior that doesn't involve carrying something might be even better. You might decide that whenever you are in a slow line, you will recite your favorite poetry or do various visualizations. Or you could decide to have the Kama Sutra or Spanish verbs as your first choice and the poetry or visualization as a backup should you fail to bring either text.

☐ When you come up with a new behavioral choice, develop an internal instruction to tie the new behavior to a specific triggering event.[2]

What's a specific triggering event? It is either the event that prompted the old behavior or the event with which you want to associate the new behavior. Standing in a slow-moving postal line was the triggering event for impatience. For your new behavior, the triggering event must be one that will occur reliably enough to bring out the new behavior.

☐ Put your internal instruction or specific operating instruction in the following form: "Whenever I stand in any line I will *always* . . ." Then add in the behavior you decide will work best for you. If you chose the Spanish verbs, the sentence would end: ". . . pull out my book of Spanish verbs and begin to memorize them."

You must also develop specific operating instructions to see that you always carry your Spanish verb book. The specific operating instruction for that could be, "Whenever I pick up my car keys, I put my Spanish verb book in my pocket too." The keys are a good triggering event, at least if you usually drive to the post office. If you walk, take a cab, or use public transportation, you will have to come up with a different triggering event, but your house or apartment keys are still a likely choice. You will make it easier to comply if you keep the book of verbs in a convenient place next to your keys.

Note the use of the word *always* in the instructions. Always use *always* in your specific operating instructions.

It is important to work with your new specific operating instructions when you are not in the situation and to keep working with them whether you encounter success or failure in the actual situation. You will experience a particular pleasure when you employ the new behavior in a real situation, and that is all to the good. Your goal, however, is to make the new behavior become your automatic response. Repetition is the key to achieving that outcome.

I once injured my back, and the doctor prescribed movement re-education: a physical therapist helped me learn specific new ways to move my body for the sake of my back. Since my existing habits of movement were completely automatic, the therapist prescribed a series of simple exercises that involved repeating specific movements. After six thousand repetitions for each movement, I was done. According to the physical therapist, this is the number of repetitions that research has shown is required to replace an old, completely nonconscious habit pattern with a new one.

You need repetitions of your new behavior to lock them in. Six thousand repetitions may not be that far off the mark. Rehearse your new behavior consistently when you are cool and unflustered. This will help you internalize the instructions and become mentally accustomed to the new choice.[3]

☐ Repeat the new specific operating instructions five times in the morning and five times in the evening, and after you complete each set of repetitions, add the statement, "I will follow these instructions very carefully." Finish by visualizing yourself doing each new behavior. Continue this exercise indefinitely, but for *at least one month* after you notice that you are consistently using each new behavior.

In addition to talking to yourself and visualizing, practice the new behaviors in real situations. Each day, create as many opportunities as possible to use your new instructions. This means that you should actually seek out lines, stand in them, and use your new substitute behaviors. When you are about to enter the situation, repeat the instruction and visualize the new behavior. There is nothing like rehearsal in real situations to increase the speed at which you adopt new behaviors and make new habits. Many people notice substantial change in a month or less.

Let me use the two other examples, procrastination and inconsistency, to give you more ideas for specific operating instructions. You could convert "When I have a deadline, I choose to work in a timely way" to "Whenever I receive or make a deadline, I will always write it in my schedule immediately and arrange my schedule then and there so that I can finish the project with sufficient time to review my work." You could convert "I *choose* to work consistently" to "Whenever I accept or begin any ongoing project, I will always arrange my schedule immediately so that I can work in a steady, consistent fashion."

After completing the first four weeks of this exercise, make an important addition to your routine. Impatience, as a description, summarizes your behavior, you note, in many situations and many different possible actions. You describe these actions with the same term, impatience, but you behave differently in these situations. What you call impatience and your impatient behavior at the post office differ from the impatience you express with your son when he has forgotten to wipe his feet before crossing the carpet. One situation involves one set of actions, the other a different set. Therefore, you must deal with impatient behavior in different situations, and come up with new behaviors for each one.

☐ For each negative personal characteristic, self-defeating behavior, or missing master skill on which you have been working, identify two additional typical situations in which you have displayed the same self-defeating behavior.

Choose to work first on the one you consider the most important to change; then develop a new, specific operating instruction that pertains to it. Remember, it must be specific, not vague, and include a new, positive behavior. Saying, "When Wallace walks in with muddy feet, I won't ever let it bother me," won't work, but a new behavior, such as singing an aria from *Carmen* or counting to 100, will work. Your specific operating instruction might include a calm sentence or two that you will say to your son about mud, floors, and existentialism. As before, repeat the new specific operating instructions five times, morning and night; repeat the statement, "I will follow these instructions very carefully";[4] and visualize yourself enacting the new behavior. Then seek out opportunities to have sane discussions with your son about muddy shoes or other topics. It's up to you to decide whether or not to flood the yard on purpose.

The transition to a new habit is not always smooth, and you need to understand why. Habits are triggered by familiar situations, and that is why we searched for triggering events. When you wish to replace an existing habit with a new one, the new response has to compete for a time with the old one, which is triggered by the same situation and held in place by many millions of repetitions. This is the uphill battle you face when replacing habits, but the technique of tying specific operating instructions to a triggering event greatly speeds the replacement process. The enormous gratification of replacing negative patterns with positive new behaviors is another powerful incentive.

Here are some other things to consider when working against self-limiting, self-defeating patterns and descriptions. Examine the payoffs you received from the old behaviors and how you have justified continuing them. When you confront something difficult, ask yourself whether avoiding it gives you the result you want. Learn to appreciate the new behaviors of taking a risk, going against an old habit, and getting out of your mode of sticking to what is comfortable because it is familiar. Lastly, stop making excuses, period.

## TASK 9: CHANGE YOUR LANGUAGE TO THE LANGUAGE OF CHANGE[5]

I once spent an evening at a dinner party with Clive, an extremely effective businessman and investor—someone with a reputation for making decisions quickly, firmly, and clearly. When he spoke, his language was remarkably free of qualifiers such as "maybe" and "sort of," and absent of phrases such as "I'll try" or "We'll see." His language said that he made things *happen,* things did not happen to him. *He* made plans, *he* set deadlines and dates, and *he* followed through. His speech expressed his style of approaching life.

Clive, at some point in the evening, mentioned that he had cut his smoking down to one cigarette per day, an interesting and unusual goal. To reach this goal he had made a plan and kept to it. That sounded like Clive's approach. When I asked whether he intended to use this method to quit smoking entirely, he said he had considered quitting, and then, in a remarkably jarring departure, added, "It will be interesting to see how *that* comes out—whether *it* goes that way. Who knows, *it* might go the other way. We'll have to see how *it* goes."

I have added the italics to emphasize the words he chose. He did not emphasize those particular words, and he may not have noticed the distinctive shift in his speech. But what a difference all of those qualifiers made! It was clear that quitting had never been his goal; it was equally obvious how "it"—the question of whether or not he would quit—was going to "come out." His language gave *it* away. When I saw him on a subsequent occasion, he had returned to smoking a pack of cigarettes a day.

Although it's a chicken-or-egg discussion to determine what comes first—language, feelings, or beliefs—it is clear that Clive's language reflected a fuzzy, indefinite view of smoking that helped keep his smoking habit in place.

We do not use language accidentally.[6] Although we employ language without being conscious of shifts like Clive's, what we say, and the words we choose, reveal what we believe, expect, and intend. Our language thus reflects our reality, especially in terms of what we consider possible. To say it another way, we use language to express the expectations we have and the limits we see. Thus, the way you use language either helps to keep you stuck or aids in your liberation. You can increase your effectiveness by using language that supports change. Create a change-supporting semantic environment and urge others around you to do the same thing.

Here are specific things to do:

▪ Eliminate loophole language that expresses and invites equivocation. "Try," as in "Try to do it if you can," is a sorry, sickly little word that insinuates itself regularly into otherwise reasonable requests and kills their power. In fact, "I'll try" in response to a request is usually a polite form of refusal. That use of *try* differs completely from the *try* that means "to test or examine." The word *try,* meaning "to attempt," is a weasel word that leaves a loophole through which you can drive a tank. If you asked Sam and Sally to come over for dinner on Saturday, and they responded with, "We'll try," I suspect you would immediately reschedule the dinner for a time when they knew they would come. Eliminate the word *try.*

The use of *try* in the sense of "attempt" actually contains an implicit directive to stop short of succeeding. When someone say "Try to," or "Just try your best," he or she is suggesting that you mount some kind of effort but not expect to be successful. In fact, to comply fully with the directive "Just try your best," you are required to stop short of bringing something to a successful conclusion. "Try your best" is the same as saying, "Don't worry, I don't expect you to make it." Think for a moment. Would "Try your best" be what you would want to say to your heart surgeon before going under the knife? The effect of "try to" is the same when you say it to yourself. Soft language with its built-in slack gives you and others permission to do less than your best.

When you talk to yourself in loophole language, you listen to and follow the implied directives. Language that expresses unequivocal intention sounds different and makes entirely different demands on the listener. With it, you create an internal environment of clear objectives and directives. For a startlingly revealing exercise, forbid yourself for one week to use the word *try* in relation to actions you are going to take. Observe the effect. You will quickly discover how often you use the word, and perhaps why you use it too. You will also *feel* how different it is to shed this semantic hideout. One patient told me that doing this exercise was like eavesdropping on her own unconscious. Also, note how different it is to *forbid* yourself to use the word *try* than it is to simply *try* not to use *try*.

▪ *Eliminate vague phrases like* kind of *and* sort of *from your language, especially when talking about what you want to do.* Vague language invites you to hold back and also says little, especially when combined with superlatives like *really.* What does it mean to say, "I sort of really want to do it?" This kind of speech carries the ambivalence virus. Its lack of definitiveness permeates your thinking and infects your ability to move on things. When you speak of goals, use definitive, unequivocal language about what your goals are and how you intend to reach them. Say, "I will do it," and say when you will do it.

▪ *Pay attention to and correct language that denies personal responsibility and personal power.* Self-imposed limits are expressed by language that puts the control of events outside yourself. Decisive people, like Clive from the dinner party, speak in simple terms and use the present tense, the indicative mood, and the active voice. Statements expressed this way sound different and mean something different. Compare the conditional tense and passive voice of "I would like it to get done today" with the present tense and active voice of "I am doing it today" or the imperative "Do it today." Sound different? Of course. It *is* different.

When you use the passive voice or make the subject of your sentence the indefinite and mysterious *it*, as Clive notably did when he began to talk about quitting smoking, you suggest that things happen independent of your will or because of external events not under your direction. Though it is true that you are not in control of everything, using that kind of speech suggests that there is no point in exercising the power you have and thus excuses you from responsibility. Though it can be momentarily appealing to evade responsibility, doing so always costs you heavily. When you reduce personal responsibility, you reduce personal power and control and engender passivity. Who needs that trifecta?

Rather than looking for ways to reduce responsibility, look for ways to embrace it and increase it. The active voice is the expression of personal responsibility and frees you to seek ways in which you can exert a directing force upon your life. Use the active voice, embrace as much responsibility for your actions as you can, and you will *feel* a noticeably greater sense of mastery and personal efficacy.

■ *Put controls on negative statements.* In the course of a day, note your particular litany of limits. "I hate public speaking." "It's too late to go back to school." "I can't plan; I'm not good at details." These are negative, limiting statements. As we have discussed, repeating them helps keep you stuck.

You can eliminate limits by reversing negative statements, using the same method I described for eliminating self-defeating behavior in task 7. Turn "I hate public speaking" into "I choose to like public speaking," and "It's too late to . . ." into "There's still time to . . ." Also, you can take any "I can't" statement, such as "I can't learn Russian," and change it to an "I haven't so far" statement, such as "I haven't learned Russian yet." Do it and sense the difference it makes. It is a gentle but effective tool to increase awareness of possibilities.

Ask others to join you in catching negative, self-limiting statements. With willing family members, housemates, or friends, turn this into an ongoing, harmless, positive game. Everyone agrees to be on alert for negative, self-limiting statements, and everyone agrees that any person who makes a self-critical, self-limiting statement must turn the

statement into a positive one. By changing your semantic environment, you will foster other change.

If you are in some situation that does not allow you to reverse a negative statement aloud, you can do it in your head, or use an alternative
method: cancel out the negative statement by simply saying to yourself,
"delete" or "cancel" as quickly following the statement as possible.

■ *Use the past tense when speaking of negative patterns.* Change any negative self-statement, such as "I am selfish," to "I used to be selfish," or
"I have been selfish in the past." Change a statement such as "I always
start something new with excitement then grow disinterested and
quit," to "I used to always start new things with excitement then quit."
This is a simple, potent way to differentiate what you have done in the
past from what is possible for your behavior now. Putting negative
habits you want to change into the past tense consciously invokes the
possibility that they have changed, are changing, or, at the minimum,
can change.

As psychologist Jim Fadiman points out,[7] you intend the future
when you use the present tense. If you say, "I am intelligent," you
mean not only that you are intelligent now but that the quality will
endure—you will continue to be intelligent in the future. When you
use the present tense for a negative characteristic, it has the same effect.
Therefore, move negative characteristics to the past tense to avoid
hanging on to them.

■ *Use the present tense to speak of positive attributes, even ones you don't
feel you yet manifest consistently.* Claim them as yours anyway. Since
you intend to keep them, it makes sense to use the present tense. Using
the present tense creates a demand for your behavior to match the
description.

The French philosopher Alain said:

Especially in the human realm itself, where self-confidence is a factor, I would calculate very inaccurately if I did not take into

account my own self-confidence. If I believe that I am going to fail, I fail; if I believe that there is nothing I can do, then I can do nothing. If I believe that my hope is deceiving me, it does then deceive me. Be wary of that. I make the good weather as well as the bad; within myself, first of all; around me too, in the world of men.

## TASK 10: ACKNOWLEDGE YOUR PROGRESS

It may strike you as curious to consider acknowledging progress as a formal task; however, some who make progress fail to recognize it, or they mistake the first steps of change for new difficulties. People fail to notice progress because they focus on current inadequacies or have incorrect expectations for their progress. They do not remember that as children they fell before they began to walk.

▶ Stacy, the vegetarian, organic gardener, and former dancer whom you met in chapter 2, observed that when she sensed frustration with her change project, she felt irritable about doing the exercises, was floundering, and began to fantasize about moving to Seattle or returning to San Diego. Replacing self-limiting habits and acquiring wisdom seemed boring, sterile, and serious, and she feared she was going to lose her individuality.

Then she understood. These exact thoughts, like lines from a script, had accompanied every major hopscotch move she had previously made. She soon concluded that this was her major self-defeating, self-limiting pattern. When she observed how truly limited, repetitive, and mechanical her thoughts were, she was shocked. She used this awakening as a springboard toward real progress.

When you begin to change, beware of justifying quitting on the basis of hidden former agendas that may spring up and negate your progress. It is important to acknowledge progress when it occurs in its earliest, most awkward forms—even when it is accompanied by irritability over a lack of progress. If you minimize or deride your progress, or attack yourself for crude first efforts, you are much more likely to shrink back from your effort. If you are a self-doubter/self-attacker, this tendency will be a liability throughout the change process. All efforts in new directions represent progress in the sense that they are necessary first steps. Instead of attacking yourself with statements such as "I am so far behind, it is a joke to think of this as progress," or "This is humiliating—it would be better just to acknowledge the truth that I am a failure," or minimizing statements such as "I am really no further along than when I started," or "It's probably too late to make a difference," simply acknowledge that you are moving, which is progress in itself.

You must also be ready to combat the fears that may arise when you realize that change is under way. Cindy, whom you met in chapter 1, had been looking for a soul mate but was troubled when she met someone who mattered. Positive changes are unsettling; it is easy to feel surprisingly threatened by them. If you are, do not worry. You can change while entertaining contradictory thoughts about doing so.

Learn to identify progress so that you will be less likely to dismiss its signs. The following simple exercise is an adaptation of a technique from solution-oriented therapy. Have your notebook handy and make an entry about this experience:

☐ Imagine that overnight a miracle happens, and upon awakening, you have strong new positive characteristics, you are rid of self-imposed limitations and self-defeating patterns, and new effective patterns are in their place. What is the first thing you would notice that would tip you off to the change?[8] Follow yourself through the day and note everything you would observe—your actions toward others, how others treat you—all the specific things that would let you know that a miracle has occurred. When you complete the fantasy, list these things in your notebook.

For example, in the morning you might see yourself consulting a schedule of things you want to complete. You might notice subtle things, such as the clothes you choose to put on, the cereal you have for breakfast, physical activities or classes, and so on. You might notice that people treat you differently, and that you treat them differently as well.

When you complete this list, post it where you can see it easily, preferably close to your timeline. Consult it every morning and evening when you do your other exercises. Any time you notice, experience, or feel anything that appears on your list, take it as a sign of progress. Your life is a series of external and internal events; each event that moves you in the new direction *is* progress. Let yourself appreciate and note it. Underscore it. To ease your move into a new way of life, acknowledge all progress, whether it is subtle or obvious.

## TASK 11: COMPLETE THE CONSTRUCTION OF YOUR MASTER PLAN

Rob wanted to develop a programming language, Johanna wanted to take up golf, and Stan wanted to be an expert in French literature. Minus a concrete plan, each stalled.

What successful architects, chess champions, and filmmakers know is that to succeed at any significant undertaking you need to know specifically how you will go about achieving it. You need a more or less formal plan with deadlines, checkpoints, goals, and subgoals. Without it, you circle the field and never get started, or you work inefficiently and feel easily overwhelmed.

It's time to fill in the rest of your master plan for achieving your vision. Whether your dream is to create a women's health information service or to develop your own employment agency, your master plan must:

1. Break down the ultimate goal or dream into projects
2. Break down each project into tasks
3. Break down tasks into manageable action steps
4. Develop a hierarchy of action steps that progress from simple to more advanced
5. Break down each action step into specific activities that can be completed in discrete, manageable chunks of time

If your aim is to be a physician in the Middle East and you have not yet attended medical school, you have numerous goals to reach before you can live your dream. These could include completing coursework requirements, preparing for the Medical College Aptitude Test, and perhaps learning to speak and write Farsi.

If you follow these five steps, you will easily generate a master plan that converts even fuzzy wishes into specific actions. Fill out the plan with all other essential details you will need to make it complete and workable. You will know it is reasonably complete when your support person can look at it and follow the steps. Your master plan can take whatever form you wish. Depending on your objective, your master plan could be as spare and simple as a one-or two-page list, or a flow chart, or a project board. Be creative. Your master plan is your tool and your map.

How detailed should your master plan be? That depends on the self-defeating pitfalls to which you are most susceptible and the plans you have in mind. People vary widely in terms of how much structure they are accustomed to and how much they feel they need. If you are like Auguste, who preferred to figure things out on the fly, you may find that you benefit from far more detailed preparation and structure than you have employed in the past. If your goal requires many separate steps, simply spelling them all out will require detail.

The master plan exists to serve you, not shackle you. It is a tool for reaching a goal, but it is not the goal itself. To be helpful your master plan needs to go beyond providing merely general guidelines and direction. The objective is to create a succinct, step-by-step recipe that leaves nothing out and ensures that your efforts are pragmatic and efficient. Make your master plan systematic and thorough enough that it eliminates "seat-of-the-pants" approximations and guesstimates.[9] Remember to employ the carpenter's maxim: "Measure twice, cut once."

▶ Ronald, who had considered being a history professor but found the denizens of academia to be pedantic, at first felt that the emphasis on planning was at odds with his freewheeling style. He was proud that he had never submitted anything to a plan. When he began to work on a master plan, first he dashed something off without much reflection, but he soon realized that he had left out many things. Once he started working in exacting detail, he discovered that thinking and reflecting actually increased his creativity. He realized that he had been limiting himself to only those choices that spontaneously occurred to him. Spontaneity, in turn, had become his self-limiting definition of creativity. By repeatedly coming back to his plan, he noticed possibilities he had entirely overlooked—an unexpected outcome. "There is a use for stepping back and looking at the whole forest," he remarked, and began to tout the benefits of planning to other group members.

To make your master plan work for you, build into it whatever quality will ensure success. If skipping steps and looking for shortcuts have been habits in the past, I urge you to go for broke on precision and detail. If, on the other hand, you have gotten stuck at the planning stage, correct that by cutting to the chase. Busywork is as big an evasion as any other form of postponing. Do not turn planning and preparation into a way of becoming terminally stuck. Respond intelligently. Develop a straightforward plan, then get started. You will always make adjustments as you go along.

In terms of the precision of your plan, have your support person take a hard look at it. Your plan should be clear enough that he or she can follow it easily. Your aim is to eliminate gaps, fuzziness, and loopholes and to trim unnecessary steps or insert missing ones; it is not to develop a fifty-page document. If you have been a terminal planner, experiment with giving yourself three hours to come up with the very best plan you can, then take it to your support person. Let him or her evaluate what additional work it may need. You can generate a master plan merely by envisioning what you want to do, the steps involved in achieving it, and the probable difficulties. Or you can do it the other way around, imagining the final destination and working backward, as Jack Nicklaus did with his golf shots. In either case, write it down.

And last, the final version of your plan should be attractive. It's okay if you started on the backs of paper napkins—many good things start there. But transfer your plan to some good-quality, durable medium, and make it neat and clean. Pay it a certain respect.

You smuggle a donkey by completing your master plan. When you plan with attention to detail, you exercise your capacity to think realistically and concretely about time, and you develop your ability to think about and simplify the process of reaching seemingly unreachable goals. Over time this kind of thinking leads to a quiet development of confidence.

▶ Lifton, who had never done any carpentry, learned that by expending patient effort, he was able to tear down a wall in a shed and double the space for a room that he then made into a writing studio. And he learned that if he spent time, attention, and energy in the same thoughtful way, he could just as surely, step by step, little by little, write an entire book.

## TASK 12: SET GOALS

People who set goals, write them down, and review them reach them faster. They also report that they are happier and gain more satisfaction from life.[10] Having goals, moreover, may be important for your mental and physical health. Dr. Carl Simonton, cancer researcher, has found, for example, that terminal cancer patients who have goals live longer than those who do not.[11] Learn when and how to set goals, and you will move toward your dream more quickly.

The benefit of setting goals comes from giving your mind instructions other than "Wouldn't it be nice if . . ." Setting a goal is like crossing the line: it gives your mind a conscious objective to focus on which to move. A long-term goal also alerts your unconscious to search for possibilities and solutions while you focus your attention on specific actions. The effects of setting a goal, therefore, are part satellite dish and part laser.

Setting goals the right way increases their effectiveness. I will describe two different types of goals, long- and short-term, that serve different objectives and involve different methods. For both, it is crucial to adhere to two guidelines. First, set only your own goals; don't allow others to set them for you, and don't set goals for others. Second, always write your goals down and then look at them often. It is good policy to keep your long-term goals private and to allow others to do the same.

A long-term goal involves a long-range objective. Stating and using a long-term goal correctly moves you toward reaching that goal even when your focus is on some other immediate project.

☐ You have already taken your dream or ultimate long-term goal and broken it down into a set of projects. Classify up to fifteen of these projects as long-term goals by spelling out the exact, specific outcomes you desire, such as "to be fluent in Chinese." Simply doing this and keeping these goals in view constitute major steps. I have worked with people who achieved goals consistently merely by writing them out on New Year's Day, putting them in a drawer, and not looking at them again until the following New Year's Day.

To work actively with your long-term goals, write down each one as a present-tense statement. For example, "to be fluent in Chinese" becomes, "I am fluent in Chinese."

Repeat each present-tense statement five times in the morning and five times at night until you reach that goal. The purpose of this exercise is to make your long-term goal function as a demand that directs you to make efforts toward meeting it.

Do *not* set deadlines for your long-term goals. The reason? If you set a deadline for a long-term goal, you may slow your progress by eliminating opportunities to find truly creative and efficient solutions that could come more quickly.

Short-term goals, on the other hand, are tools for reaching immediate objectives in brief time frames, such as one week. An example of short-term goal planning might be to make six telephone calls, have two informational interviews, or read a certain book, within a week. A short-term goal has a specific objective and an unambiguous deadline for meeting it. It differs from a long-term goal in one additional striking way: you deliberately make it public.

☐ Here is how to set short-term goals. Select a specific objective you wish to accomplish within one week and write it down. Announce your goal to your support person and check in with your results one week later. Look at your goal every day, and take the actions necessary to reach it. Schedule for it. Make doing it a nonnegotiable imperative.

### TASK 13: BUILD IN BACKUPS

Psychologist John Enright tells this story. Many years ago, when the California bar exam was held just once a year, it began at 8:00 A.M. on the appointed day and no one was admitted late to the examination room. If you wanted to take the exam and did not want to wait a year, you saw to it that you arrived on time.

According to Enright, the number of people who arrived late, year after year, was exactly zero. People who wanted to take the bar exam took precautions against anything that could possibly make them late: gas tanks were full, provisions were made for unreliable cars, or people stayed in nearby hotels. Obviously they used more than good intentions: everyone developed some kind of backup for every contingency or emergency.

In any situation in which the chances of failure must be reduced to zero, you need backup strategies. NASA's manned spacecraft program was built on a policy of multiple redundancies, that is, more than one backup for every component on the spacecraft. The lack of a backup for the famous frozen O-ring on the space shuttle *Challenger* resulted in disaster, and as a result, additional backups were later put in place.

Multiple redundancies are a good idea for you as well. Build them in ahead of time. The last thing you want to do is experience setbacks that you could have prevented. Protect your work. Do not squander anything. Be ready. New habits need backup support at every turn. Good intentions are not a backup. They typically fail because most of the time you are operating on automatic pilot.

Although the Fifteen Tasks are designed to anticipate generic problems and build in solutions, backups prevent the specific problems to which you have previously been prone. When Stacy recognized her self-defeating pattern of hopscotching from one career to the next, she decided to develop a practice of devoting time each week to planning what she would do the following week. Small, regular doses of planning made her efforts much more efficient and prevented long, bleak periods spent doing deadening tasks she had put off. If you realistically plan in advance and have backup strategies in place, you will not be surprised, lose time, fall victim to frustration, or use emotional flatness as a reason to quit.

What are some examples of backups?

The best backups come from knowing how and when you have previously quit or escaped and then deciding in advance what you will do when such a moment arises again. Let's say that you know that when you get stressed, you usually drop projects and forget about them for weeks at a time. You decide that as a backup you will call your support person as soon as that kind of frustration starts to build. So far, so good. Now let's say you find yourself stressed out, but you are unable to reach your support person. This is a critical moment. Without another backup or two, you are at risk. You need to have *at least* one more *rehearsed* backup strategy in place in case the first one fails. Don't imagine you will stay cool and improvise successfully on the spot. Improvising opens the gates for old, automatic behavior patterns, such as fleeing the situation. Know your next step in advance.

Commercial pilots, no matter how often they have flown a particular aircraft, still follow a prescribed checklist before takeoff to avoid sloppiness and lapses of attention. To see to it that you do not miss any exercise, develop some version of your own daily checklist.

► Nadine, 33, decided that overkill was the most prudent strategy when it came to reminders and checklists. Without them, she feared she would not follow through, and she refused to accept failure. She put a copy of a checklist on the nightstand in her bedroom and Post-it note reminders where she could see them: on the bathroom mirror, the steering wheel of her car, the refrigerator door. She even taped a tiny reminder on her toothbrush handle. The message, "Do not go to bed without completing and checking off all items on your list," greeted her everywhere.

## TASK 14: SELECT AND COMPLETE A SPECIFIC PROJECT

Preparation and planning are necessary and satisfying. But sinking your teeth into the actual project is completely different. It is the launch, the actual nuts and bolts of action. The first walls on your cathedral now begin to rise.

To become a designer with your own line of jewelry may involve classes, an apprenticeship with a designer or work in a design firm, as well as courses in finance and business. Other dreams, such as mastering the cello, involve fewer discrete steps. By now you have taken your dream and broken it down into a series of interrelated projects. Select one to work on first. If you have a series of life goals instead, pick one, or a major project related to one.

Choose a project that makes sense in terms of some sequence and presents a moderately difficult challenge given your current knowledge and master skills. If the project you choose is too simple, you will gain little from the exercise. But if it is too demanding, you will set yourself up for discouragement, if not a back-of-the-room-style dramatic flameout or fluke success. You learn little from either situation. I strongly encourage you, therefore, to choose your project well and to not be hasty.

Let's follow Stacy, because when she reached this task, her dream was still unclear. Having struggled longer than many to identify her dream, she needed even more tenacity in selecting a project.

▶ After spending a month on task 2, Stacy had rediscovered a fascination with what she called "settings" in restaurant interiors, gardens, private homes, and even stage sets. At first she was reluctant to expand on her interest because she could not see where it might lead.

Stacy's resolve was tested—this was another moment at which she could have stopped, hopscotched to some new path, or otherwise squandered what she had invested. With encouragement to continue, however, she decided to devote three hours each Thursday evening to finding out about settings. Her plan was skeletal: she would explore the subject and then proceed based on what she discovered.

Her first schedule looked like this: "Thursday, November 10. Search the net 8:30 to 11:30 P.M. for information concerning interior design."

This step doesn't look momentous. In fact, there is no one right way to go about discovering or exploring an interest. What was important, however, was to begin and persistently put in the time in a systematic way.

In the course of Internet searches, stints at a university library, and visits to her favorite restaurants and gardens, Stacy realized that her real fascination was with lighting. She then made lighting her new focus of interest and moved to informational interviews with interior designers, gardeners, stage managers, and architects. The key to this progression was setting aside the necessary three-hour block of time and specifying in advance how she would use it each week.

For her project, Stacy chose to volunteer to develop a simple lighting scheme for the winter production of a local choral group. Three months later she volunteered to design the lighting for a friend's café. Nine months later Stacy was shadowing the lighting director of a regional dance group, radically expanding her base of knowledge, and investigating career possibilities in this area. One year later, having made another considered change of direction, she began work on a short documentary film about the effects of lighting in dance.

"I could never have possibly imagined that I could hang on and complete something like this," she said.

There are a couple of important things to note here. Stacy was adaptable. As she progressed, she used the positive side of adaptability to remain open to emerging opportunities. A hopscotcher in the past, she did not simply leap and leave things unfinished this time. As she stuck with it, she learned that her interests could evolve. Moreover, she went from a series of specific projects and actions to arrive at a dream.

Changes on which you have worked now get put into practice.

### TASK 15: THE ALL-OUT PUSH

The All-out Push is both an attitude and a set of practices you need not only to carry you through the completion of your project, but also through and beyond the final stages of your change effort. The goal is to ensure success and eliminate the possibility of failure. The method is to exercise the maximum control over your life.

Manage your time. A major element of your All-out Push is good time management. To stay on task and get the most from your time, live on schedule. People who achieve their dreams construct their lives according to a reasonable schedule. Knowing how to schedule is an art, while keeping a schedule is a matter of setting up specific operating instructions.

Your schedule must address your goals and the demands of your personal life and include time for both. Do not begin an All-out Push on a project by sacrificing your personal life or any other essential aspect of your life. Instead, become more covetous of, and efficient with, time. When you live on schedule, you leave nothing to chance and leave nothing out.

Juggling and making room for all of the things you want to include in your day is a science. When is the optimal moment to exercise, bathe, rest, listen to music, read, or study? It may differ from one day to the next. The purpose of scheduling is not to introduce uniformity or rigidity; it is to ensure that you have time for everything. If you need to improve your time management skills, practice making schedules; include in them time to work on schedules. With practice, you will become better at making realistic schedules, and your resulting actions will stem more from considered choices and less from pointless improvisation.

▶ Bryan, the freelance journalist, whose All-out Push became a crusade, found pleasure in clear planning and the structure of focused, relentless, and unceasing effort after a life of delays and false starts. His first goal toward his newly fleshed-out dream of working in broadcast journalism was to land a steady job in print journalism, even if he started at the bottom. Instead of continuing to look for some big break, he decided to follow a systematic plan and to acquire habits that would help him to achieve his dream.

His first project was to refine his writing skills. He enrolled in a journalism class at a local community college, pulled out his old journals, and began writing half an hour per day. To ensure his success, his All-out Push included a new schedule of getting up an hour and a half earlier to start his day with visualizations and other exercises. He put friends on notice, and while he worked, he unplugged the phone in the study he had created. Instead of yielding to the temptation to move to Los Angeles, he stayed put and avoided another costly disruption.

Proust's narrator in *Remembrance of Things Past* has this to say about beginning his literary work in earnest:

I intended to resume the very next day my solitary existence, but with a definite purpose this time. I would not even let people come to call on me at my home during my working hours, for the obligation to accomplish my literary task took precedence over the duty to be courteous or even kind. Doubtless the friends who had not seen me for such a long time and who had just met me again and thought me in good health once more would be insistent. They would come with their importunate demands when the toil of the day—or of their lives—was done or interrupted [because] the subjective chronometers allotted to men are not all regulated to keep the same time; one strikes the hour of rest while the other is summoning to work.

Take drastic measures. You must make a complete, unequivocal commitment to do what is necessary to reach your dream. Alert friends and acquaintances as to the best time to call. Control outside intrusions. Discipline yourself about the time you spend online, including e-mail. Unplug phones or at least turn down answering machines; put the outside world on hold while you attend to what is most important. Maintain positive practices and all other exercises that support your dream.

Bryan's All-out Push was a serious response to what had become a grave situation. If you break every bone in your body, you don't question the need for a body cast or complain about the tight fit. Bryan needed to break major self-limiting patterns. His past goals had been diffuse and ever-changing. As he clarified his goals and became truly devoted to reaching them, he found it perfectly reasonable to take drastic measures.

How long should you remain in the body cast of the All-out Push? As long as necessary. How long is that? To break through barriers that previously held you in check, to ensure rapid progress in developing new behaviors and master skills, and to maintain and consolidate the gains you make, stay in the All-out Push mode until new habits become second nature and past limitations are crowded out of your life.

Use the All-out Push mode anytime you are truly serious about completing a project. Adopt it and stay with it. Progress is the inevitable outcome when you repeat a set of steps with your new skills. Since a number of projects lie ahead, you may be in the mode for a while. You are finally on your way to your dream.

Do you need to stay in the All-out Push mode all the time? You decide when you want a break. Some people celebrate completion of a major project before beginning again. Don't drop the thread of your exercises or your positive practices, however. As a minimum, remember the five-minute rule in relation to both.

You are the only person under your direct control. Use your resolve. Make the All-out Push. Be consistent like you've never been consistent before.

# And Beyond

# Altitude Sickness
# and Other
# Predictable Problems

The tragedy of life is not that man loses but that he almost wins.—Heywood Broun

▶ After finding a buyer for his business of building handmade guitars, Fritz, 36, went to work on his five-year plan to build a boat in his backyard and sail around the world. Fritz had never sailed until the previous year, when he helped a friend pick up a boat in the Gulf of Mexico. He had served as a deckhand while his friend took the boat through the Panama Canal and on to California.

Fritz was willing to take sizable calculated risks. He had but one small sailing experience and had never constructed a boat. But he had worked with wood to make guitars, had paramedic training from work as a volunteer fireman, and was resourceful, careful, and good at detailed planning and solving problems. He laid out his steps: he enrolled in sailing and navigation courses, purchased materials and onboard equipment, and began constructing his boat. All was going according to plan when he began to run into problems.

After two years' work, he discovered that the epoxy resins he was using to hold the wood together were failing. The boat was literally coming unglued. Fritz, however, did not come unglued. Even though he could not salvage the boat or the two years he'd put into it, he did not abandon ship. He was committed to sailing around the world, so he switched gears. He sold a piece of property he owned and eventually bought a boat. He was out to sea within his five-year time frame.

Fritz's dream was no more special than your dream. What is noteworthy was how he continued in the face of a major setback. Being adaptable is a major plus when it is backed by other redeeming qualities. If you combine adaptability with tenacity, resourcefulness, ambition, a willingness to take appropriate risks, and a devotion to being meticulous when necessary, you have a formula for overcoming obstacles.

I would love to be able to tell you that once you begin the All-out Push you go on to achieve your goals and dreams in one uninterrupted, trouble-free, storybook straight line. More commonly, however, life continues to be life—a maze of contradictions, challenges, complicated choices, and surprises. If, like Fritz, you respond resiliently, you gain additional self-sufficiency from bumping up against these aspects of life; occasionally you even come out ahead on your plan.

When you allow yourself to live life fully, absorbing both its conquests and its defeats, you begin to touch on the totality of your potential. But since your habits are new, they are somewhat fragile and require tender care during this transitional period. For this reason, to safeguard the progress you have made you must act wisely and at times forcefully.

Maintenance, the stage of consolidating your gains, is just as active and as vital as the action stage. To ensure that you lose nothing you have gained, you need to stabilize the new base from which you move. You must arrange your life so that it supports your changes. Like tender garden shoots and newborn babies, new habits demand special precautions and care. Nurturing and protecting are the tasks of the maintenance phase.

In this chapter, we examine how you can solidify gains and introduce techniques to strengthen them and prevent relapses. The issues addressed include dealing with predictable and unpredictable setbacks, staying on course, assimilating and managing the effects of change, controlling the pace of change and staying on schedule, dealing with rapid change, and managing the problems that come with progress, including increased demands. But beyond maintaining the gains you have made, this chapter deals with completing the work on the project you began in task 14 and extending it to fulfill your dream. The chapter closes with a look at the question of whether it is possible to strive too much and with an examiniation of traditional warnings that suggest caution.

## Stuff Happens

Even if you sailed through the Fifteen Tasks, setbacks are an inevitable part of life and of change. Difficulties arise routinely during any project, and this is as true when you feel you are making real progress as when you were first building new skills.

If you are prepared for turbulence and understand it, setbacks are fodder for further growth. You can always count on experiencing some setbacks. They may be the consequence of things you do or fail to do, or they may be something entirely unexpected, such as the unreliable epoxy resins. They could involve sickness or death—in other words, real suffering—as opposed to any neurotic invention or self-limiting stance. Occasionally, they can stem from the actions or decisions of others.

When you are the source of the setback, seek immediately to understand your role; decide to *learn* from the hitch in your progress, then make necessary adjustments. The answer will always be that you either lacked information or momentarily fell prey to some old self-defeating tendency. Find out which it is, and take charge of your emotional response to the situation. Talk through the situation and your emotions with someone, and then accept the situation without attacking yourself. Attacking yourself costs time and self-knowledge and reduces your effectiveness for moving ahead.

Instead, purposefully cultivate optimism[1] and a tranquil mood, which will allow you to be more resourceful and creative as you find good solutions to your problems. Obstacles, interruptions, and digressions are inevitable signs of a lively existence. Decide to draw energy from setbacks, and use them to become even more formidably committed. From the chance to overcome them you can derive joy and strength.

If a setback you experience is due to an external source, complain to someone in a position to do something about it, and do not be shy.

▶ On January 19, in the year of our Lord 2001, my trusty Macintosh G3 PowerBook laptop stops responding to my tapping while I am working on a February 15, 2001, deadline for my manuscript. The screen goes black.

The problem is tiny; the little sleeve at the back of the computer into which I insert the power cord has come loose inside, and the computer is no longer receiving current from the cord. I am told by the local repair facility, Livingstone Systems and Service (L2S), that it should not take long to repair, perhaps ten days at most, but the computer will have to be shipped to Amsterdam. To make my deadline, I will have to rent another computer for the interim.

I decide to pay extra for a "flash devis"—a quick diagnosis and cost estimate for what I am promised will be a quick repair. When I hand over my computer, however, the real problem begins. Ten days pass, then three weeks, and I do not have an estimate. When I inquire repeatedly, I am told not to worry. I still receive no estimate. For a month I am not able to communicate by e-mail due to mysterious problems on my rented Mac, so I send nothing to my editor. I miss my deadline. Finally, L2S says they are ready to send my computer for repairs and quote a mind-boggling price. But when I investigate with AppleCare France, they say my laptop was repaired and sent back to the local dealer within days after I dropped it off.

Besides the unconscionable delays, I now have some detective work to do. I discover that L2S had the computer repaired without giving me a written estimate, quoted to me a repair cost greater than what I would pay for a new computer, and is now pretending that it has not sent the machine away to force me to pay a large return fee. I refuse to pay the ransom, and only after several calls to Apple corporate headquarters in Cupertino, California, do I secure the release of my machine.

As a final touch, when I pick up my computer, it does not work. The original power cord, which was functioning perfectly when I took the computer in for repair, is now damaged.

Even in the face of an outrage, if you spend energy grumbling to others or indulging in self-pity, you merely steal energy that you need to put into rectifying things. Do not fall for victim mentality. That trap for some can be incredibly seductive. Be wiser. Keep working to create a real life. Travel lighter. Let others gnash their teeth.

When a problem arises to which there is no solution, such as the death of someone you love, seek support, grieve, talk through your feelings, and then begin to move again when you are ready. Seek out people who support you, your new gains, and your new life. Changing brings wonderful people across your path. Seek support in these affiliations and from old friends.

Setbacks, of course, slow the rate of your progress, at least in terms of your project. You wanted to be *there*, but you are still back *here*. Remember, however, that these setbacks may not be setbacks for you in terms of your overall progress. Guard against impatience; refuse to submit to its destructive force. As soon as you allow yourself to have an ambition, you will face setbacks and delays. Fortunately, impatience is something you can learn to overcome. In a way, life itself teaches you. Make peace with the pace of things over which you have no control.

Though it may not be fun to do things methodically and not be rewarded, learn to appreciate doing your part well no matter what else happens. Besides, you don't have to get everything you want, and you do not have to like everything about life! At times you need to be insistent with yourself; whether or not you feel like doing something—

whether or not you receive gratification at some specified moment—you must persist. Life is punctuated by rewards and by punishments; you can't live only the dramatic highs. That's all there is to it.

The saving grace is that your triumph will be sweeter when you prevail in the face of hardships. When you work and persist despite setbacks, you appreciate your capacities more. You feel bigger and stronger, sturdier and more formidable. And you like yourself even more.

## Staying on Track

A central chore of maintenance is to stay on track while new things are happening. There are various elements of staying on track beyond being ready for unexpected nasty surprises. At the beginning of *The Divine Comedy*, Dante's narrator says that in the middle of his life he has awakened to realize that he took a wrong path somewhere, and he laments, "I cannot tell how I entered it, so full of sleep was I about the moment I left the true way." In *The Wizard of Oz*, Dorothy and her friends are making perfectly good, if uneven, progress on their journey to find the Wizard when they get sidetracked, lose their way in the field of poppies, and pass out. When they awaken, they right themselves and begin again. In Homer's *Odyssey*, Odysseus' men get distracted in the land of the lotus-eaters and forget their mission. All of these vague drifts from purpose seem to happen almost without notice, and from no apparent cause other than some kind of entropy or momentary lapse.

This kind of twist in literature and fairy tales is so common that we can take it to express some universal aspect of existence, a truth about human experience—some fundamental quality about our nature and the nature of our journey, something embedded in our unconscious minds. We wander out into the poppies and must reawaken, or we stay there with our goal-directed efforts having ground to a halt, and we remain stranded.

As mentioned before, in his journal, Emerson referred to the distractions that derailed him as "idle curiosities" that stole his time. They could pop up anywhere and anytime. In addition, at age 34, he mourned that he was aging, that friends around him were already dying, and that he had found no sponsor.

Part of maintenance is to simply stay on task. This means that you know the task and must keep it in front of you at all times.

Even if you are ambitious, you may notice that reaching particular objectives often takes longer than anticipated. Wandering from the task is a major cause. You are not alone in this. Experts at planning—be it the L.A. subway system, the Sydney Opera House, or the "Chunnel" connecting France and Great Britain—notoriously underestimate time and budget. This tendency to be overly optimistic about what can be completed is known as the planning fallacy.[2]

The standard interpretation of the planning fallacy has been that it stems from wishful thinking and a lack of realism. The suggested solution has been to become more realistic and stretch out any estimate of the length of a project. That solution is like creating a deadline for a long-term goal: you unnecessarily extend the time it takes to reach it because with less sense of urgency, you move more slowly. A better solution is to pay a different kind of attention to the way you use the time set aside for working on a project. When you sit down to work every day, know what you are going to do with that block of time and be sure to accomplish it. Before beginning work, do the following simple exercise:

☐ Five minutes before, see yourself getting organized by visualizing yourself gathering together the materials and resources you need, then envision yourself beginning work and going on to complete the work.

Research reveals that this deceptively simple exercise, done before you begin work, greatly improves your ability to keep pace with your time estimate by increasing your efficiency and keeping you on track.

There are two obvious ways in which you can get off pace: by delaying starting (procrastinating) or by getting distracted (going off course) and not finishing what you intended to complete for that work session. This five-minute visualization is effective at dealing with both forms of derailment.

In addition, take the following steps:

☐ As you begin your All-out Push, make the following addition to your timeline: a new section that extends from your current position to some *indefinite* point by which you believe you will be living your dream. Don't build in extra time. Make it an efficient interval. Put this timeline in the space below the life timeline you have already created, like a blow up of a detail of a photograph. This puts the current segment of your timeline in clearer relief as you begin the period of the All-out Push.

Record deadlines for completing the specific projects associated with reaching your dream, but do not establish a deadline for reaching your dream. In this blowup detail, leave that date open-ended. Your timeline will help you keep time in mind and maintain a realistic sense of urgency.

For survival reasons, we respond strongly to information we take in through our eyes. We say, "I see," when we understand something, because at that moment understanding seems as straightforward and trustworthy as our visual sense. We are no longer in the dark. On a more literal level, seeing something presented visually often allows us to "see" it in the sense of understanding. Your timeline, a representation that allows you to see in graphic form something conceptually complex, is a powerful tool. A timeline helps you understand something most of us habitually deny—the passage of time.

We say we are aware of time in the sense that we have to be someplace at some hour. But the big sweep of time usually takes us by surprise, as if someone sneaked in during the night and rearranged the furniture. Though we witness our own aging and watch our children grow up, these changes happen gradually, almost imperceptibly.

One of the main benefits of your timeline is to help you *see* time and evaluate it more effectively. One of the many benefits of keeping its deadlines is to be develop your confidence in your own reliability. Look at your timeline daily, and you will remain in contact with where you are in relation to your goals.

☐ Do the following about once a month: set a deadline with more work to do than usual, and then keep that deadline even if it requires staying up late. Sure, I know that you may have done this when you were in college. This time, however, do it deliberately to increase your capacity to accomplish things through intense, focused efforts.

Making promises and then keeping them is fundamental to real achievement. If you do not keep your word, you do not consider yourself reliable and will not take your own statements seriously. This weakens you. Perhaps you have weakened yourself in just this way by not keeping deadlines or by breaking past promises to yourself. Use this exercise to create a new track record.

A special caution, however, about extra work. Upon crossing the line and starting your All-out Push, you may notice a sudden tendency to overwork. This is a self-defeating trap. Studiously avoid it. Overwork is often an attempt to make up for a lack of efficiency, and it can create a reason for withdrawing from your effort. Pace yourself.

Make sure to have pleasure in your life. The many SLHPPs who do not have pleasure in their lives have more difficulty with task 1, positive practices, than with writing down their negative characteristics. Furthermore, upon breaking through old self-limiting barriers, some find such exhilaration and pleasure in work that they feed on the new high, tend to stay up late, become overtired, then function poorly for days. Savor the beginning of your new life, but stay in balance. Do not flame out then swear that the mission is impossible, that you are not cut out for achieving, or both. This is simply building in failure from jump-street.

And then there is the issue of consistent effort. I have met SLHPPs, usually flashers, who contend that they work best in concentrated, intensive bursts followed by rest. I remain skeptical of this approach, but people vary greatly. Experiment to find the equilibrium that works for you. There is nothing sacrosanct about that balance. It can change. What works well for you this month may not next month, and you may need to make an adjustment.

Most important, work from a well-thought-out plan, your blueprint. You can change the plan as long as the change is considered and not based on whim.

Even with these steps, it is easy to miss the big sweep of time and find again and again that it takes you by surprise. Marcel Proust's narrator in *Remembrance of Things Past* says: "In theory one is aware that the earth revolves, but in practice one does not perceive it, the ground upon which one treads seems not to move, and one can live undisturbed. So it is with Time in one's life."

To stay on track you must attend to time and what you do with it. And you must always strive to prevent problems before they arise.

## Relapse-Proofing

Remember my physical therapist who prescribed six thousand repetitions of each new movement when I injured my back? He wanted the new movements to be so well established that I would perform them automatically, without thinking. He wanted me to overlearn them until they were automatic. Overlearning takes a while.[3]

You must decide that getting off schedule for any reason—illness, an upwelling of old self-defeating behaviors, hitting a wall and running out of energy—does not have to mean that you have failed or that there is reason to abandon your effort. If you experience flagging enthusiasm or a crisis of confidence, don't panic. Your new behavior is just new, that's all, and it is not yet overlearned.

But beyond this, there are techniques for relapse-proofing. Strategic family therapists, for example, have developed a method for dealing specifically with recurrences of old patterns by scheduling planned relapses. On a date selected by a family in advance, *they deliberately reenact old negative patterns*. If the family's quarrelling over their daughter's curfew used to lead to slammed doors, shouting, and sulking, the family purposely reenacts this sequence. The bizarre juxtaposition of old behavior and new awareness, of consciously choosing and intentionally engaging in previous negative behavior, creates a clear comparison between old and new and makes a memorably preposterous farce of the old pattern. I urge you to do the following version of this exercise:

☐ Plan a day, once a month for three months, when you deliberately think through your worst versions of settling for less and engage in them, perhaps even in a slightly exaggerated way. Do it for fifteen minutes, and pay attention to how it feels. See how you used to hold yourself back. The old pathways still exist. Pay attention to how it feels to take them. Then write up this experience in your journal.

Since setbacks, lapses, and even dreaded relapses are a normal part of progress, preparing for them in this way helps you recognize them for what they are: old overlearned behaviors that, without adequate reflection, automatically and quickly lead to others.

A planned relapse increases your awareness and prepares you to deal with a possible recurrence. The exercise will help you catch yourself much faster if a relapse occurs. At the same time, rehearsal reduces the likelihood of a relapse, as well as the length and seriousness of any that might happen. Specific sequences of events contribute to the triggering of an old pattern. The exercise of intentionally enacting this pattern helps you deal with it much more effectively and quickly should it arise again.

Another version of relapse-proofing comes from research on maintaining abstinence from smoking and excessive drinking in high-risk-for-relapse situations.[5] For example, a man trying to overcome a drinking problem is asked to rehearse mentally his step-by-step approach to dealing with his friends on Superbowl Sunday. This research demonstrates that through such rehearsals, people can develop and refine the specific coping skills they need to avoid temptations.

☐ Do the following exercise daily for one month and as often thereafter as you feel will be helpful. Take each escape route you identified in your self-appraisal, and visualize three situations in which you previously used this escape and could be tempted to use it again. For each of these situations, mentally rehearse, step by step, positive substitute behaviors.

If you experience a setback, you could choose to step back from your mission. Resist being so drastic. Instead, choose to keep things simple. Pick yourself up, learn from the failure, zero in quickly on what was missing from your preparation, your plan, or your resolve, and then begin again. Go back to the drawing board briefly, if necessary, and adapt your plan by closing off previously undetected escape routes, or develop new targets for growth. But do not delay. Do not make the setback more than it is; keep the cost of the setback low. Fear multiplies in the vacuum of avoidance. Use the strategy of getting back on the horse after the fall.

This is definitely a time to consult with your support person or your constituency. They will assure you that they have failed too. Those who do not milk failure for what they can learn from it squander a major opportunity.

## Both Sides of Progress

Of course, progress itself brings problems in its wake. We have touched on this before, but it bears repeating here: advantages always contain within them disadvantages. Strengths always harbor corresponding weaknesses. The physical attributes that support your excellence in classical dance have a way of eliminating your possibilities of success in sumo wrestling, and vice versa. Attaining higher ground means leaving lower ground behind, and sometimes lower ground looks as if it wasn't so bad after all.

I love Manhattan. "Manhattan is fast-paced, hectic—something is always happening." Say that sentence in one tone of voice, and you appreciate part of its attraction. Say the same sentence, changing not a word, in another tone of voice, and you convey weariness about the relentlessness of Manhattan. Manhattan's advantages contain its disadvantages. What makes Manhattan unique is also what many seek occasional relief from, for the city makes demands in exchange for what it offers.

Life is complicated in this way. Downsides accompany the upsides of *every* situation, *every* choice, and *every* intention; progress comes with a price too. Think of progress as exchanging tired, colorless problems for new, far more engrossing ones at the next level. The new game is more absorbing than the old game, but you are never short of puzzles to solve.

▶ When Sebastian, 39, went from acting in a few regional theater productions to taking a small role in a locally produced film, he discovered that participating in the move raised all kinds of puzzling questions.

Though he had a passion for acting, professional acting had always seemed so uncertain and unreliable that he had long ago set aside serious considerations of pursuing it as anything other than an avocation. And he disdained the idea of Hollywood-style film work as devoid of artistic achievement. Now, with good notices for his work, he faced a pleasant career crisis he had not anticipated.

You reach goals by taking appropriate steps. You exert, observe, revise, and progress. When you reach goals, you must deal with the consequences. These consequences are far and away more positive than negative, but you also face things you did not foresee.

There is a wonderful Chinese story of a man whose horses run away. His neighbors and servants appear to exclaim over his misfortune and shower him with pity. In response, he only says, "Could be good, could be bad." Some time later his servants tell him that as fortune would have it, his horses have returned, bringing many fine wild horses with them. To this the man responds, "Could be good, could be bad."

Soon the man's son is thrown trying to tame the horses and breaks a leg. Neighbors and servants come to exclaim over the misfortune and offer pity, but the man only says, "Could be good, could be bad." Some time later the army comes to town to take young men away to war, but the son cannot go because of his broken leg, and the father says . . .

Success inevitably brings complications. When you make serious changes, you move on many levels simultaneously. You cannot make one serious change in your life without feeling its effects everywhere else. You are made up of intricate and complex systems; when you make changes in one of the systems, the others inevitably shift. When the pace of change is slow, adjustments are spaced far apart and the effects of progress are less upsetting and troublesome.

Let's say you want to read every book in print on Italian Renaissance art, a goal that is largely personal, does not depend immediately on others, and does not have many divergent steps. Even so, reaching that goal will change you, ever so slowly. It would be impossible for you to experience the beauty of the art over time and not change internally. Furthermore, the process of fulfilling your aim might lead to interesting inconveniences along the way. You might decide to learn Italian in order to read art texts available only in that language. You might decide to travel in order to see the art in person.

Your decision to secure books would put you in contact with librarians, book dealers, and experts in art history generally and in the Italian Renaissance period specifically. The acquaintances, the conversations, and the journeys to meet booksellers would mark you. Moreover, your endeavor would be increasingly difficult to conceal, for you would have to make many additional contacts and increase your own notoriety in the field. As you gained a more complete knowledge of Italian Renaissance art, people would solicit your opinion. The change would transform your life.

Greater achievement brings about greater demands. Success brings increased expectations, responsibilities, and scrutiny. That is the price of success throughout life.

In the beginning of life you have no fear of change or greater demands. All children spontaneously delight in going after what they want, trying and mastering new things, and doing things independently, when and where they can. This can be observed in an infant younger than six months old.

When I put my firstborn daughter to bed each night, the last thing I did was pull the handle of a tiny music box suspended above her crib that played a soft, tinkling rendition of Brahms's "Lullaby." When she was a newborn, the furthest reach of her tiny outstretched hands could not possibly have grasped this handle. As time passed and it came within her reach, she made flailing sweeps in its direction, then progressively more refined movements.

When she pulled that handle down for the first time, successfully releasing the melody trapped in the tiny box, her entire body convulsed with exhilaration. Reveling in her accomplishment, she pulled it down again and again. The next night, and each night thereafter, it was she, of course, who pulled down the handle.

Had I placed the music box in her hands would it have meant as much to her? I am certain the answer is no. Her joy arose from reaching it on her own, a joy she could have felt only by striving repeatedly, persisting, and improving, until she finally accomplished something she had set out to do on her own. By reaching for that handle, she learned that she could succeed with her own effort.

You used to shy away from increased demands. *Used to.* That need no longer be the case. You can guarantee that you never miss a shot by never shooting the ball, but what is it like to be the one who says, "If the score is close, give me the ball?" Experiencing fear only means that you are leaving behind the comfortable and familiar. You are raising the standard and moving up another level. Fear arises when one is faced with risk, but progress comes with taking prudent risks.

Following your interests by developing your knowledge and skills is the natural path to progress. Maintaining balance, however, between dependence, independence, interdependence, and demands takes ongoing work and wisdom. To arrive at a life that is profoundly satisfying you must go beyond what is merely easy and accept increasing demands as the cost of progress.

Years after my eldest daughter had grown out of the crib, I came home from a farmers' market one Sunday morning with a box of oranges. She watched me squeeze oranges by pushing down the handle of a small juicer. She asked to try, and quickly mastered the juicing process. Pleased with her new skill, she offered to finish the job. For the next three mornings she enthusiastically volunteered to squeeze the oranges.

She took such delight in juicing oranges that on the fourth morning I asked her whether she would like the job to be her chore. Kiss of death. Chores were compulsory, yucky. She abruptly lost interest. She enjoyed squeezing the oranges when the task was voluntary. Things changed when obligation, or demand, entered. At this stage a responsibility was still a burden, and a demand something she preferred to avoid rather than embrace.

Knowledge and skills demand responsibility. Shifts in expectations are simply one more change to which you must become accustomed. It need only be for a while that you fear or reject the demands that your new knowledge and skills will bring. This is a transitional phase. You are now a more capable person, and you will stretch to tolerate or even welcome new expectations, just as you have with every other new step of growth in your life.

You have all you need to meet new demands. Don't worry if people's expectations start to get ahead of your capabilities, at least as you perceive them. You must learn to endure this as you make your progress.

Professional tennis player Lindsay Davenport, who made a slow, steady rise to the top of the world rankings, said that at each level, from joining the professional circuit to winning a Grand Slam event, she had to become accustomed to the idea that she was playing at that level.

▶ Fred, 45, a corporate executive, thought he knew how he would feel when he solved his problem with public speaking. Although he had recently received a standing ovation for a talk, his feelings about speaking successfully in public were still not quite what he had imagined, and for a time, despite very favorable results, he continued to cling to the idea that public speaking was difficult for him.

Fred's problem was not meeting others' expectations but meeting his own. Fred had imagined that if he were an effective speaker, he would feel an otherworldly calm and a confidence that would erase any anxiety. Not surprisingly, although he acknowledged he had made progress, Fred's feelings did not match what he had anticipated feeling. It took him longer to accept his progress, because to embrace success he had to overcome patently unrealistic expectations. These expectations were, in part, a self-protective method for reducing stress. As long as he continued to regard himself as short of his goal, he felt less pressured to produce good results.

Learn to view new problems as new possibilities to learn. If you do not, you will remain superficial, shallow in your understanding, and uncreative in your responses. You will also face unnecessary surprises. With proper reflection, you will unlock what you need to learn.

## Quick Change Artistry

Unexpected success is at least as unsettling as failure, particularly when it comes quickly. When you do not build up to success progressively, you have no framework to accommodate it. You may have heard accounts of lottery winners who, wanting to escape the unaccustomed expectations of wealth, rid themselves of their winnings. But in any field, from athletics to corporate life, abrupt transitions leave people seriously unprepared.

The solution is not to cower or to exert some kind of extraordinary white-knuckles control. If you find any change so threatening that you impose rigid strictures on yourself, you can miss out on opportunities to move in new directions. After all, avoidance is avoidance, and you make any change more difficult to accept by avoiding it. Carefully select the changes you want to make in order to feel a level of control.

► Stacy could not have imagined the combination of exhilaration and fear she felt on beginning work on the documentary dance film. Suddenly people treated her as a serious artist, and she got requests for advice and offers of help from film students who heard about her project. She had to manage her time in the face of demands she had not anticipated. She also noticed that she struggled in conversations when people referred to her as a filmmaker. She liked the sound of that identity but had not internalized it yet.

When you succeed at new things, you have to integrate the new success into your view of yourself. Even if you always retained a belief in your abilities, actualizing goals and dreams is new territory and gives talent a different meaning. To be gifted is one thing, to be accomplished another. Stacy kept experiencing jolts from people's responses to her as well as from their expectations.

When Jesus walked on the Sea of Galilee toward the boat where his disciples fished, Peter saw Him coming and, at Jesus' beckoning, leaped out of the boat and onto the water to meet Him. Peter took a few steps, then looked down and sank like a stone. In the moment Peter stepped out of the boat, he also stepped out of what he had understood as reality. Once he realized that what he was doing was impossible—that he was literally and figuratively in over his head—he abruptly sank.

Peter ran into an irresolvable contradiction between reality as he understood it and what he found himself doing. He was unprepared, and having no way to understand what he was doing or to stretch his reality to accommodate his experience, he resolved the contradiction by sinking.

Surprises reflexively bring up resistance and the impulse to return to earlier, more familiar patterns. When you are surprised, you contract in order to protect yourself. If your goals involve activities that could bring external attention or sudden success, it is better to plan for trouble to reduce the shock. If change comes quickly, you are then better prepared to ride out the discomfort and stay on course. Otherwise, you will resist the success you achieve and find some way to undermine it.

When you begin to change, your notion of who you are has to keep pace with, and adapt to, your new capacities, or you will experience the Peter effect. If you change rapidly, it is difficult to maintain control but extremely important that you do. Remain supple. If you think that a happy life is a trouble-free one, you will experience disappointment even when you succeed. Do not resist, freeze, or clutch. If you lose control, do not stop backing yourself. Steady yourself, and get back to your plan.

▶ Sylvia, 31, who had never attended college and who questioned her intellectual abilities, was bewildered when she began to advance at a car rental agency. Having moved up quickly from handling rentals to overseeing the resale of rental cars in her region, she viewed her success as accidental and undeserved. It did not mesh with her previous history.

She felt self-conscious and ill at ease in meetings and at company socials because she feared that she would reveal her lack of education through some gaffe. She pulled back in these situations, and people generally ignored her. She interpreted both the inattention *and* any attention paid to her as proof of her inadequacies: if no one noticed her, it was because she was unworthy; if someone did notice her, it was probably because of some mistake in her behavior. Worst of all, when people were cordial, she viewed them as either pitying or patronizing her.

Sylvia's picture of herself had not caught up with her new situation. She experienced the Peter effect and, before long, found herself doing small things to not only slow down her ascent but undo her progress— for instance, being less cooperative with management and late with reports.

When changes come too fast, you experience them as shocks or blows. There is no time to recover from one before the next one arrives, and instead of assimilating them, you only react to them. The effect is like being pummeled. Anyone unprepared for the onslaught can easily feel out of control.

Many of the negative consequences of rapid change stem from having insufficient time to reflect before having to make some choice. The challenge of rapid change is that you need more control at a time when it is harder to maintain it. You therefore cannot wait until you are in the moment, hoping you will think clearly, because you will not have had enough time. You will be better able than Peter to adapt if you prepare as much as possible ahead of time. Though you cannot conceive of or control every possible future outcome, plan ahead.

First of all, if demands increase quickly, remember that this is *your* life. Respond to demands by being the one to set the pace for meeting them. Do not allow success to eat you. Do not let others' ideas of success be your undoing. At the same time, pay careful attention to your own demands and expectations. See to it that they remain realistic. Be disciplined enough to take the time you need to savor your new life and appreciate it fully. Stay in touch with your own overall vision or aim, and when surprises come, stay in contact with your support person and constituency to maintain stability. Keep your own intentions in the forefront of your mind and keep moving on them.

Second, make the public reaction to your dream or project secondary to the intrinsic rewards of attaining your goals. This is obvious, but I say it anyway: public opinion is fickle. Rapid ascents in public opinion are easily followed by equally rapid descents. If you make public opinion the measure of the importance of your success, you set up an inevitable crash.

In addition to these general preparations, you can prepare concretely for rapid change with the following simple exercise, which is yet another use of visualization. This time the focus is on finding solutions in advance and practicing them.

☐ Apply thoughtful attention to the double-sided aspect of success seen in the Chinese story of the missing horses. Imagine achieving some success rapidly and visualize the various possible outcomes. Mentally rehearse how the success or change will arise and how you will deal with the accommodations it demands. See yourself taking those steps, including slowing things down and consulting your constituency or other advisers.

Write in a special section of your notebook a record of what you visualized and the steps you took. This is another way to rehearse your responses and keep a record of your solutions.

## A Natural Progression

Reaching the other goals embodied in your dream ultimately requires the same careful, thorough preparation and the same decision to go to work, with or without your doubts about your talents and skills. You begin small, add exercises and practices, and grind through the period when you feel inept and clumsy and seem to make no progress. Eventually your habits and skills shift. Then you accelerate your program.

The key is not to focus on a makeover of your entire life or on a laundry list of changes, but to make small, crucial revisions of your routine—like Max's use of an alarm clock—that will produce sweeping outcomes. That small change increased Max's sense of inner strength, and by providing experience in exercising his will, it broke his self-limiting conventions, increased his confidence that he could reach external goals, and made him open to change.

Work on external goals, like Stacy's lighting scheme, in turn creates *internal* changes. When Stacy prepared for the choral group's show, she augmented her store of knowledge and skills, increased her self-confidence, and greatly enhanced her belief in her ability to continue to work in the face of setbacks.

Applying concentrated effort to anything—a mud pie, a math problem, a woodcutting, organic gardening, a business issue, basketball—requires attention and volition, capacities that are then built up, just as physical exercise builds up physical capacities.

When you strive, fall back, and return to the battle, you acquire skills that help you reach new goals; you grow into a new sense of yourself. As you repeat this cycle, building skill atop skill, you can soon tackle and finish things you used to be afraid to start. You build momentum—a powerful force. Take advantage of it after you complete one project by going on to the next one.

For whichever project you turn to next, set up your master plan as a series of tasks and action steps. To construct your master plan, I suggest that you include the following tasks, adapting them to your particular project by visualizing what other tasks you will need to do, step by step, to accomplish the project. Finally, break down each task into finite, manageable action steps. Following this formula religiously will make reaching your dream a tangible reality in a matter of time.

1. Maintain positive practices: Continue to devote an hour per day to ongoing positive practices, and be sure to follow the five-minute rule for interruptions.
2. Cultivate resolve. Use the visualization exercises to further strengthen your resolve and see yourself complete steps. Never drop this task.
3. Develop a timeline. A timeline provides a visual guide to progress and a clear representation of how a particular project fits into your life.
4. Conduct a self-appraisal. The stakes are higher now, and this is not the moment to shortchange your efforts by retaining unnecessary limits. Assess current skills and self-defeating patterns, determine traps and escapes, and make plans for dealing with them. Compare your current answers to your previous self-appraisal. You may notice that something not of concern in the past now seems pressing because of new demands.
5. Eliminate self-defeating behaviors; shore up weaknesses and plan countermeasures and backups. Replace any remaining self-limiting habits, close off escapes, develop redundant backups, and strengthen master skills.
6. Assemble resources. In an organized way, assemble materials, tools, and other resources. Develop a constituency of human resources to provide technical assistance. If you

want someone to be your support person, make the choice based on your experience and previous recommendations.

7. Fill in gaps. Set up the mentoring, coursework, and advanced training you need to complete this project.
8. Engineer your physical environment and control your time. Adapt and fine-tune your workspace to the specifications of your task. Be drastic about controlling your time. Develop and firmly keep a schedule of appointments with yourself for crucial activities. Systematically devote the time necessary to your campaign.
9. Set realistic long- and short-term goals.
10. Begin your All-out Push.

As you reach your goals, what you once considered impossible becomes increasingly a part of daily life. You find your own methods for enhancing your effectiveness. But as you proceed you may wish to try out the advanced tools detailed in the remainder of this section. They are designed to increase the intensity and focus of your efforts and to provide more forceful ways to make progress on lingering self-limiting patterns. Because they are powerful, use them sparingly and thoughtfully.

## Extreme Goals

Extreme goals serve as a wrecking ball for breaking down any remaining limiting beliefs and internal structures. Setting extreme goals combines the elements of the All-out Push with "impossible" time frames. By judiciously using extreme goals and intense scheduling, you break through inefficient patterns and disrupt old, limiting ways of thinking. If you have difficulty completing a specific action step or regularly bog down with a particular activity, cut the time you spend on it and force yourself to complete it within a new, impossible time frame.

▶ Even after she completed the Fifteen Tasks and began to achieve major successes, Meredith, 28, retained certain limits that at first she did not recognize. She continued, for example, to do certain things inefficiently because she believed that they were inherently difficult and that she could not do them quickly. She was driving the car with the emergency brake on.

She noted particularly that she spent too much time on e-mail, but thought it impossible to do more efficiently. Urged to use an impossible time frame for e-mail, Meredith cut in half the time she had been allotting to it and in six days was able to keep to this new schedule more than 50 percent of the time.

Though people push past limits by using extreme goals and impossible time frames, this tool is not a prescription for living. Use this tool strategically and sparingly. Otherwise, you run the risk of overwork.

▶ Lifton, having finally begun real work on his novel, knew that his progress was still blocked by his belief that the road to his long-delayed goal had to be hard and torturous. He had, after all, delayed it.

Lifton experimented with some very drastic extreme goals and impossible deadlines for completing drafts of certain chapters. He pulled some all-nighters, and on one occasion stayed up for thirty-three hours. He found that he could push past certain obstacles by occasionally using these time frames. He learned that he had created imaginary problems and reasons not to succeed.

Lifton's choice was his own; I cannot recommend that you go to this extreme. You may even want to consult your physician about the advisability of using extreme deadlines at all. Under no circumstances should you use them at night if you must drive a car the following day. You must also realize that this is a tool with a limited application, not one to be used in an ongoing way.

Although you need not go to Lifton's extreme, I suggest that you experiment with less severe demands and shorter impossible time frames. If you decide you will complete a report or an updated version of your CV, you can permanently break limited views of your capacities in one intense work period. The results are greater efficiency and a surge in confidence.

## Harness the Power of Procrastination

If you have ever procrastinated but somehow finished a quality project, you may have experienced a sense of heightened awareness and clarity of mind while completing it. You tapped into a state of consciousness that some SLHPPs find so addictive that they make delaying a habit just to experience this exceptionally efficient state of mind.

Procrastinating, of course, becomes a trap. When you fail to start a project in a timely manner and leave things to the last minute, you finish because time expires. You may feel relieved upon completing it, but you feel anxious before you begin. Besides using procrastination as a form of self-handicapping ("I did pretty well for the amount of time I had"), some SLHPPs use procrastination to cut through perfectionist tendencies and limit wheel-spinning. Although procrastination can evoke a kind of clarity and creativity, it is ultimately self-defeating: your project suffers because you do not have the time to add the good ideas that could come from your creativity. You may produce something passable or good, but you cannot take it to the final stage of excellence.

Rather than procrastinate, use a version of extreme goals to tap into and harness this clarity and efficiency whenever you sit down to work.

☐ Create an early, imperative, extreme deadline for a project that is not due for a while. If it is due in one week, set the deadline for tomorrow at noon. Then, alternate periods of intense work with rest until you reach the deadline. Force yourself to create a finished project of the best possible quality by the deadline. Then stop and step back from the project. Twenty-four hours later, go back and edit, correct, polish, and improve your work, but again set an early, extreme deadline. Step back again and repeat the process one more time. Do not dismiss this method by saying, "This won't work because I will know there really isn't a deadline." You may surprise yourself and be able to do it the first time. If not, perfect the method.

To use this method, before you begin work, think back to some previous time of working intensively and with heightened clarity to meet a deadline; in detail, notice your physical sensations and your mental outlook and relive the experience. Then, retain the physical sensations and outlook of urgency that accompanied that state, bring the feelings back with you, and begin work on the project in front of you.

▶ Jeremy, 29, a best-or-nothing, found that using this method increased his efficiency both for making sales contacts and for doing the associated paperwork. He discovered that boredom disappeared when he worked at an intense pace. Having previously put off looking at correspondence until the last possible moment, he now followed up immediately on the day of any sales contact and gave himself a five-minute time frame for completing it. His efficiency and the quality of his writing took a quantum leap forward.

Experiment with setting early deadlines for projects and meeting them. When you create early deadlines, you invoke the efficiency and clarity of the "back-against-the-wall" experience without the downside of actually having your back against the wall.

There is nothing unreal, however, about the success that such efficiency and clarity help bring about. Besides changing you and your life, that success also changes your direction.

▶ When Fritz unexpectedly had to purchase a boat before going to sea, he needed income for the ongoing costs of his voyage. So he took on passengers, who served as crew and paid him in advance for passage. Faced with the task of selecting crew members and supervising them, Fritz had to learn to be the captain and to deal with its consequences.

When he arrived in Turkey, he became so enamored of what he saw there that he stayed for months. He became fascinated with Turkish rugs and for the next few years learned enough about them to become a dealer in textiles, sailing back and forth to the United States with shipments, extending his knowledge, and developing new skills. With each change, he remained in one way consistent: he considered his possibilities, decided what he wanted to do next, and then planned well.

Meeting goals leads to a desire to meet new ones. But should there be a limit to how far you go?

## Altitude Sickness

Climbing teams now regularly ascend Mount Everest, but that effort is still no walk in the park. It requires intensive preparation, training, and expert support and guidance; even then, when you get near the top, you can run into serious problems. Your body, no matter how much you prepare, is acclimated to lower altitudes. At the very high altitudes of Everest, people suffer altitude sickness, and lingering symptoms can cause serious problems.

The primary symptoms of altitude sickness are headaches, blurred vision, and occasionally nosebleeds. It stems from moving abruptly from lower to higher elevations—from where air pressure and oxygen are more concentrated to where air pressure and oxygen are less concentrated. Symptoms dissipate in about a day as the body accommodates to the new altitude. At the very highest altitudes, particularly on Everest expeditions, people adapt at differing rates, and some do not adapt completely.

Regardless of how quickly you may have changed, the greater the change, the greater the separation between you and the majority of people. You have arrived, at whatever speed, at a kind of rarified atmosphere where fears of isolation and loneliness may arise. If you reach a very high level of knowledge about Italian Renaissance art, you may have few friends with whom to share the full extent of that knowledge, but fears of separation from friends are largely unfounded. You never lose any real relationship by moving forward with your life.

In the maintenance stage, and at every point thereafter, be on the lookout for the subtle ways in which you limit yourself and the new fears that arise as you progress. Some fears seem to have lain beneath the surface, submerged logs waiting to damage the hull of any vessel you might launch. At times a brooding fear can caution you against going too far beyond your station or seeking too much. Disregard that fear.

Nearly every major cultural tradition has stories that warn of the destructive nature of pride and the folly of presumptuousness or ambition unaccompanied by wisdom. Attempting to climb too high, venture too far, set oneself as equal to God, or avoid His injunctions always leads to one's undoing.

In the Grimms' fairy tale "The Fisherman and His Wife," the warning is to be careful of what you wish for because you just might get it. In stories from the East, difficulties getting the genie back in the bottle similarly suggest that hastiness, a wish to find magical solutions, and a lack of foresight bring results we do not anticipate or want. The Greeks warned of the danger of human ambition in the story of Icarus, who fashioned wings of feathers and wax and dared to fly too close to the sun; the wax on his wings melted, and he fell to earth. They warned of the dangers of pride or hubris in the story of Oedipus, who attempted to escape the oracle's prophecy and in the process fulfilled it by killing his father and marrying his mother. In each of these stories, the consequences are built into the heedlessness of the actions themselves.

In the Judeo-Christian tradition, God directly punishes attempts to set oneself equal to God. Lucifer, the highest of the angels, is cast from heaven for this, and Adam and Eve are expelled from Paradise for disobediently eating from the Tree of Knowledge. This story and others from the Old Testament suggest that if left unchecked, man would recognize no limits to his power. By eating the fruit, Adam and Eve develop self-awareness. If they were to likewise eat of the Tree of Eternal Life, their transformation into gods would be complete. For this disobedience they are banished, and angels are sent to guard the entrance to the east side of Eden. After the great flood, already a punishment imposed by Jehovah, people on earth remain united by a shared language and common purposes and begin to build a tower to reach into the heavens. The Lord then says, "And now nothing will be restrained from them which they begin to do." To prevent this power from emerging, He confounds their language and scatters them.

How shall we take these warnings? Could it be that they merely express superstitious fears of the unknown, of going too far or flying too high? Many human fears have turned out to be superstitious. In the twentieth century people feared the effects on the body of traveling more than sixty miles per hour, then the effects of traveling faster than the speed of sound; the four-minute mile was also considered an impossible barrier. So perhaps the stories express only fears of the unknown.

But the stories of the Greeks say that human pride and presumptuousness, hubris, leads to destructive outcomes. Man should not attempt to soar too high or to escape the consequences of his fate, because he lacks the necessary wisdom to govern this power.

The Old Testament stories contain striking references to Jehovah feeling threatened by the possibility of man's unlimited potential. No one with a minuscule awareness of current events or recorded history could deny that in the hands of humans power and abilities can be misused and lead to hideous consequences. Wisdom and justice often suffer when that kind of power is exercised.

In view of these warnings, what conclusions may we reach? In terms of limits, it is true that we do not eat of the Tree of Life but are born and fated to die. There seems to be little we can do about this particular limit. But exactly what would be the point of longer life?

As individuals, can we increase our capacity for reflection and sound judgment and reduce the damaging risks of egocentricity, prejudice, and reflexive adherence to conventions? In any such effort, we must be extremely mindful and disciplined and follow a path with our hearts as well as our minds.

At a minimum, we must be aware that everything in our environment is systemic and that our actions never affect us alone. We do not operate in a vacuum. We must appreciate that a change in one part of the whole creates corresponding changes elsewhere in the system. We must develop reciprocity in our relationships. We must be wise stewards, neither fearless nor cowardly. We must humbly submit ourselves to transformation and gain a more profound understanding of life.

If we seek not power but intrinsic rewards, such as wisdom and personal development, our strivings will be more profound and less egoistic and potentially lethal. Though we must heed warnings, we should not put unnecessary limits on our lives. Remember the lessons of Katherine Butler Hathaway's journey. She joyously took her life to the limit and plunged ahead despite one mistake after another. Act as she did—always as a novice, always ready to learn.

At this stage, as at any other, failures are the fuel for growth. Mistakes signal that you willingly pushed the edges of what you know in order to learn new skills. Being unafraid of failure will not only help you keep growing but, paradoxically, will help prevent a relapse into old patterns. When you accept failures as part of growth, you are far less likely to be frustrated by setbacks and to misinterpret them as proof of failure. When you correctly see setbacks for what they are—an essential element of your growth—it is ludicrous to throw in the towel. As you acquire wisdom, though, the direction of your strivings may quite naturally begin to change.

# 9

# Defying Gravity

At first our dreams seem impossible, then they seem improbable, but when we summon the will, they become inevitable.

—Christopher Reeve, from a speech given at 1996 Democratic Party
National Convention

You've accomplished something major. You've taken the wraps off your talent, removed limits, rid yourself of self-defeating habits, built master skills, and committed yourself to completing a series of serious projects. Savor it. You are on your way to your dream, and it doesn't get much better than that. Or does it? Is there more to learn? When you reach your dream, what then?

Your dream is a beginning or an end point, depending on what you decide. If you decide to go on from there, whether your dream remains the solitary consuming passion of your life or leads to new directions, you will never be short of satisfying things to do. You will live something rare and exquisite: a life that you have fashioned around a central aim.

For most people, their dream is a long-range objective. You may wait until you reach your dream to know whether there is more you want to do. You may be ready, however, to make a different kind of progress once you have set things in motion and settled into a comfortable rhythm.

That progress, which moves everything in your life to another level, is what we examine in this chapter as we look at the next steps in your evolution. Here I suggest a shift in perspective and intention that will significantly accelerate your general growth without additional exercises or new specific goals. This shift in perspective is to view life and its events as a school; the task, a natural extension of your work to date, is to imbue daily activities with the same quality and level of self-expressive attention you use for activities related to your dream. I describe this shift through examples that show why this new perspective automatically raises the standard for your activities and shifts your relationship to them. The remainder of the chapter examines a range of possibilities that will allow you to soar beyond your previous dreams.

## Your Next Quest

You enter life needing to complete two tasks if you are to survive independently: learning the world and mastering necessary skills. To manage the tasks, you were born with temperament, talents, and an amazing cerebral cortex. Evolutionarily, the human brain is overkill; its capacities exceed what is necessary for mere survival. Like a Ferrari used to deliver mail, it is conspicuously overqualified for the task. To what use could that extra mental horsepower be put? With instruction and proper study, might we all reach an elite level? How many Solomons, Buddhas, or Einsteins sleep within us? In the West we still do not put much emphasis on controlling our minds and directing our attention. We're not encouraged to look under the hood of that Ferrari, so we don't develop an owner's manual.

In Life 101, life itself is a school, class is always in session, and you are enrolled. Life presents universal elements with which to grapple—birth, aging, death, relationships, and choice points—along with a pressure cooker of additional puzzles in random events and the twists and turns of your particular life story. How you react to them influences their outcome, what you learn from them, and your next lessons. Your intentions and goals, combined with how well you pay attention and use your abilities, influence continuously what you get and who you become. If you exploit the possibilities and learn, the school is your pass to freedom. If you turn away from those possibilities, the school is a prison sentence, and you are left to pass time in the yard.

Your life is of uncertain duration, but it belongs only to you; you do not have to return it to a rental facility, and no one can tell you how to live it. If you do not learn, however, you are likely to repeat some partial solution again and again. In Martin Scorsese's *Raging Bull*, Robert De Niro plays Jake LaMotta, a professional boxer whose relentlessness brings one brief moment of success but whose inability to adapt destroys his life. Abraham Maslow once summarized succinctly the problem of incomplete knowledge: "If all you have is a hammer, everything starts to look like nails." This is the prison of limited insight and understanding. Rita Mae Brown has said, "Insanity is doing the same thing over and over again and thinking you'll get different results." LaMotta hammers away sufficiently well with his fists to become the world middleweight boxing champion, but he hammers away insanely at those who care for him with the same intensity, until he loses them all. In the end he is still standing, but he is alone.

The school of life presents stiff challenges, unadulterated joys, deep anguish, and at times unspeakable horror. It is how you respond to what life offers you that determines what and how much you learn, or whether you learn much at all. In *Next Stop Wonderland*, when a young woman's life is jolted by the death of the physician father she loves, she is left alone to deal with her mother's superficial values. She struggles to regain her footing, abandons her plans to study medicine and become a nurse, and lives with the regrets and misgivings of one who has given up an opportunity. And yet the film expresses the hope of her redemption.

To gain any kind of mastery of life, you must open up to its lessons. If you adopt the point of view that life is a school and make it your goal to learn and understand all you can, you will transform your life.

Having completed the Fifteen Tasks, you have a model for how to approach future ventures. You can adapt some version of this method to any objective, including self-mastery. But all of life, if approached appropriately, is an opportunity to learn.

At some point you may want to pursue more actively the implications of life as a school, filled with a rich and diverse curriculum. The external world can be explored and conquered, but it is your internal world that selects and guides your efforts. By making shifts in your perspective and intentions, it is possible to alter everything in your life.

This shift is separate from perfecting your personality or eliminating defective habits and limiting outlooks. To function optimally you have endless skills to master and polish. If you keep at it, you will receive countless benefits. But to arrive at the fullest expression of your potential you cannot stop at eliminating negative habits and shoring up weaknesses. To transcend the ordinary you must launch a different, more personalized effort, accepting only the small additional risk of following your heart.

You may have intuitively known this—to be truly alive you need to give your life your personal stamp. And partly for this reason you may have rejected overly regimented paths. But it is easy to throw out the baby with the bathwater. The most common self-defeating error is skipping not only the stifling rigidity of conventional choices but also the step of rigorously laying the foundation for expressing your own vision. Without that foundation, you are caught short. Dance innovator Martha Graham said it takes ten years to master the basics before one can really begin to dance. True creativity requires skills, discipline, and development, as well as talent. That kind of discipline has excellence as its aim.

The shift in focus I am suggesting does not require additional exercises or new external goals. Instead, it involves changing the way you approach your daily activities by changing the kind of attention you give them. Instead of focusing on some future point when you will reach your dream, lend importance to *everything* you do every moment of every day. Attend to each activity as if it were holy work or the quintessential expression of your dream.

Some decisions are transformational. Deciding to make all of your actions equally important to your dream is one of them. As soon as you begin to pursue your daily activities this way you change. If you continue to apply this attention, you greatly accelerate your development while retaining your current schedule of activities. You simply change your approach to them and in some way likewise your approach to yourself.

If you have always searched for instant gratification, you will receive it with this activity. There is no wait. Treat each moment as if it were your dream. Make dream moments. If you make everything you do equally important and do not rush distractedly through what you consider unimportant things, you immediately leave the ordinary. Every moment counts. Pay attention to the small things, and they become grand. It is a way of treating yourself warmly, gently, and generously. When you make all your moments matter you make your life matter.

If you want to make your life a dream—to make it your work of art—simply apply this different kind of attention to ever-widening ranges of activities and see what happens. Your life will be energized; everything will be fresher. Follow the career of any serious artist and you see natural evolution. To make art of your life is what Katherine Butler Hathaway called "to make of one's self the poem," and what you express in the poem of your life will change effortlessly and continuously.

As I have said, no prescription applies to all—no rules can dictate what you finally do with your life or how you express yourself. I have often seen SLHPPs take the limits off their lives and spontaneously begin to elevate previously mundane aspects of their lives with this kind of attention. If they used to eat in a rush standing up, they now sit down in the dining room, bring out the good silver, and take a little longer to savor the moment. They create occasions with their attention. They make all of life an occasion for celebration. The way they think about the ordinary stuff of life is as different as each individual, but they are all devoted to shaping the smallest details of their lives into personal expressions of an ideal.

These actions do not arise from dissatisfaction or a feeling that what they have is not enough. They stem from a wish to extend the addictive pleasure of mastery. It's as if they have discovered a formula: if aiming for a dream brings such happiness, why not aim to express your heart's desire across the board, all the time?

You may recognize a similarity between what I am suggesting here and my workshops on work in which I presented mundane tasks as exercises in attention. The instructions to work slowly and pay attention to body movements were designed to increase attention to the task and make it a vehicle for a more attentive and meditative way of working. The antidote to boredom is always attention, whether the task is doing a calculus problem or trimming your toenails, but this perspective elevates what you do to a kind of nobility. At the same time it increases your pleasure in doing it, an effect that has no obvious downsides.

Proceeding in this way inevitably leads to more balance. If your dream has revolved around spiritual and personal development, the external things in your life will be targets for this new approach as well. If external accomplishments have been at the heart of your dream, you will give new attention to the subtler internal aspects of your existence. Of course, by now you know that the work I have suggested has been deliberately designed to blur conventional distinctions between internal and external so that each side of life enhances the other.

## How to Raise Your Standard of Living

To begin to raise the standard for your life, consider starting with one of life's big givens—time. Gaining control over time is basic to gaining control over your life. How would you treat time in order to elevate it?

The most clichéd remark people make about time is that they never have enough of it, almost as if to suggest that others get a different ration than they do. This comment, however, is usually a tip-off that they do not control or exploit the time they do have. The time you have never varies, but your subjective experience of it varies based on what you do with it. Time can drag on or fly by depending on your point of view. Many people who say that they do not have enough time do little with the time they do have. They fail to respect time, or they do not really want to acknowledge its existence. People are continually in denial about time. They truly try to block it out of their minds.

If you shift to the perspective that time is precious, that it is finite, not infinite, and that you must honor it and treat it as treasure, your orientation changes. Time is invaluable and irreplaceable. How you spend it defines your existence. That does not mean that you have to hoard it. You can be generous with it. But when you give time, you give up a piece of your life. You can no longer treat time as if it were nothing, nor can you "kill time."

Instead, ask yourself, what do I want to do now? What is the one thing most worth doing? Do I want to spend my time this way or another way? How shall I spend this day of my life, this hour, this moment? How can I most profit from this time? There is a science of living with an awareness of time in order to make the most of your life, to extract the greatest and most profound pleasure and meaning.

This includes building in leisure time to free yourself from obligations and to experience pleasure in activities or rest. Without this elevation of time and an accompanying intention to make the best use of it, you barely advance past a childlike conception of life.

Many in each new generation of retirees find that they have not developed their interests, talents, and potential, and therefore they experience a crisis as to what to do with their newly abundant time. This crisis can be sidestepped by learning early on how to use leisure time for richly rewarding activities. Set a very high standard now for what you do with your time.

In this light, examine the common expression "pastime." Do you want leisure activities that serve to merely "pass time"? Or do you want to exploit joyously the time you have for everything you can wring out of it? Examine the common expression "to kill time." If your time is your life, killing time is killing off your life piece by piece. Consider the notion of being entertained. Can you not find pleasure in something substantial—a film, a piece of music, a play—that raises questions about the meaning of existence, or must you be merely distracted by the standard rehashed drivel served up by entertainment factories?

Just asking.

If you have a storehouse of lively, compelling interests from which you extract meaning and a packed schedule of profoundly rewarding activities, you have a very good formula for spending your time. Use your leisure time to find real relaxation and deep pleasure and simultaneously to increase your personal development. These two goals are complementary, not mutually exclusive. At the very least, you can never be bored with a good library, a hungry mind, and a devotion to probing deeply.

Time is related to another of life's givens—death. Perhaps more than anything else it is the denial of death that underlies the denial of time. In any case, both forms of denial are equally strong. To remain clueless about either one results in a dangerous naïveté that cancels out reflection, evaluation, and real choice. If you casually give time away, reflexively saying yes to every social invitation or night out, rather than treasure it, you become a slut with your time. If you always consider the same two or three activities pleasurable, you are on automatic pilot about time. If, on the other hand, you are aware of the limited nature of time, you will naturally treat it with respect. Be on top of your time—know where you are going and what you are going to do when you get there. Otherwise, you can be either easily distracted or limited to the imagination and desires of the person at the other end of the phone line. In many teaching traditions it is said that to really live you must first become aware of your own death—the fact that your time is finite.

At the end of the day a real sense of fullness and satisfaction results from having done several things well. If you elevate time, you will prepare for the time you have and be ready to use it. People who lead full and happy lives think about their time, packing it with the mixture of activities that pleases them, including study, play, and challenges. They do not hang out to see what happens. Instead, they create positive routines and structures and eliminate negative ones. And they finish things so as not to, as Amiel emphasized, let the unfinished affairs of this day rob from the next one.

To master your time you need to be conscious of it. Let's say you want to have friends over for a long evening. How can you maximize the benefit of the time you will share? You will have dinner and talk, but what will enhance the time spent together and make it most rewarding for all? And consider how, and when, you will bring the evening to a close. This is not to tie yourself in knots planning some kind of spectacular evening. Spending five minutes of precious time considering this will make the five hours you spend with your friends far more pleasurable and satisfying.

Reaching goals means paying attention to time. I have known people who worked regular daytime shifts but went to bed at 7:00 P.M. in order to awaken and have silent, uninterrupted time at 3:00 A.M. I have known artists and writers who sleep during the day in order to work between midnight and 6:00 A.M. These solutions worked for them. The goal with time is to make it work for you—not only for projects and large-scale goals but for your entire life.

When it comes to the simple, inescapable chores of living, the issue remains the same. What is the best way to insert the garbage can liner anyway? Whether you are sewing on a button, polishing silver, or cleaning the oven, if you elevate the value of your time, you must invest attention in it regardless of the task. The formula is the one mentioned before. Give your attention to each moment and each act. Slow down. Do not be distracted. You will be more efficient. In this way, you will transform neutral or even unpleasant tasks into pleasure.

A final note about time and this kind of attention: You need rest and sleep. Your biology is highly rhythmic, and some people are more sensitive than others to interruptions and variations. If you experience sleep difficulties, pay attention to your rhythms and adjust them to a more regular schedule. If you go to bed each night and get up each morning at about the same time, you are likely to sleep much better. If, on the other hand, your sleep time is completely random, you are working against your biology and spending most of your time jetlagged without having boarded a plane. If you value your time, you'll want to be in good condition to enjoy it.

If you experience difficulties paying this kind of attention to time because your mind wanders, there are methods to develop more discipline and control over your attention. Attention is the basis for order and for running your own life instead of merely being pushed along by unexamined conventions and habits. Without attention, focus, and the ability to concentrate, you literally cannot learn, much less attain mastery. At a minimum, the school of life teaches that lesson.

In the West we are less familiar with the control of attention except as a consequence of the fad diagnosis, attention deficit disorder (ADD). According to Eastern notions, attention is a weak function that needs development, not medication. Attention is considered a matter of personal responsibility and closely related to health. For this reason, practices from the Japanese tea ceremony to martial arts increase control over attention by making it a primary focus. For various reasons, including unfamiliarity, people are sometimes hesitant about approaching these practices. But stripped of their religious connotations, kung fu, tai chi chuan, aikido, tae kwon do, chi gong, meditation practices of various kinds, and even yoga are *attentional technologies* and can be practiced with that in mind. Not all attentional technologies come from the East. Various orders of the Catholic Church have developed techniques and meditative practices that have similar effects.

If you are put off by the philosophical basis of any method for developing attention, do not be put off by the goal. These methods work as focusing devices, and if versions of them were introduced routinely to children and others currently medicated for ADD, they might in many cases eliminate the need for medication and its potential long-term side effects.

As an alternative to following some formal method of meditation or martial art, simply follow the practice of clearing your mind of thoughts. The instructions are simple, but doing it is at first difficult. To achieve anything you have to ignore the initial difficulties and continue. The instructions are to sit quietly or lie down and then let go of all thoughts. Let your mind become blank. If you begin to resume thinking, notice it and let go again. In this way, you will progressively gain volitional control over your attention and learn to direct your mind. Although it is difficult, you will slowly get better at it, over time and with persistence.

Another attention-focusing device is to close your eyes and sense a body part, perhaps your left or right foot or elbow, and then, as you open your eyes and begin normal activities, maintain attention there. Doing this exercise continuously requires posting reminders everywhere that direct your attention back to the task.

Having done both of these exercises extensively, I can tell you that they provide maddeningly clear evidence of how fragile our attention is without training. I can also tell you that the more you repeat these exercises, the more progress you will see. As a bonus, they are a useful source of information on your current ability to tolerate frustration.

Deep muscle relaxation exercises also increase attentional control. Start with these if you want to ease your way into work on attention. Herbert Benson's book *The Relaxation Response* is an excellent resource. A variety of excellent nonsectarian audiotapes, available from various outlets, teach deep relaxation and other simple attention-focusing techniques.

Another method for developing increased attentional control, when approached properly, is study. An unfortunate fallout of most schooling experiences is the way in which students come to regard study. School gives study a bad name. Study in school means test preparation, and the test itself is often a bizarre and random examination of one's grasp of information. Once the link is made between study and exams, study is associated with the feelings that accompany exam preparation. This is a great loss. Study, besides being a tool to focus attention and a route to self-development, is intrinsically pleasurable and results in the profound reward of increased knowledge.

People who make study part of a lifelong pattern develop extraordinary capacities. To struggle with a math problem, plumb deeply the meaning of a serious work of fiction, or memorize an epic poem is to focus attention intensely and engage in an effort of mastery. Twentieth-century French philosopher Simone Weil said that the attitude of study and the process itself are major tools for self-development because they require a focused attention that increases capacities. Specifically with regard to study she said, "No true effort of attention is wasted, even though it may never have any visible result, either direct or indirect."

When you read a book like the newly translated Roger Martin Du Gard's *Lieutenant-Colonel de Maumort,* have a notebook nearby to jot down thoughts and questions, or insert Post-it notes beside passages to which you want to return. Making such notes increases your pleasure by forcing you to pause and reflect. You deepen that pleasure by coming back to these passages to study them, asking yourself questions and making connections between them. Any serious painting, piece of music, or literary work is replete with complexity and truth that demands and rewards repeated reflection and focused attention. To study, discuss, or write about a work leaves a lasting mark on your consciousness and geometrically extends your understanding and satisfaction.

If you devote yourself to making each moment excellent, you accelerate your progress across the board. That extends to your relationships and to what constitutes the basis for all good relationships— self-knowledge. The process is circular: self-knowledge helps you have profound relationships, and relationships themselves are paths to self-understanding.

If you don't know yourself, how can you really get to know someone else or function in an optimal manner? If you repeatedly experience the same patterns and problems in relationships and do not quite understand why, there is much for you to learn. If someone asks you why you behaved in a certain fashion and you cannot put your finger on why you are probably adhering to unconscious patterns. The problem is that though we hear the injunction "Know thyself," we barely know what it means, much less how to go about fulfilling it. Surely we must examine ourselves to know ourselves, and sometimes we feel that by solving some little piece of the puzzle we gain understanding. But how do we get past the light-bending prism of our prejudice and our faulty assumptions?

You know what I am going to say: it takes time and systematic effort. To understand yourself, much less the rest of the world, is a long-term, probably lifelong effort, but what were you going to do with the time anyway? The opportunities exist; the question is how to make the best of them. Each person, like the pilgrim Kaminita, looks out at the world through his own window.

Until you embrace the role of student of life, you continue to see the world from your vantage point and cannot achieve a clear, broad view. One good tool for broadening your outlook is long-term psychotherapy; group therapy is also worth considering. But it is imperative that you find an excellent therapist. Ask for referrals or recommendations. Then begin with an agreement for two or three appointments. If you do not feel a good connection or sense that the person will help you, move on to another therapist.

Rather than set out thinking that you will attain wisdom, gain self-control, and learn aesthetic, intellectual, and moral judgment, begin with a sense of modesty and humor. Achieving self-mastery is an exhausting process; you have to know how to laugh and see the humor in your flawed efforts. Otherwise, the seriousness gets ponderous. Go about your progress with pleasure and fun in mind. If you set out down the path of self-mastery, you will probably get lost anyway. You learn to master yourself through the lessons in Life 101.

If you want to set new goals, you might begin by transforming the master skills into arts, and then extend the list to include the topics we have now covered. Consider devoting yourself to:

- The art of patience (related to tolerating frustration)
- The art of persistence and tenacity
- The art of consistency of effort
- The art of thoroughness and follow-through
- The art of finishing
- The art of reflection and contemplation
- The art of planning
- The art of perfecting
- The art of attention
- The art of friendship

You could then use the passages from Amiel as a guide to using skills beyond those of mere survival. When you sustain your demand for excellence by investing excellence in each moment, you inevitably move toward greater self-mastery. Amiel's suggestions concerning order demand and create excellence. They give standards as goals. Aiming to improve even one area is a sufficient place to start. Dispatching in an orderly way your obligations, relationships, and interactions with the world requires focus. These are the benefits of living an ordinary, non-esoteric life mindfully and well.

Amiel had another definition of order and self-mastery: "To employ one's capital and resources, one's talent and one's chances profitably." This means that elevating your financial activities can be another avenue. What would that look like for you?

> ▶ Greg's persistently unrealistic approach to his finances over the years became a source of real concern to his family and friends. He had no dependents, but it was clear that he literally never had money set aside. In fact, with some exquisite sense of balance, he managed to be always slightly behind, so that when he completed an editing job or other project and got a lump sum, he had already spent it and had none left over to save.

Some friends confronted him, leading to his visit to the Maximum Potential Project.

This is not a book about financial advice, and external events sometimes play a part in financial problems. Nevertheless, some aspects of money are simple. To handle your finances you need adequate, realistic reflection, know-how and sound advice, and a long-range perspective. This is one area in which you should not try to hit a home run every time you come to bat. And don't make things needlessly complicated. Save the fancy stuff for when you go from nickel to dime millionaire.

Of course, you must have enough money to meet your needs. Spell out your financial goals. You need not be greedy or impecunious. With money perhaps more than most things, people get what they ask for and earn about what they actually expect to earn. If you do not make much money, do you expect or want to earn more? It is difficult to focus on other areas if your financial survival is in doubt. If you have not been making sufficient money, learning to do it is a discipline that can be an avenue for growth. Make a master plan, and follow through as you would with any other goal. Get advice through sensible, useful resources, like newsletters, books, and, of course, advisers. Select them with care.

Since financial problems can pull your focus away from other goals, take a close look at yourself if you are perpetually in financial difficulty. The problem may express another set of self-limiting habits and serve as an excuse not to move forward. Deal with the fears and make adjustments to your lifestyle as needed. Financial goals are easier to meet when you eliminate negative and fuzzy thinking in this area.

Do not be afraid of money.

"To be able to dispose of all one's forces, to have all one's means of whatever kind under command"—Amiel's journal entry could suggest a number of things, but he must have included among them the intellect, the will, and perhaps the physical body. What would seeking excellence in these areas involve? To "dispose of" is to deal with a matter in order to settle it. To "dispose" means to position something for use. Consider what it would mean to you to put all your forces to use and to have your means under command.

As a fundamental requirement for order, Amiel included "to keep one's word and one's engagements." Making and keeping promises to yourself is the way to build your sense of confidence in your own reliability, but it applies to those with whom you have contact as well. It is vital in all of your dealings that your word means something. Make it a rule to speak with impeccable integrity or not at all. You will increase your personal power and enhance your ability to achieve your highest aims. If you wish to defy gravity, speak this way. Be clear and direct. Do not be evasive or vague. Speak simply, and say what you mean.

If you make appointments with others, keep them and be punctual. This is a matter of not only courtesy but integrity. If you are habitually late, you are saying that your time is more important than the time of others. Keeping one's word and one's engagements is a basis for reciprocity in relationships. Developing reciprocity is the key to taking relationships beyond the ordinary. But do not keep score about whose turn it is to give. Make your aim in relationships to take them to the highest level. Move away from seeing relationships as revolving around you and your needs. Do whatever is necessary to develop this type of order in relationships and this aspect of self-mastery.

If you set a high standard for self-knowledge and cultivate the position of student, you will develop deeply meaningful relationships. Develop a goal of truly knowing and understanding the motives behind your actions. If you find someone who has a similar commitment, the two of you can develop a relationship based on what Maurice Maeterlinck refers to as sincerity—laying out your faults for another person in order to neutralize their potentially damaging effects.

Maeterlinck suggests that "until we attain this sincerity, our love is but an experiment: we live in expectation, and our words and kisses are only provisional." The goal of sincerity is not to eliminate personal defect and develop a kind of otherworldly moral impeccability: "Thus understood sincerity's aim is not to lead to moral perfection. It leads elsewhere, higher if we will: in any case to more human and more fertile regions." What Maeterlinck considers higher is a kind of honest acknowledgment and confession that eliminates what are considered conventional moral inadequacies. For this purifying sincerity to develop and serve as a foundation for happiness, both people must deeply engage in the original work of conscious self-observation, developing "a consciousness and analysis of all of life's actions."

If you want an extraordinary life with extraordinary relationships, accept Maeterlinck's challenge. Most who have tried to practice sincerity, even "toe-in-the-water" style with a lover or spouse, have found it reduces defensiveness and promotes profound intimacy. This kind of advanced work is reserved for rarefied moments. It is work of devotion and the stuff of dreams.

Here is Amiel again, this time on what constitutes order in connection with relationships: "To take the measure of one's duties and make one's rights respected." This economical statement summarizes essential elements for conducting a relationship on a day-to-day basis. The emphasis on responsibility cuts in both directions, as indeed it must for relationships to have a proper foundation.

To Amiel, it is equally important that you discharge your duties and see to it that your rights are respected. In fact, to see that your rights are respected *is* to discharge your duties. It is useful to evaluate your personal strengths and struggles in these two areas. How do you stack up against the standard? Is one easier than the other? Are both difficult?

You might consider that all relationships have obligations, responsibilities, rights, prerogatives, and privileges. Can you say with clarity what those are for you and for those with whom you have a relationship? They should shift based on the nature of the relationship.

You can turn the question of the different aspects and demands of any relationship into an interesting and potentially enlightening activity with a spouse, family member, partner, or business associate. To do this, everyone should write down what he or she considers to be his or her obligations, responsibilities, and so on; then each person should write down what he or she considers to be the other's obligations. Exchange papers and discuss what you have written. A number of misunderstandings can be clarified with this exchange, and I encourage you to do it. Even if you do not do the exercise with someone else, make it a regular activity for yourself. It will bring precision to your thinking.

Another exercise is to consider in which relationships you defer control, share control, or take control. Depending on your various relationships, you should have opportunities for each form of dealing with control. Closely examine the roles in which you excel most and least and the ones in which you are most and least comfortable. These considerations alone will improve your relationships.

In your relationships, consciously develop the courage and the ability to play your role to the fullest. Each type of role is important. Each is a school. Practice making your wishes, requests, and directives clear, but also ask questions and say what you need and want and, if appropriate, what you require in each role you play.

▶ By doing this exercise, Doug, the father who had trouble making clear demands to his daughter, Amy, found that he had approached each of his personal and even some business relationships in the same way: as Doug, warm human being and great guy. Seeing that he had different roles to play in different relationships and recognizing that each required different aspects of his character and made different demands helped him make necessary progress.

Approach any activity with the right intention and mindful attention. The payoff is immediate. You are more interested when you are engaged and you get more out of the activity. You also find more to give. What would it look like for you to raise the standard at work?

▶ Brandon, a 36-year-old bored middle school science teacher, gained permission to create a vegetable garden on the school grounds that gave all schoolchildren an opportunity to do cooperative vegetable gardening. The students built raised garden beds, began composting, and tested different gardening conditions to determine which gave the greatest yield. Brandon's original intention was to teach environmental awareness and some agriculture and horticulture in a hands-on way, but the garden became a source of personal pride for the children and the school and transformed his own teaching experience. Brandon, feeling under paid, had been giving the minimum to his teaching. He discovered he had been cheating himself.

In terms of work, we have for too long honored spectacular displays of natural talent and raw potential over hard work and painstaking achievement. Jack London boasted that he wrote everything in a single draft. If so, what might he have accomplished with some polishing? The effortless grace of Fred Astaire resulted from hard work. Though he began dancing at age seven, he put in twelve-hour-per-day rehearsals with Ginger Rogers (from which she emerged with bruised and bloodied feet). Our cultural emphasis on talent seems to have an additional side effect: if we lack prodigious gifts, we excuse ourselves from trying and become spectators only. But you can be among the people who seek out new activities to extend their mastery, who take up guitar or expand their aesthetic experience through art, music, literature, architecture, or gardening. You could write that novel. It doesn't matter if it's never published.

You could get everyone in your apartment building or on your block to write a play, and then cordon off the street and have a three-day festival of original theater with the neighbors playing the parts. You could paint or write poems. You could start a project to beautify a park or educate an at-risk student. You no longer have to be trapped by the feeling that you must be the best at something in order to do it. The greatest pleasure comes from engaging yourself and from making each moment express the best of you.[1] No one else can do that but you.

Wouldn't it be great if you started something and it caught on? Wouldn't it be great if in every city and every town people were holding events that they created on their own out of the joy of doing it and out of the joy of life?

You can do it. You can do anything. You no longer have to hide. You do not have to be your own worst enemy.

## Another Look at the Progression of Development

When you complete any project, you will have further extended your skills and your horizon of possibilities. And when you complete your quests, achieve your goals, and arrive at what you dreamed, what then? Attune your ear, and in the rabble of loud voices you will hear whispers of how to move beyond what you have already achieved. Those voices may come from within yourself or from external sources.

There is a point to your existence. Seek it. If you continue to work on both inner and outer goals, you will focus increasingly and naturally on your inner development.

For guidance here, you can look to abundant resources: prophets, spiritual texts, ancient wisdom, art, music, philosophy, literature, poetry, and essays. Too often voices that speak the truth straightforwardly have been muffled or drowned out. Profound teachings about how to live life have been co-opted and distorted by those claiming an exclusive franchise for dispensing and interpreting wisdom.

Many are repulsed by the packaging of that which cannot be owned or dispensed, that which no one can claim as their own; they therefore turn from the message, losing it and the messenger too. Setting prophets apart on lofty pedestals makes their teachings seem attainable only for their closest adherents and their ideas applicable only to those few who are temperamentally disposed to, or otherwise mysteriously able to, follow them. This, I believe, has been a historic form of laziness, an easy out from the challenges presented by the teachers of wisdom.

You were born with potential for a reason. You did not dream of having a real life without the possibility of actually having it. Once you decisively break through limiting beliefs and self-defeating habits, you have room to breathe and a chance to shape how you live. You do not have to acquiesce to the commonplace. You can reach your dream and go even further, defying gravity and soaring well beyond what you previously considered possible.

Changing is difficult, but it is only difficult. The reward is finding your real life for the first time or getting back your real self. You can leave behind your fearful, pinched adherence to that "place by the window" where you simply "walk up and down." You can have the larger room, the grander view you deserve: it's yours for the making.

To have the life of your dreams and avoid regret, consider:

If no one else is doing it, it might be the thing to do.

If it defies practicality, it might be the thing to do.

If you feel afraid, assess the risk. If there is danger to your health, or to your person, move on. If not, keep exploring your curiosities, evaluating the results, and building on your progress.

Under the heading "Creative Breath," Katherine Butler Hathaway wrote in one of her last entries in her journal: "Something wonderful is happening to me . . . that same feeling of surprised, delicious excitement. . . . To be humble, submissive to universe, selfless, yet make of one's self the poem, the lovely interpretation, medium for mysterious heightened sense of life."

Bon voyage.

# Acknowledgments

This book would not have been possible without the support of the people who have generously contributed to it. While developing the Maximum Potential Project and writing this book I have been sustained by relationships with excellent clinicians and friends. I want to take the opportunity to thank as many of them as possible.

The ideas for this book have their origins in practical ongoing work with hundreds of people. I wish to express my appreciation to them for their courage in taking the necessary risks to change direction and their willingness to share their experiences. My first observations of the beneficial effects of practical, multifaceted approaches to change came from my work with the Concentrated Employment Program (CEP) in Fresno, California. Though this experience considerably predated my launching of the Maximum Potential Project, I want to express my thanks to the staff of CEP, and in particular to Alex Esmael, Ken Woods, Chuck Pollock, and Carl Scholars for their special contributions and friendship.

In the earliest stages of the Maximum Potential Project four people in particular offered valuable assistance. Rebecca Jewell contributed her experience of working with underachieving children; Phillip Erdberg provided dependably stellar advice on clinical instruments for assessments; Juliann Kaufmann contributed her enthusiasm, clinical skills, excellent data collection, and heartwarming constancy; and Bonnie Miller was resourceful, dauntless, idealistic, and practical in leaving no stone unturned in searching for approaches to solving logistical and clinical problems. I would also like to express my appreciation to Cloe Madanes, who served as consultant during the early days of the project and taught all of us much about taking necessary risks.

As the project matured, Andrea Shaw played the invaluable simultaneous roles of project coordinator and clinician. I am especially thankful for her cheerful and untiring devotion to going beyond the call of duty in search of excellence in all things large and small. Special thanks go also to Robert Lincoln for his pioneering contributions to work with adult underachievers, and to Terrence Patterson for advice on strategy. I would also like to thank my longtime clinical associate and friend Kris Picklesimer for his nurturing friendship over the years and consistent, unswerving collegial support at the Lafayette Therapy Center. It would be hard to imagine that anyone else could play either role better.

Many thanks also to Jon Douglas Lindjord and Peggy Schalk for their suggestions, enthusiastic support, unstinting generosity, and excellent, conscientious work videotaping talks and presentations, and to Renn Vera and Maureen Taylor of Family Talk, KQED-FM San Francisco, for their interest in work with underachievers and for repeatedly inviting me as a guest on their program to discuss the project. And thanks to Stuart Margulies for the lengthy and valuable talks we shared on interventions and approaches.

I would like to express my appreciation to Lisa Wagner and Robert Thur, who read and commented on extensive passages of early versions of the manuscript; to John Gallo, Tim Crouse, Ken Walton, and Andrea Shaw, who likewise read and commented on specific sections; and to Jim Cameron for his expert advice and opinions on sections related to temperament. Most of all I must express my profound gratitude to Gwyneth Cravens, who spiritedly, tirelessly, generously, and joyously worked under difficult circumstances to make an invaluable editorial contribution and provide a great deal of other support and counsel. To receive both her creative and sound technical advice and warm friendship was a sustaining source of inspiration.

Several people helped to ease my transition into Paris. I want to express my appreciation to Laurent and Isabelle Massing-Charpentier for their warm welcome and many kindnesses. Special thanks to Irene Assayg for generously providing me emergency accommodations, and to Pierre Bolzak and Brigitte Gueryraud for providing assistance of every imaginable kind, always as if it were nothing. Many thanks to Abdelmounine Amar of Gingko Boutique Macintosh, Paris, for his help during the disappearance of my computer, to Ralph Cutillo for logistical support, and to Elodie Denis for technical consultation.

Finally, I want to express appreciation to my agent, Eileen Cope, for her professionalism and excellent practical help; to Monica Crowley for helping put a final polish on the text; and to Cal Morgan, my editor at ReganBooks, who championed this book from the beginning and who had much to do with shaping its final form. To be able to work with an editor such as Cal, who understood the ideas, knew how to make them more comprehensible, and as a bonus is a warm, personable human being, has been a dream.

To Gudrun Mazoyer, I send special, personal thanks for everything—absolutely everything.

# Notes

## Introduction

1. Haberman, C., "Highfalutin but Hardly Proud of It," *New York Times*, October 10, 2001.
2. Balch, S.H., Zurcher, R.C., 1996. *The Dissolution of General Education Requirements: 1914–1993.* National Association of Scholars, Princeton, N.J.
3. International comparisons actually suggest that *most* U.S. children are underachieving because at all ability levels they perform more poorly than children in many European and East Asian nations. See Stevenson, H., Chen, C. & Lee, S. 1993 "Motivation and Achievement of Gifted Children in East Asia and the United States." *Journal for the Education of the Gifted,* 16, 223–250; and Stevenson, H. & Stigler, J. 1992 *The Learning Gap: Why Our Schools Are Failing and What We Can Learn From Japanese and Chinese Education.* New York: Simon & Schuster.
4. Cravens, G. 2001. Personal communication. Grade inflation has been widely reported and discussed. For one overview of issues related to grade inflation see Wilson, B. P. 1999 "The Phenomenon of Grade Inflation in Higher Education," Meeting of the Governor's Blue Ribbon Commission on Higher Education, Longwood College.
5. The story of grade inflation and the 2001 Harvard graduating class was widely reported. For two representative articles see Rothstein, R., "Doubling of A's at Harvard: Grade Inflation or Brains?" *New York Times*, December 5, 2001; and

an editorial, "Why Grade Inflation Is Serious," *New York Times*, December 9, 2001.

6. The story of the flap over reading levels was related by Richard Beery at a continuing education workshop concerning MMPI-R sponsored by the California Psychological Association, September, 1997, Emeryville, CA.

## Chapter One

1. For further information on underachieving among gifted students see Reis, S. M. 1994, April. "How Schools Are Shortchanging the Gifted." MIT Technology Review, 39–45; Ross, P. O. 1993. *National Excellence: A Case for Developing America's Talent*. Washington, DC: U.S. Department of Education, Office of Educational Research and Improvement; and VanTassel-Baska, J. 1991. "Research on Special Populations of Gifted Learners." In M. Wang, M. Reynolds, & H. J. Walberg, Eds. *Handbook of Special Education: Research and Practice: Vol.4. Emerging Programs*, 77–101. Oxford, England: Pergamon Press.

2. Ford's 1998 buyout program for underachieving managers is referred to in Simison, R. 1999. "Ford Decides to Teach Workers New Idea: 'Shareholder Value,' " *Wall Street Journal*, January 13, 1999.

3. For a thorough discussion of self-defeating behavior and a review of the literature on tradeoffs and choices see Baumeister, R., Scher, S. 1988. "Self-Defeating Behavior Patterns Among Normal Individuals: Review and Analysis of Common Self-Destructive Tendencies," *Psychological Bulletin*, 104, 3–22.

## Chapter Two

1. See Baumeister, R.F., Bratslavsky, E., Muraven, M., and Tice, D.M., "Ego Depletion: Is the Active Self a Limited Resource?," *Journal of Personality and Social Psychology*, 46, 1129–1146. In addition see Volume 54, Number 7, of the *American Psychologist*, which in its entirety is devoted to research findings concerning the preponderant role of nonconscious, involuntary behavior in everyday life.

2. For a theoretical description of the way we construct our worlds see Kelly, G. A. 1955. *The Psychology of Personal Constructs*. Volume 1. New York: Norton. Much of the discussion in this chapter is in keeping with Kelly's theoretical outlook.

3. We pay conscious attention only when we are first learning. James, W. 1890. *The Principles of Psychology*. Volume 2. New York: Holt.

4. For a discussion of the power and influence of our beliefs once they are in place see Frank, J. D. 1961. *Persuasion and Healing*. New York: Schocken.

5. Kelly (1955).

6. See Bargh, J., and Chartrand, T. 1999. "The Unbearable Automaticity of Being," *American Psychologist*, 54, 461–479.

7. Thomas, A., Chess, S., and Birch, H. 1968. *Temperament and Behavior Disorders in Children*. New York University Press: New York.

8. Gardner, H. 1983. *Frames of Mind: The Theory of Multiple Intelligences*. New York: Basic Books.

9. These observations are from a taped interview with James Cameron. Cameron, J. 2001. Personal communication.

10. Coopersmith, Stanley. 1967. *The Antecedents of Self-Esteem*. San Francisco: W.H. Freeman.

11. See Haley, Jay. 1974, *Uncommon Therapy: The Psychiatric Techniques of Milton H. Erickson, M.D.* New York: Grune & Stratton.

12. For an introduction to and overview of research on the topic of self-talk see Braiker, H.B. 1989. "The Power of Self-Talk," *Psychology Today*, December, 23–27; and Levine, B.H. 1991. *Your Body Believes Every Word You Say: The Language of the Body/Mind Connection*. Boulder Creek, CA: Aslan. The role of self-talk in athletic performance has been extensively examined. For example, see Orlick, T., and Partington, J. 1988. "Mental Links to Excellence," *The Sport Psychologist*, 2, 105–130.

13. A number of studies support conclusions similar to the ones we drew from the school experiences of the gifted individuals with whom we worked. See Bloom, B., Ed. 1985. *Developing Talent in Young People*. New York: Ballantine Books. Csikszentmihalyi, M., Rathunde, K. & Whalen, S. 1993. *Talented Teenagers: The Roots of Success and Failure*. New York: Cambridge University Press. Cox, J., Daniel, N., and Boston, B. O. 1985. *Educating Able Learners: Programs and Promising Practices*. (Austin: University of Texas Press. Goertzel, V., and Goertzel, M. G. 1962. *Cradles of Eminence*. Boston: Little, Brown. Gross, M. 1993. *Exceptionally Gifted Children*. London: Routledge. See also Ellen Winner's 1997 review of the research literature on giftedness and schooling: Winner, E. 1997. "Exceptionally High Intelligence and Schooling." *American Psychologist*, 52, 1070, 1081.

14. Winner, E. (1997).

15. For a discussion of the lack of motivation in underachievers and low self-esteem about their intellectual capacities see Butler-Por, N. 1987. *Underachievers in School: Issues and Intervention*. Chichester, England: Wiley. Note that all beliefs such as Kendra's become self-fulfilling prophecies.

16. For discussions concerning fostering talent in the gifted see Bloom, B., Ed. 1985. *Developing Talent in Young People*. New York: Ballantine Books. Ericsson, K. A., Krampe, R. T. & Tesch-Romer, C. 1993. "The Role of Deliberate Practice in the Acquisition of Expert Performance," *Psychological Review*, 100, 363–406.

17. See Snyder, C.R. 1993. *The Psychology of Hope*. New York: Free Press.

18. Uncertainty about how one has attained previous and possible future successes appears to be key ingredients in eliciting self-handicapping. See Berglas, S. 1985. "Self Handicapping and Self-Handicappers: A Cognitive/Attributional Model of Interpersonal Self Protective Behavior," in Hogan, R. Ed. *Perspective in Personality* Vol 1, 235–270. Greenwich, CT: JAI Press. See also Goldberg, C. 1973. "Some Effects of Fear-of-Failure in the Academic Setting," *Journal of Psychology*, 84, 323–331; and Harris, R.N., and Snyder, C.R. 1986. "The Role of Uncertain Self-Esteem in Self-Handicapping," *Journal of Personality and Social Psychology*, 51, 451–458 for research demonstrating the deleterious effects of fear and uncertainty.

19. For a further discussion of gifted children moving away from their gifts see Winner, E. 2000. "The Origins and Ends of Giftedness," *American Psychologist*, 55, 1, 159-169.

20. Cameron, J. 2001. Personal communication.

21. See Koditz,T.A., and Arking, A. M. 1982. "An Impression Management Interpretation of Self-Handicapping," *Journal of Personality and Social Psychology*, 43, 492–502.

22. Self-handicapping is described by Berglas (1985) and Baumeister, R., Scher, S. 1988. "Self-Defeating Behavior Patterns Among Normal Individuals: Review and Analysis of Common Self-Destructive Tendencies," *Psychological Bulletin*, 104, 3–22. The cause of self-handicapping appears to be insecurity about how you will perform, especially when that uncertainty is coupled with high expectations for performance.

23. Coopersmith, S. "Studies in Self-Esteem," *Scientific American*, February, 1968.

24. For a discussion of excuses and their functions see Snyder, C. R. Higgins, and Stucky, R. J. 1983. *Excuses: Masquerades in Search of Grace*. New York: Wiley.

## Chapter Four

1. Lecky, P. 1945. *The Theory of Self-Consistency*. New York: Island Press.

2. See Bargh, J., and Chartrand , T. 1999.

3. The information on change in this chapter is a distillation of what I have observed in my work as a practicing psychologist and specifically with underachievers. A rich psychological research literature exists on change, a complete review of which is beyond the scope of this book. For one overview see Prochaska, J., Norcross J., and DiClemente, C. 1992. *Changing for Good*. New York: William Morrow and Co.

4. Katherine Butler Hathaway. "Past Present." *Nations*, October 25, 1993.

5. Prochaska, J. O., DiClemente, C. C., & Norcross, J. C. 1992. "In Search of How People Change: Applications to Addictive Behavior," *American Psychologist*, 47, 1102–1114.

## Chapter Five

1. For an excellent introduction Milton Erickson's way of thinking and his approach to psychotherapy see Haley, J. 1974. *Uncommon Therapy: The Psychiatric Techniques of Milton Erickson*. New York: Grune & Stratton.

2. For an overview of learned helplessness and how attributing one's failures to an enduring lack of talent or capacity leads to the conclusion that future efforts are useless and doomed to failure, see Abramson, L. Y., Seligman, M. E. P., and Teasdale, J. D. 1978. "Learned Helplessness in Humans: A Critique and Reformulation," *Journal of Abnormal Psychology*, 87, 49–74.

3. The work of Agassi's team and his tennis comeback has been widely reported. For two representative articles see Finn, R. "Agassi Revival Reaches a Peak In French Open," *New York Times*, June 7, 1999; and Finn, R., "It's Agassi in (What Else?) a Comeback," *New York Times*, September 13, 1999.

4. This story was related to me by Gwyneth Cravens who studied with Erickson.
5. For an overview see Sommer, R. 1969. *Personal Space: The Behavioral Basis of Design.* Englewood Cliffs, NJ: Prentice-Hall.
6. See Assagioli, R. 1994. *The Act of Will: A Guide To Self-Actualization Through Psychosynthesis.* London: Aquarian/Thorsons.
7. Rilke, Rainer, Maria. (1949), *The Notebooks of Malte Laurids Brigge.* Translated by M. D. Herter Norton. New York: W. W. Norton & Company.

## Chapter Six

1. People's visions of themselves in the future influence their current self-conceptions and actions. See Markus, H., and Nurius, P. 1986. "Possible Selves," *American Psychologist,* 41, 954–969.
2. For an excellent comprehensive review of the effective use of imagery, see Taylor, S., Pham, L. B., Rivkin, I. D., Armor, D. A.1998. "Harnessing the Imagination: Mental Simulation, Self-Regulation, and Coping," *American Psychologist,* 53, 429–439.
3. Nicklaus, J. 1976. *Play Better Golf.* New York: King Features.
4. Taylor, et. al. (1998), cite nine studies that have demonstrated that when people imagine hypothetical future events and are then later asked to rate the likelihood of those events occurring, they are more likely to believe the events will actually occur following mental simulation than following other kinds of thinking about those hypothetical events. One such study is Koehler, D. J. 1991. "Explanation, Imagination, and Confidence in Judgment," *Psychological Bulletin,* 110, 499–519.
5. Taylor, et. al. (1998).
6. See Kohn, A. (1993), *Punished by Rewards.* New York: Houghton Mifflin.

## Chapter Seven

1. The instructions in this section draw heavily on Peter Gollwitzer's work with what he refers to as implementation intentions. See Gollwitzer, P. 1999. "Implementation Intentions: Strong Effects of Simple Plans," *American Psychologist,* 54, 493–503.
2. A wide variety of different studies from different contexts support the notion of the importance of repetition over time. For one discussion of practice over time see Dempster, F. N., (1990) "The Spacing Effect: A Case Study in the Failure to Apply the Results of Psychological Research," *American Psychologist,* 43. For an overview of overlearning see Baldwin, T. T., and Ford, K. J. 1988. "Transfer of Training," *Personnel Psychology,* 41.
3. Golwitzer, P. (1999) emphasizes the importance of this self-instruction because his research shows that it plays a crucial role in the effectiveness of specific operating instructions by increasing the likelihood that they will be followed.
4. My use of the term "the language of change" refer to something different from Watzlawick's usage in his 1993 book, *The Language of Change: Elements of Therapeutic Communication* (New York: W.W. Norton & Company), though the emphasis on language and its effects is similar. A vast literature exists in philosophy, communications theory, family systems theory, and psychology concerning how

language and communication influence individuals and systems, even thinking. For but one introduction see Watzlawick, P., Beavin, J., and Jackson, D. D. 1967. *Pragmatics of Human Communication: A Study of Interactional Patterns, Pathologies, and Paradoxes.* New York: W. W. Norton & Company.

5.  Watzlawick, P., Beavin, J., and Jackson, D. D. (1967).

6.  Fadiman, J. 1989. *Unlimit Your Life: Setting and Getting Goals.* Berkeley: CelestialArts.

7.  This is the so-called "miracle question," the technique most associated with solution-focused therapy. For more information on solution-oriented therapy see DeJong, Peter, and Berg, Insoo Kim. 1997. *Interviewing for Solutions.* Pacific Grove, CA: Brooks/Cole; and de Shazer, S. 1985. *Keys to Solution in Brief Therapy.* New York: Norton.

8.  Much has been written about the benefits of setting goals, types of goals, and how to set them. The usefulness of goals has been studied in a variety of settings, including health care, organizations, and athletics. For one overview of goal-setting see Fadiman, J. 1989.

9.  See Snyder, C.R. 1993.

10. See Simonton, O. Carl, Matthews-Simonton, S., Creighton, J. 1978. *Getting Well Again: A Step-By-Step Self Help Guide To Overcoming Cancer for Patients and Their Families.* New York: J. P. Tarcher.

11. The exercises which follow involving replacing self-limiting behavior were based upon Jonathan Chamberlain's 1978 book, *Eliminate Your Sdbs: Self-Defeating Behaviors.* Provo, UT: Brigham Young University Press. With the author's permission, we adapted his methods to our work with SLHPPs.

## Chapter Eight

1.  Optimism can be learned, and learning it can be worthwhile. See Seligman, M. E. P. 1991. *Learned Optimism.* New York: Knopf.

2.  See Taylor, et. al. (1988) for a brief overview of research on the planning fallacy and the use of visualization. The technique I suggest is drawn directly from her work.

3.  See Baldwin, T. T., and Ford, J. K. (1988).

4.  Strategic family therapy stems from the work of Milton Erickson and a planned relapse is a paradoxical technique. For an anlysis of paradoxical techniques in strategic therapy see Coyne, J. C., and Biglan, A. 1984. "Paradoxical Techniques in Strategic Family Therapy: A Behavioral Analysis," *Journal of Behavioral Therapy and Experimental Psychiatry*, 15, 221–227. For an introduction to Erickson's approach, see Haley (1974).

5.  Brownell, K. D., Marlatt, G. A., Lichtenstein, E., and Wilson, G. T. 1986. "Understanding and Preventing Relapse," *American Psychologist*, 41, 765–782.

## Chapter Nine

1.  Csikszentmihalyi, M. 1990. *Flow: The Psychology of Optimal Experience.* New York: Harper & Row.